To Alan,
my oldest friend
— and lover of history!
Mike

From Anvil to Pulpit

Rev. Robert Collyer D.D., Lit.D.

Bronze bust by Frances Darlington originally in Ilkley Public Library

From Anvil to Pulpit

The making of Robert Collyer: Yorkshire Blacksmith – American Preacher

Mike Dixon

ISBN 978-1-5272-9325-0

Cover design by jo hill: www.artstar.london
Published by Michael F. Dixon, 2 Tarn Villas, Ilkley LS29 8RH
mikedixon@blueyonder.co.uk
Printed by Inky Little Fingers, Churcham, Gloucestershire GL2 8AX

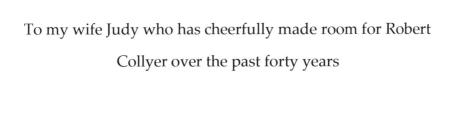

To my wife Judy who has cheerfully made room for Robert Collyer over the past forty years

Collyer's former Unity Church in North Dearborn Street, Chicago (2014)

Table of Contents

Foreword

Robert Collyer was a household name in Chicago and New York in the second half of the nineteenth century. Not only was he widely recognized as a formidable preacher and orator, but also as a man of action and courage. It was Collyer who took the Chicago Relief Fund to the victims of the Iowa Tornado in 1860 and, during the Civil War, to the bereaved families after the massacre in Lawrence, Kansas. In the War he served as a Chaplain and 'Nurse', and as a champion and rallying point for the Union cause. Subsequently, he was a major channel for aid after the Great Fire in Chicago. As a pastor in New York, he was recognized as one the leading churchmen in the city and an agent for social change. Yet, prior to his appointment as an outreach minister in Chicago in 1859, Collyer had worked as a factory hand in Pennsylvania, making hammers. Before that he lived in England, working as a blacksmith in a Yorkshire village, from where he emigrated to America at the age of twenty-six in 1850.

Collyer's life exemplifies the social and economic pressures that drove young men and women to leave their homelands in Europe for America's 'land of opportunity' and the potential for success when an individual took this opportunity. After enduring poverty and factory labor as a child, Collyer became increasingly aware that in England his life would be forever constrained by his position as an uneducated artisan. His frustration and unfulfilled ambitions were common to many people who chose to emigrate, but his story is remarkable in many other respects. Without theological training and qualifications, he was appointed a minister in the Unitarian church in Chicago and was soon acclaimed as a gifted and charismatic preacher. Without medical or nursing training he brought care and comfort to wounded and dying soldiers carried from the battlefields, and confronted death and disease as he sought to relieve suffering among Confederate prisoners-of-war held in Chicago. Later, he faced the personal tragedy of the destruction of his church and home in the Great Fire. Finally, despite little formal education, he became a nationally renowned speaker on the American lecture circuit and moved in the highest literary circles in the country.

Following his appointment as Minister-at-Large in Chicago, Collyer and his volunteer helpers set about relieving poverty, finding work for the unemployed, and promoting good citizenship. At the same time, he took an increasing part in the preaching and pastoral work of the church and within two years was appointed foundation minister of the new Unity (Second Unitarian) Church in Chicago. The former blacksmith, factory worker and itinerant preacher now had to grow into the role of church and civic leader in a great city. He had to equip himself to become not only a pastor and pulpit figure but, more controversially, to champion the abolition of slavery, the freedom of the press, Women's Rights, and the orderly colonization of the West. After twenty years in Chicago, he continued his ministry at the Church of the Messiah in New York. There he added to his national reputation, gained access to the highest echelons of civic and literary society, and continued to press for social change.

A memorial bust of Robert Collyer in the Second Unitarian Church, Chicago, bears the inscription; 'A man he was of cheerful yesterdays and confident tomorrows'. This was a fitting tribute to his final years, but many of his yesterdays were far from cheerful. He was a man racked with self-doubt who suffered periodic bouts of depression. He endured constant tension between his lack of formal education and the high standing he enjoyed in the communities in which he served. In his lifetime, Collyer surmounted the peaks of fame and success, but he struggled through many lows on his long and eventful journey. It is a struggle that reminds us of universal truths about the supremacy of determination, persistence, and faith.

1: A bell for Cornell

As you set out for Ithaca
hope your road is a long one,
full of adventure, full of discovery.
From a poem, Ithaca, by Constantine P. Cavafy, 1863-1933

The horse-drawn cab toiled up the hill from the railway station in Ithaca and entered the grounds of Cornell University. Reaching the main entrance of Sibley Hall, the Reverend Robert Collyer stepped down and announced himself to the hall porter. A few minutes later the University President, Charles Adams, appeared and greeted him warmly.[1] After a polite enquiry about his journey from New York, Adams introduced Collyer to his host for the afternoon, Dr. Robert Thurston, Director of the Sibley College of Engineering.[2] Dr. Thurston invited Collyer inside, where they joined other members of the Faculty for refreshments prior to the gathering in the Main Hall.

---

[1] Cornell University was founded in 1865 by two Unitarian educationalists, Ezra Cornell and Andrew Dickson White. Charles Kendall Adams (1835-1902) was inaugurated as President in 1885. http://www.cornell.edu/president/history_bio_adams.cfm.

[2] In 1870, Hiram Sibley, a wealthy businessman from Rochester, New York and one of the original trustees of Cornell University, provided funding to erect a building to foster engineering studies — the Sibley College of Mechanical Engineering and Mechanic Arts. The Ithaca campus now includes more than 260 major buildings on 745 acres. See http://www.mae.cornell.edu/index.cfm/page/about/history.htm.

An hour later, the assembled staff and engineering students struggled to hear the words of Dr. Thurston as he introduced the principal guest. Thurston seemed overawed by the occasion; the gathering of University dignitaries and the stature of the visitor rendered him unusually hesitant. The focus of his oration, Robert Collyer, was an ageing but erect, well-built man with a strong-featured face softened by smiling eyes and framed with bushy side-whiskers and a mane of silver-grey hair falling over his collar. Collyer had been invited to Cornell to inaugurate the Fewston Bell, his gift to the University, and a bell with which he had an unusual and far-reaching connection.[3]

The bell originally hung at West House Mill, a linen factory in the Washburn Valley, Yorkshire. On six mornings a week, from 5.30 am, its insistent ringing filled the valley, summoning the reluctant child-laborers to their flax spinning-frames. Collyer was one of them, one of the scores of children trapped before their time in the unrelenting grind of labor. The bell was a chilling reminder of those days. Now its peal would summon young people to a different kind of toil.

Collyer's association with Cornell began eighteen years before this visit, in 1871, after the Great Fire in Chicago had consumed and destroyed not only his Unity Church, but also his house and virtually all his possessions. After the fire, a wave of sympathy swept across America, and into Europe. Donations large and small were sent to both the main Chicago relief fund and directly to Collyer for him to disburse. Among them came an offer of $1000 from the students at Cornell, subject to the proviso that, "the Rev. Robert Collyer shall make for them, with his own hands, and in a proper and workmanlike manner, one small, sufficient and substantial horseshoe."[4]

Collyer fashioned the horseshoe at a forge in his neighborhood, and having fulfilled his side of the bargain, Cornell replied with great generosity. Over following months, bank drafts totaling $2250 were received in Chicago. In June 1872, Collyer travelled to Ithaca and handed over the horseshoe to Vice-President Russel, who responded on behalf of the students.[5] Collyer confessed that the horseshoe, stamped as it was with "Robert Collyer — Maker", was not the best example of his work, after all it was the first horseshoe he had produced for twenty-two years, but it was certainly the most valuable.

---

[3] 'A Bell for Cornell, Robert Collyer's unique present to the University'. *The New York Times,* Feb 1, 1889

[4] 'Robert Collyer D.D.', *The Cornell Era, vol* XXIX; no. 24; April 24, 1897.

[5] 'Cornell University', in *Chicago Tribune,* Jun 14, 1872.

Cornell University campus in the 1920s. The view is dominated by the McGraw clock-tower. The Sage Chapel is in the center almost hidden by trees. (Author's collection)

Two years after the opening of Cornell's Sage Chapel in 1873,[6] Collyer was able to fulfil a long-standing invitation to deliver the sermon at one of the weekly services. His compelling and charismatic preaching was so well-received that he was persuaded to give an annual sermon each Spring, thereby joining a distinguished list of preachers who occupied the Sage Chapel pulpit. Through these yearly visits he became increasingly friendly with President Andrew White and his successor, Charles Adams. It was Adams who had instigated the presentation of the bell.

The Fewston Bell (as it was called at Cornell) came to Collyer in an unexpected way. From time to time he received copies of a Yorkshire newspaper, the *Leeds Mercury*. Sometime in 1870, he read that the great industrial city of Leeds needed more drinking water for its rapidly expanding population. The city authorities had bought a large tract of land in the Washburn Valley, about eighteen miles from Leeds, with the aim of building a reservoir. The purchase

[6] The Sage Chapel was the gift of Henry and Susan Sage. Their eldest son, Dean Sage, endowed the fund that continues to bring notable religious leaders of all denominations to speak at the chapel. see http://www.curw.cornell.edu/sagehistory.html.

included the site of West House Mill, by then abandoned and in partial ruin.[7] Collyer wrote to an old friend who served on Leeds City Council and asked, 'when they break up that wicked old bell ... secure me a piece and send it over.' Although it was some years before the mill was finally demolished, his request was remembered. By this time, Collyer had moved from Chicago to New York, but the Leeds friend had tracked him down and the entire bell arrived, unannounced, at his apartment.

The Sibley School of Mechanical Engineering, now Sibley Hall, at Cornell University, ca 1883-1894. The first building, built in 1870, was the western part in the center. An identical second building was built a short distance east of it in 1894 and opened just prior to Collyer's visit. (Photo from Cornell Engineering via Wikimedia Commons).

The bell had been delivered free of charge as a gift from the Corporation and Council in Leeds. However, the bell was substantial, heavy and certainly not a thing of beauty.[8] There was no question of keeping it in the house, so the bell was transferred to the shop rented by Collyer's younger brother, John, who had followed Robert to America and settled in New York. Several years later, when Collyer was up at Cornell for a Sage Chapel service, President Adams mentioned

---

[7] Fewston Reservoir was built between 1874 and 1879. West House mill was demolished in 1877-78 and stone from the mill used to build the boundary walls around the reservoir.

[8] The bell was made from heavy cast iron and measured 18 inches high and 15 inches diameter in the mouth and had a clapper with a rope attached (from a description in the catalogue of Cornell University Memorabilia, p. 140).

the establishment of a new mechanical engineering school. It occurred to Collyer that he might usefully dispose of the old bell to the University where it could hang over the workshops. Adams received the idea readily, even though Collyer, with characteristic honesty, told him 'it used to be the most infernal clang in all the world.'[9]

The Fewston Bell in Kimball Hall. (Courtesy of Mr. Gould Colman, Cornell University)

[9] On 21 January 1889 Collyer wrote to President Adams describing the history of the bell and informed him; 'That old bell would be sent up the road on Saturday by my brother in whose shop it lay.' Original letter in The Department of Manuscripts and University Archives, Cornell University Libraries (39/5/949).

Now on the Sibley Hall platform, Collyer stood patiently, transferring his considerable weight from foot to foot. Eventually, Director Thurston reached the culmination of his eulogy, and turning towards Collyer, invited him to sound the bell. Collyer moved forward and pulled the rope with some trepidation. The deep, metallic notes reverberated from the high ceiling and filled the Hall with sound. Its ringing sent a quiver of recognition down Collyer's spine. The clanging bell transported him across the years and the miles. He was again a timid child of eight years old, rubbing sleep out of his eyes and dragging on his factory clothes as the bell sent out its hated message across the Washburn Valley. Even when the last peals had died away, he stood transfixed by the powerful memories that its sound had unleashed, memories of harsh times in the mill intermingled with happier recollections of his boyhood home in Yorkshire.[10]

[10] The bell was first hung in Sibley College in 1889. When Rand Hall, part of Sibley College was opened in 1912, the Fewston bell was moved there, and in 1975 transferred to Kimball Hall, a machine shop belonging to the engineering department. In 1994, at the author's request, the University Archivist, Mr. Gould P. Colman, went to locate the bell only to be told that it had been transferred along with the machines to the Theory Center. However, it did not arrive at its destination. After its removal from the Kimball Hall mounting, and while the foreman was preparing to relocate the bell, it was stolen. All trace of the bell has been lost.

2: West House Mill

West House Mill ruled the lives of the Collyer family for thirty-two years across two generations. Robert Collyer's parents worked there as children. Later, his father was the blacksmith in the mill-forge. In turn, Robert worked there from the age of eight until he was fourteen, at which age he left the mill to learn the blacksmiths' trade in the nearby village of Ilkley.

The mill was one of several built for flax-spinning in the Washburn Valley.[1] The need for water-power drove the prospective factory owners further and further into upland valleys to find sites for their new mills. Considerations such as accessibility and the potential workforce were secondary to the availability of a constant and abundant water supply. Thus, the mills came to be located on the banks of rivers in the remote upper dales, usually some distance from the nearest town or village. Worker's cottages had to be built around them, thus forming small, isolated communities.

West House Mill was unusually large for the times, but otherwise a typical example of the isolated factory at the heart of a hamlet housing the mill-

---

[1] The valley of the River Washburn lies north and east of Otley, near Leeds. The valley is 14 miles long and now contains four reservoirs, Thruscross, Fewston, Swinsty and Lindley Wood, that interrupt the flow of the Washburn before its confluence with the River Wharfe near Leathley. The valley includes the villages of Thruscross, Blubberhouses, Fewston, Timble, Norwood, Lindley, Leathley and Farnley. Rickard's Report for Factories in the West Riding 1835-6 indicates that there were five flax mills in Fewston Township alone.

workers.[2] It was built at the end of the eighteenth century alongside an existing corn-mill, so as to share the established water-rights, and, with its associated buildings, came to dominate the most picturesque part of the Washburn valley.[3] The mill was situated on the north side of the river at the foot of steeply rising ground called Hardisty Hill. It was an extensive four-story building with cellars and a floor in the roof space, the whole forming a forbiddingly impressive building that stood like a monolith in the valley bottom. In addition, there was the Owner's house, a large warehouse, a coach-house and stables, numerous cottages and two 'apprentice houses'. Power was provided by two large water wheels supplied from the River Washburn via a complicated system of by-washes, culverts and goits (open water-channels).[4]

The building of West House in a sparsely populated rural setting meant that workers had to be drawn from far and wide, and housed in cottages erected by the mill owners. This put a further strain on the precarious finances of the enterprise, although there was some small return through rents. A cheaper and more abundant source of labor was the orphanages and poorhouses of the major cities from where the factory owners sought young children to serve 'apprenticeships' in the mills[5]. It was in this way that Robert Collyer's parents arrived at West House Mill. They were both orphans. Robert's father, Samuel Collyer, was born on March 27, 1797. Samuel's father, the first Robert Collyer,

---

[2] West House was situated just off the Harrogate-Skipton turnpike road close to Blubberhouses Bridge, about 8 miles from Harrogate and 12 miles from Skipton.

[3] In the 16th century West House Mill was a fulling mill, i.e. for the scouring of woollen cloth, and was later a corn-mill. With the decline in milling in the 18th century, many corn-mills were sold for conversion to textile mills. At West House, however, the corn-mill continued to function alongside the flax-spinning mill, the latter being built in 1797 by Thomas Colbeck, William Holdsworth and John Holdsworth. For a detailed description of West House Mill see Calum Giles and Ian H. Goodall, *Yorkshire Textile Mills: The Buildings of the Yorkshire Textile Industry 1770-1930* (London: Her Majesty's Stationery Office, 1992), and the file on *West House Mill, Fewston,* Ref BF063849, in the Historic England Archive, London.

[4] Bernard Jennings ed., *A History of Nidderdale* (Huddersfield, Yorkshire: The Advertiser Press Ltd, 1967), 232. The larger West House wheel was made of iron, 36 feet in diameter and buckets 10 feet broad; the smaller wheel was wooden, 33 feet in diameter and had buckets 11 feet broad.

[5] The apprentices at West House were to be taught 'weaving or flax-dressing'. Katrina Honeyman, *Child Workers in England 1780-1820: Parish Apprentices and the Making of the Early Industrial Labour Force* (Abingdon and New York: Routledge, 2007), 137.

was a sailor in Nelson's fleet. Samuel would recount how he sat on his father's shoulders to see the procession escorting the great admiral's body up the Thames for burial in St. Paul's Cathedral.[6] Samuel's father went to sea again soon after this event and was lost overboard in a storm. His mother died shortly afterwards, leaving her family of five children in the care of a poorhouse in the City of London.

West House Mill and Blubberhouses Bridge from an ink and watercolor painting attributed to Dean Wolstenholme Snr (1757-1837) in the author's collection.

Robert Collyer's mother was called Harriet Norman, a name that allowed Robert to claim in later life that he had 'Norman' blood in his veins. Harriet's father, Thomas Norman, was also a sailor. His home port was Yarmouth although the family lived in Norwich. Harriet was vague about the details of her early childhood, but she told Robert that her father was also lost at sea, and sometime later, the four children in the family were placed in an orphanage in

---

[6] Nelson was killed at Trafalgar on 21 October 1805. His burial did not take place until January, 1806. After lying in state at Greenwich Hospital his body was brought by barge up the Thames for a highly elaborate state funeral at St Paul's Cathedral.

Norwich. Collyer used to say that; 'we have no family tree to speak of, only this low bush.'[7]

Between 1797 and 1814 various partners in the West House Mill business would travel to London, and other large cities, to recruit child-workers. In London, they visited the orphanages and poorhouses in the parishes of Lambeth and Southwark and selected suitable children. If the children 'agreed', those selected were indentured there and then to the mill-owners, to serve an apprenticeship. For their part, the owners undertook to house, feed and clothe the apprentices until the girls were eighteen and the boys were twenty-one. They also entered into an obligation to teach them the three R's (Reading, 'Riting and 'Rithmetic) and the boys some craft by which they might earn their living when they were 'free'. The Parish Churchwardens, the Overseers of the Poor and the mill-owners present at the time, signed the indentures.[8] Two Justices of the Peace witnessed the documents. By this process, in 1807, Robert's parents came to be apprentices at West House Mill; Samuel, aged ten, from the City of London, and Harriet from Norwich, aged nine.[9]

On their arrival, they were dispatched to their separate accommodation, Samuel to the boys' High Apprentice House situated about half a mile from the mill up the Hardisty Hill road, and Harriet to the girls' Low Apprentice House lying away from the road down a narrow lane to the east. Amidst the confusion of accents in the dormitory, Samuel soon identified other friendly London voices. One such was John Wells, a boy of thirteen, who had come from Southwark three years earlier.[10] He took Samuel under his wing and they became firm friends. The two boys also became friendly with Harriet Norman, and the three became close work- and play-mates.

---

[7] Robert Collyer, *Some Memories* (Boston, American Unitarian Association, 1908), 2.

[8] An indenture which apprenticed Frederick Simpson, aged 12, to West House Mill, drawn up on November 17, 1804, is signed by six partners, namely Thomas Colbeck, Rowland Watson, Francis Watson, Jacob Wilks and Jonathan and William Holdsworth, (personal communication, Sheila Gallagher, East Surrey Family History Society).

[9] Similar arrangements for child apprentices prevailed in the textile mills of the U.S.; see Edith Abbott, *A Study of Child Labor in America* in *American Journal of Sociology* (Chicago: The University of Chicago Press, 1908), 14: 15-37.

[10] John Wells was in the care of the Parish of St George the Martyr, Southwark, and was indentured to the owners of West House Mill on November 20, 1804, (personal communication, Sheila Gallagher).

The former High Apprentice House on Hardisty Hill following its restoration. Now a private house. Photographed by the author in 2011.

At first, the mill enjoyed increasing prosperity. The long wars against France and the collapse of French power led to a fall in the price of flax while yarn prices remained steady. There was a boom between 1813-15 during which time the mill expanded. The owners installed a steam engine to maintain power when, in a dry summer, the water supply failed, and added a weaving shed and bleaching house, so that West House became one of the few mills in Yorkshire able to undertake all aspects of linen manufacture. Unfortunately, the boom was short lived. In the immediate aftermath of the Napoleonic campaign, the linen industry became a victim of the overall economic slump, and one of the casualties was West House Mill. The owners, Colbeck, Ellis and Company went bankrupt in November 1816.[11] While in administration, the work-force was reduced, though some were re-deployed. Samuel Collyer moved from the weaving shed to the mill-forge where he worked under the

[11] Jennings, *History of Nidderdale,* 215.

blacksmith, Jacky Birch.[12] About the same time, Harriet finished her apprenticeship. The friendship between John Wells and Harriet now blossomed into romance. The two were married and, in 1819, they had a child - William. Tragically, John Wells died after only two years of marriage. Samuel Collyer began to court the young widow, and the couple were married at Fewston Parish Church in March 1823.[13] There must have been a late snow-fall that year, for Harriet used to tell of walking back from the church with the snow so high that the newly-weds walked along the tops of the walls on Busky Dike Lane.

Part of the former Low Apprentice (Girls) House off Hardisty Hill. Photographed by the author in 1990.

[12] Birch came to Fewston from his family home in Lofthouse in Nidderdale.

[13] The marriage took place on 10 March 1823 and was conducted by the Rev Christopher Ramshaw. The witnesses were John Pullinger and Thomas Robinson. Ramshaw was Vicar at Fewston from 1790-1843, (Fewston Parish Church Register, entry 170, p 57).

On marriage, Samuel and Harriet were able to move into one of the mill cottages, and soon afterwards Harriet became pregnant. A few months later, however, Samuel got into a dispute over wages and decided to leave the mill. Gathering up their few belongings, the couple, together with Harriet's son William, walked across Denton Moor to Ilkley and then over Ilkley Moor to Keighley in the Aire valley, about 15 miles. There, Samuel managed to get a job at the anvil in Hattersleys' textile-machinery works. Thus, it was that their child, Robert, was born in Keighley on December 8, 1823.[14] Within nine days of Robert's birth, however, Samuel got news of a better wage offer at West House and the couple decided to return. Robert, wrapped in a bundle of blankets to guard against the harsh winter weather, was carried by his father over the moors back to Fewston.[15]

The family set up in another of the West House mill cottages, and this was to be Robert's home for the next 14 years. It had two rooms downstairs and an attic above, open to the roof. Over the following few years, this tiny cottage also became home to four more Collyer children, Martha (born 1825), Thomas (1828), John (1830), and Maria (1832). Until William started work, this ever-enlarging family had to be clothed, fed, warmed and sheltered on Samuel's wage of 18 shillings a week (20 shillings=£1). Harriet managed the household economy by dint of hard-work and thrift, and a large measure of 'grit'.[16]

Looking around the cottage, thick white lime covered the interior walls reflecting the light from the small deep-set windows. A mahogany bureau shone like a dim mirror through much polishing that owed more to Harriet's 'elbow grease' than beeswax. Above it, a wooden rack held the willow-pattern pottery, kept sacred for Christmas and the village feast in the summer. The room had chairs for the company, but the children sat on stools, and in the far corner stood a tall clock that was always too fast for Robert at bedtime, and too slow as mealtimes approached. There was also clean linen and soft calico to wear next to the body and to sleep in, and once a week a good, sound scrubbing in a tub in front of the fire, with yellow soap that got in their eyes, and a rough, shaggy towel to dry them down. On the small fireside range, a pot would

[14] Robert was baptized at Fewston Parish Church on 29 January 1824 also by the Vicar, Christopher Ramshaw, (Fewston Parish Church Register)

[15] Collyer, *Some Memories*, 5.

[16] Collyer always valued the word 'grit' – one of his favorite lectures was entitled 'Clear Grit'. For Collyer, the word combined qualities of strength and determination with echoes of the native rock of the Yorkshire Dales, Millstone Grit.

simmer for hours, soup and dumplings in the evening, coarse oatmeal porridge in the morning. There would be a little meat, but not at every dinner. When there was meat, the meal would always begin with the challenge from Harriet that those eating the most suet pudding would get the most meat. This generally meant the children were so stuffed with pudding that there was meat left for the next day. There was oatmeal, skim-milk, white bread, with a thin spread of butter on a Sunday afternoon, and tea of a peculiar pedigree. Robert always believed that the clean linen, the weekly scrub, the white purity of fresh lime laid on the walls every year by his mother's hands, and the food she gave them laid a foundation for health that carried him through life. In ripe old age Collyer was able to boast that "I have never been one day sick in my bed these fourscore years or, so far as I can remember, had my breakfast there".[17]

West House Mill from an old letter head. The mill was reliant on horse-drawn wagons (front-center) to bring in flax bales and take away finished linen cloth.

There were about forty mill-owned cottages in the hamlet around West House[18], interspersed with more substantial properties. The Collyers' cottage was one of a short row that stood on a raised terrace. Outside the cottage, there was a neat patch of grass with a single rose-bush at its centre and a plum-tree whose fruit in summer never fulfilled the promise of the blossom in spring. At one end of the row, a mill foreman, Thomas Scotson, had a house of some dignity, thick clad with ivy where the sparrows nested in great numbers and made a cheerful racket on summer mornings. The western end of the row butted against the house of Michael Robinson, the factory manager. He was the son of Thomas Robinson, the village blacksmith whose smithy stood near

[17] Collyer, *Some Memories*, 7.

[18] A sale notice of 1843 gives the number at 37 (author's collection)

the old Toll Bar on the Harrogate-Skipton turnpike. Michael could not 'thoil' (tolerate) the hammer and anvil, and instead took to school more keenly than the rest. He learnt to such good purpose, that when Colbeck and Ellis wanted someone to bring the water from the High Dam to the new overshot wheel – a very delicate and difficult bit of work – 'that lad o' Robinson's' took the contract. He did this job so well that the Company held on to him, and when Colbeck and Ellis failed in 1816, and the property passed into the hands of the Craven Bank in Skipton, the whole management of the factory and estate passed into his hands. Mr. Robinson's house, complete with a bow window framed in roses, seemed a grand place indeed to Robert's young eyes but even this paled by comparison with the Owner's house.[19] Situated above the old corn mill, Mr. Colbeck had erected a handsome double-fronted property with elegant bay-windows and high, carved-stone doorcases.[20] The house was enclosed by a well-stocked garden and orchard, and flanked by stables and a coach-house. The close proximity of this grand residence to the mean cottages of the workers bred resentment in some, but for the Collyer family there was a largely unquestioning acceptance of 'them and us'.

Up Hardisty Hill, beyond the main cluster of cottages and the apprentice houses, stood the workhouse, a large building considering the size of the hamlet, where the old and infirm were accommodated at the expense of the parish. At the foot of the hill, near to Blubberhouses Bridge, stood a small coal-gas works that supplied the mill and many of the cottages with light, while opposite the gasworks was a further row of twelve mill-workers cottages.

---

[19] Details of the Robinson and Gill families together with personal reminiscences of Blubberhouses in a lecture given by Collyer on the opening of the Robinson Library are taken from William Grainge, *The History and Topography of the Townships of Little Timble, Great Timble and the hamlet of Snowden, in the West Riding in the County of York* (Otley, Yorkshire: William Walker & Sons, 1895), 129-172.

[20] The house was later converted into two semi-detached dwellings, West House Villas. Following purchase by Leeds Corporation in 1870 the two houses were amalgamated and became Skaife Hall. In the early 20th century Skaife Hall was the residence of a Colonel Galloway who had the cricket pitch made where the mill had been. He had house parties and held matches among his friends with well-known cricketers. He became MP for a Manchester Division and left the district in 1924. After a few years as a holiday retreat, the Hall was abandoned and fell into decay in the 1930s, (Historic England Archive, London).

Close to the junction of the Harrogate-Skipton and Otley to Pateley Bridge turnpikes stood the Frankland Arms, an inn built early in the century by Sir Robert Frankland, a wealthy land owner in the area.[21]

The Frankland Arms on the Harrogate-Skipton turnpike road. From an old postcard in the author's collection.

Westwards along the turnpike road stood the Toll-Bar house and Robinson's smithy. The toll-house collected dues from those that passed on the road, travelers in horse drawn carriages, tradesmen in their carts, and farmers and drovers moving animals – although many drovers favored the upland routes where pasturage was readily available and no dues had to be paid. While it had an inn, a chapel, a smithy and a gas-works, the hamlet did not have a proper school. For his education, Robert Collyer had to go further afield.

[21] The Frankland Arms closed for business in 1903 and was demolished in 1907. David Alred, *Washburn Valley Yesterday* (Otley,Yorkshire: Smith Settle, 1997), 34.

3: School and Work

Poor as they were, Robert's parents put great store by education – 'you must pay so much a week or go ignorant'.[1] So every week, from Robert's fourth birthday, they willingly handed over the few pence needed to buy him an elementary education. At four, he started at a 'Dame' school in the village (at nearby Scaife House), where Miss Horsman fostered Robert's early attempts at reading. A little later he went to a school with a master, a severe man who reprimanded Robert by striking the top of his head with a gnarled, stick-like finger. Fortunately for Robert's peace of mind, and the top of his head, this master soon left the village. Robert was then considered old enough to walk the two miles to Fewston village and therefore able to attend Willie Hardy's school. Willie was one of Fewston's most colorful characters.[2]. Noted equally for his badly crippled legs and his incomparable fiddle playing, Willie was in big demand at all the local social events. Perched on a high stool, he held court in the upper room at the Smiths' Arms in Fewston, urging on the dancers with his merry tunes.

Willie's school was held in his house, where the living-room also served as the school-room. By the hearth, with its wood-burning stove, stood the small round table for the family meals, flanked by the usual high-backed chairs. The center of the room was occupied by three or four benches, or 'forms' as they were called, for the younger scholars. Along one side, by the window, stood

---

[1] Holmes, *Life and Letters,* 1: 32

[2] William (Willie) Hardy was born on 11 July 1808, the son of Joseph and Grace Hardy of Fewston.

the 'desk', accommodating ten or a dozen of the older or 'head' scholars, who sat face to face. In all, there would be between twenty and thirty scholars. Mr Hardy sat at one end of the room, in his comfortable armchair – although in winter the chair was placed much nearer the stove! On a table at Willie's right hand rested the end of a long hazel rod. The narrow end of this rod had a loop attached, and it hung from the ceiling, above the heads of the youngsters. When necessity required, it was easily unhooked, to be brought down with a thwack on the head, or shoulders, of any luckless offender, even if he was sitting in a distant part of the room.[3]

Willie Hardy was a good teacher but found Robert a bit of a dunce with figures, although he was enthusiastic about reading. Collyer appears to have had a natural leaning towards the printed word. He attached great significance to the occasion when he purchased his first book. Holding a big George III penny in his hand, Robert peered through the window of the small village shop and spied a jar filled with boiled sweets that he dearly loved. However, sitting next to the jar was a tiny book. The cover read 'The History of Whittington and His Cat' with the name of the publisher prominently displayed 'William Walker, Printer, Otley: Price, One Penny'.[4] Robert resisted the sweets and chose the book. He read it over and over until the paper was reduced to rag, but this little book was the seed of a personal library that grew to over three thousand volumes. In later life when Collyer visited London he always went up Highgate Hill to call on an old friend, and invariably stopped to look at the milestone on which Dick Whittington allegedly sat when the bells tolled him back to his destiny as Lord Mayor of London.

Learning at day-school was supplemented by the Congregational Mission Sunday School. The Collyer children went twice every Sunday, with no rewards and no picnics to bribe them into attendance. Collyer claimed that nothing outside of the training of home could compare in pure worth to the

---

[3] From Thomas Parkinson, *Lays and Leaves of the Forest: A collection of poems, and historical, genealogical and biographical essays and sketches, relating chiefly to men and things connected with the Royal Forest of Knaresborough* (London: Kent and Co., 1882), 212

[4] *Dick Whittington and His Cat* is a favorite English folk tale based on the real-life Richard Whittington (c.1354–1423), a wealthy London merchant who became Lord Mayor. The tale describes how Dick rose from poverty in childhood to earn a fortune through the sale of his cat to a rat-infested country. Disappointingly, the story has no basis in reality.

teaching he received over ten years in that good simple Sunday School.[5] The family's allegiance to the old parish church at Fewston, where his parents were married, and the children baptized, was an occasional matter, and they only went there at Easter and Whitsun (Pentecost). The vicar, the Rev. Christopher Ramshaw, provided more entertainment outside of the pulpit than enlightenment in it. He was noted for his wild scrapes such as the occasion he shot the ears off a donkey when under the influence of drink. Apparently, he mistook the donkey's ears for birds popping up over a wall.[6]

Fewston Parish Church and graveyard photographed by the author in 1990.

Rare visits to the Anglican church apart, the Collyer family attended services with great regularity in the small 'dissenting chapel' up Hardisty Hill. The Congregational Mission, like several in the dales, was too small to support its own minister. The services were taken by students from Airedale College who got ten shillings and sixpence for the Sunday, and were given hospitality by old John Pullan and his wife, at the Manor House – the so-called 'Ministers'

---

[5] The location of the Congregational Mission Hall is in doubt. The Sunday School may have been located in Hardisty House which stands near the Hardisty Hill Road. The Methodists built a small chapel nearby in 1838.

[6] quoted by Moncure Conway, *Harper's New Monthly Magazine* (May 1874): 823.

Tavern'.[7] Come rain or shine, the students would walk the twenty miles from the College near Bradford to Fewston on a Saturday and make the return journey on a Monday.[8] At the Sunday service the young men all looked alike, wearing white 'chokers' stiffened with whalebone pads that held their heads in a 'lofty' position. Despite their best efforts, the students rarely managed to hold the children's attention and it was always a relief to them when a 'proper minister', like Mr. Hastie from Otley, occupied the pulpit.[9] The Sunday School was a different matter. Here Mr. William Gill demanded the children's constant attention, and out of respect, or possibly fear, they certainly gave it. William Gill, a stone-mason through the week, was a serious and Puritanical man who pursued his calling as Sunday School superintendent with single-minded zeal. Yet, his sincerity and enthusiasm came shining through the stern exterior and he was a true disciple and valued teacher. The Gill family lived in a terraced cottage near to the Collyer's, and Robert came to know the four sons. The youngest of these, Robinson Gill, became a particular friend in later life.[10] He was to follow an older brother, Edward, to America where he became a successful businessman in New York.

Thus, Robert's education was shared between the school-teacher, Willie Hardy, the Sunday-School superintendent, William Gill, and his parents. Collyer had pleasing recollections of his father, "He never thrashed me but once – for striking my sister – and then cried because I would not yell, begged my pardon, gave me sixpence, and took me to a grand 'tuck out' at a club dinner, which was so good that I would have taken another thrashing for the like".[11] Although he deeply admired his father for his skill at the anvil, his quiet strength and his generosity of spirit, it was Robert's mother who provided the

---

[7] The Airedale Independent College was formed in 1826 from the Idle Academy, a small 'college' for the training of Congregational ministers. Thomas Whitehead, *History of the Dales Congregational Churches.* (Keighley, Yorkshire: Feather Brothers, 1930), 63

[8] from Thomas Whitehead, *Illustrated Guide to Nidderdale and a History of its Congregational Churches* (Keighley, Yorkshire: Feather Brothers, 1932), 123

[9] The Rev James Swift Hastie was minister at Otley Congregational Church from 1829 until just a few years before his death in 1878. G. S. Briggs, *Congregational Church Otley 1821-1921 – A centenary retrospect* (Privately published, 1921)

[10] William Gill married Elizabeth Robinson, one of the Robinsons of Swinsty Hall. The surname Robinson was given to their youngest son as a first name. Robinson emigrated to America in 1851 at the age of twenty one. (Grainge, *History of the Timbles and Snowden,* 44)

[11] Conway, *Harper's Magazine,* (May 1874): 822.

fulcrum around which his childhood revolved. She was his comforter, guide and teacher and the tender disciplinarian who shaped his faltering progress. She did this without recourse to physical punishment; indeed, she claimed that she "never had to speak sharply to Robert......(he) was always a dutiful son and did his part well by us".[12] A 'well-made' if not pretty woman, she had survived her years in the mill with limbs straight and her health intact. She was strong in voice and spirit, and faced up to adversity, intolerance or rudeness with the same steely determination and unbending confidence in her own judgement. She could neither read nor write, such was the poverty of the education provided by the mill-owners as their part of the apprenticeship bargain, but this deficiency never affected her children's young lives.[13] Her bedtime stories were written in the vivid pages of her mind. The beguiling tales of romance, gallantry and adventure were part of an oral tradition that wove the salty escapades of her sea-faring father and her mother's rustic folklore into some fresh and vivid story of her own creating. Her stories transported them to places and situations that would fill a whole library of books. Robert's father was not much of a reader either.... he would occasionally read a bible passage at the chapel and if he came to a difficult place-name would substitute 'Jerusalem', whatever the context. The impoverished home held only four books, the Bible, Bunyan's *Pilgrim's Progress,* the *Young Man's Companion,* and *Robinson Crusoe.* Nevertheless, feeding the children's minds was sometimes a lot easier than feeding their bodies.

Food was strictly rationed, yet there always seemed to be enough, and at certain times there were even 'extras' to be had. Christmas was, of course, such a time, but the build-up was not without its warnings of frugality. Collyer recalled seeing his mother sitting by the fireside staring deep into its flickering warmth and with a sigh and a shrug declaring "I fear we shall have no Christmas this year".[14] A shiver of disappointment would pass through the children, but this always proved to be a false alarm. The wolf never came so close to their door as to devour their Christmas. First, there would be a bit of malt and some fresh yeast from the maltster. Then Harriet's hands would mix, knead and shape the spice-cakes and a loaf of yule bread. After they had 'risen', they were placed in the range-oven and the fire stoked up. Before long, warm

---

[12] Conway, *Harper's Magazine* (May 1874): 826

[13] In the Fewston Parish Church Marriage Register, Harriet Wells has simply 'made her mark' in place of a signature. This is taken as evidence that she was illiterate.

[14] Collyer, *Some Memories,* 9.

baking smells filled the house, carrying hints of nutmeg and cinnamon and promises of festivities to come. There was always enough money for a whole cheese, albeit a small one, and beef was ordered from the butcher. In this way the various elements of the Christmas fare were made ready. The previous year's charred yule log was retrieved from the out-house. It would be used to start the fire on Christmas Eve, and at the end of Christmas Day another partly-burned log saved to serve the same purpose the following year.[15]

Meanwhile up the valley at Thruscross, the singers and the little band of musicians would rehearse their yuletide repertoire.[16] By Christmas Eve the old familiar words had been recalled and the old tunes refreshed. Before dawn on Christmas Day, the choristers set out down the dale meandering through each hamlet and calling at every farmstead. At each house the familiar carols rang out and those inside waited for two or three verses before opening their doors and extending a warm welcome inside. At West House they called at those cottages where they knew hospitality would be extended. One such was the Collyer's cottage where the hearty voices of the carolers contributed to a hubbub of chatter that filled the tiny house with festive noise. Threading her way through the press of cold overcoats, Harriet carried a large plate piled with yule loaf and thin slices of cheese, no doubt hoping that many had already had their fill at earlier ports of call. Certainly, the food would be keenly welcomed by other callers, for Christmas Day always brought another kind of visitor to the cottage. These sang with thin, reedy voices, their carols tuneless and half-remembered. The old and infirm, the destitute widow and the orphaned waif called in the sure knowledge that on this day, if on no other, the knock on the door would be met with some food or a coin to sustain them on the threshold of another year of misery and hardship. Each left singing the same old refrain:

"God bless t'maaster of this hoose
An' t'mis-ter-ess also,
An' all yer lahtle bonny bairns
'At round yer table go."[17]

---

[15] The tradition of the Yule log is an ancient one and was probably introduced by Norsemen who burnt oak logs to honour their god Thor. George Collard, ed., *A Yorkshire Christmas.* (Stroud, Gloucester: The History Press, 1989), 91.

[16] The village of Thruscross also provides evidence of the Norse influence in this part of the Dales. The name is probably derived from 'Thor's cross'.

[17] from Richard Blakeborough, *Wit, Character, Folklore and Customs of the North Riding of Yorkshire* (London: Henry Frowde, 1898), 67

Shortly after his eighth birthday, Robert started work in the mill. It would be difficult to devise an environment less suited to human health than that found in a flax-mill. The spinning process started with the breaking and 'heckling' of the raw flax bundles.[18] The bunches of flax were fed between great crushing wheels 'from which it emerges bruised and pliable from the tremendous pressure'. The heckling came next. The bunches were tied to iron rods which were moved into the center of the machine. The steel teeth or heckles, set in a circular frame-work, revolve rapidly, and rend and comb the flax. This was a dusty and unhealthy process and some of the girls chose to wear handkerchiefs over their mouths. There is hardly a moment of inactivity; the flax had to be taken up in locks, screwed into its frame, placed on the heckling machine, taken off, and the supply constantly renewed.[19]

The fibers were then roughly carded (combed) and separated into long and short fibers. The short fibers, the 'tow', were further carded and eventually went into the making of coarse linen used for sacking and the like. Bundles of longer fibers, the 'lines', were put through rollers with the ends of the lines overlapping, then through drawing rollers which produce an endless sliver. The sliver passed through more drawing rollers causing it to lengthen ('doubling and drafting') and then twisted into a 'rove' or loose thread which was wound onto bobbins ready for the spinning frame.

The flax would not spin without being thoroughly wet. On the spinning frames, the roves passed through a trough of hot water at the back of the spindles. The rapidly revolving spindles picked up the wet yarn and threw a constant spray of water over the front of the frame.[20] The machines were placed so close together that the workers were showered back and front and within a short time their aprons and overalls became completely sodden.[21] Added to this, the hot troughs gave off clouds of steam that hung in the still, fetid air, and

[18] The flax entering the mill has already undergone 'retting' in which the outer sheath is partly rotted in water to loosen the inner fibers.

[19] Angus Reach, *The Yorkshire Textile Districts in 1849* (Helmshore, Lancashire: Helmshore Local History Society, 1974), 27

[20] The first efficient flax spinning machine was invented in 1790 by Matthew Murray of Leeds.

[21] from Frederick Engels, *The condition of the working-class in England: From Personal Observation and Authentic Sources* (reprint of 1892 English edition, Moscow: Progress Publishers, 1973): 201; and from William Dodd, *The Factory System Illustrated in a series of letters to the Right Hon. Lord Ashley. Appendix A; Mr Drinkwater's report on flax mills* (London: John Murray, 1842), 239

condensation streamed down the filthy walls. The noise from the heckling room, and the belts, pulleys, cogs and frames in the spinning rooms, was incessant and deafening. The machinery was totally unguarded so that hair and clothing were frequently caught in the gears and pulleys of the frames or on the fierce barbed cylinders of the hecklers. Inevitably fingers and limbs were dragged into the mangling machines, to be followed by amputation, or worse.

In this maelstrom of noise, water, steam and machinery, Robert was employed as a 'doffer', running between the spinning frames removing the full spindles and replacing them with empties. The working day started at 6am and finished at 8pm on five days in the week; on Saturdays they worked two hours less. The workers were given a short break for breakfast at 8am, one hour for dinner from twelve to one o'clock, and a further short break for tea at four o'clock. In total the children worked seventy-six hours a week and for this the youngest (including Robert) received only two shillings per week (equivalent to about £10/$20 in today's values).[22] The mill was closed on Sundays and Christmas Day. However, the workers were not paid for Christmas Day. Holidays were non-existent; in theory they were allowed one full day, two half-days and three quarter-days per year but only the one day was paid leave, the part-days had to be made-up by working in the dinner hour, 'to keep the wages regular'.[23] The up-shot of this was that few took their part-days, most preferring to keep their much-needed breaks.

The doffers were not allowed to sit down at work, a rule enforced by the leather strap of the Overseer. Corporal punishment was frequent and applied for all manner of real and imagined misdemeanors. The children devised a system of look-outs, nods and winks to signal the imminent appearance of the Overseer so that, at least for a short time each day, they could perch on one of their frames and take the weight off aching legs and feet. However, the system of look-outs was far from fool-proof and a beating was the penalty for a warning signal not given or missed. Unfortunately, some of the older girls could see that benefits were gained by showing favor to the Overseers. The girls, some as young as thirteen or fourteen, would take their dinner break with one or other of the Overseers, quietly slipping away together to find privacy in

---

[22] See 'A note on money' in Jerry White, *London in the Nineteenth Century* (London: Jonathan Cape, 2007), xvi.

[23] Details taken from answers to queries addressed by the Commissioners for the North Eastern District to Mill Owners, May 1, 1833. The answers for the West House Factory Company were given by Michael Robinson.

the warehouse.[24] There among the bales, the miserable girls lay with their masters knowing that the strap would not touch a back that had been caressed by an Overseers' hand. However, even favors from the Masters could not alleviate the grinding malevolence of the mill. Deformity and disease knew no favorites.

Chest problems were almost universal. Barking coughs and the hawking of phlegm punctuated the dank air of the spinning rooms. In many instances a persistent cough heralded the onset of 'consumption', and when the first blood-stained spittle appeared, there was an awful inevitability that soon another young life would end in exhaustion and coma.[25] Deformities were also common. By the time the workers were in their mid-teens, most had bow-legs through the strain of continual weight-bearing coupled with malnutrition. Add to this the maiming results of injury, the wasted bodies and the sallow wrinkling of the skin, and all were old before their time. Young women of twenty with bent backs and lined faces looked twice their age.[26]

For Robert, the Factory Act of 1833 came as an act of God.[27] At a stroke of the legislators' pen, the hours that children were permitted to work was cut so

---

[24] It was claimed in the Reports of the Factory Commissioners (1833 and 1842) that the heat and confinement of the mill caused precocious sexual development. Charles R. Fay, *Life and Labour in the Nineteenth Century* (Cambridge: Cambridge University Press, 1943) 179. William Dodd writes in the *The Factory System Illustrated etc.*, 104, "And some (females), instead of having kind paternal masters to guide their wandering steps in the right way, are under those who too often avail themselves of the power they possess over these poor unhappy beings, of the weaker sex, to gratify their own evil and corrupt propensities, and by their conduct and example, spread an immoral contagion around them."

[25] Consumption was the old term for pulmonary tuberculosis. This was one of several respiratory diseases associated with flax mills; see Charles Turner Thackrah, *The Effects of Arts, Trades and Professions and of Civic States and Habits of Living on Health and Longevity: with suggestions for the removal of many of the agents which produce disease and shorten the duration of life* (London: Longman, Rees, etc., 1832), 39

[26] The illnesses and injuries associated with flax spinning are taken from Dodd, *Factory System*, 26.

[27] Between 1819 and 1833 a series of Acts sought to set hours and ages for children employed in textile mills. None of the Acts was effective, but Parliament gradually learned how to create industrial legislation. The major breakthrough came in 1833 when, in the tradition of Tory paternalism, Lord Shaftesbury passed a Factory Act that provided for professional inspectors armed with the power to enter factories, examine

that a child of his age (ten years old) could work a maximum of nine hours per day – fifty-four hours a week. A child had to be thirteen before working the full stint. This gave Robert three years with some precious relief from the slave conditions of the mill, four hours less each weekday and two hours less on Saturdays. Thus, in the summer time there were extra hours for outdoor play - if he had the energy, and if not, four hours of daylight for reading without resort to candle-light. He saved up every penny he could and bought a few more books including Goldsmith's *England* and *The History of Sanford and Merton*, a popular children's book.[28] His mother never remembered a meal in which he did not have a book open on the table, reading while he ate.[29] The books in Robert's small library were read, and re-read. He developed a life-long love of simple English words and was able to achieve great heights as a preacher with little Latin, and still less Greek. Occasionally, his reading was enlivened by a borrowed book brought into the house by his father. In this way the poems of Burns and the plays of Shakespeare first came into his hands.

The reduction in hours ended when Collyer was thirteen, and the prospect of exhaustion, disease and deformity, which he had thus far escaped, became an ever-present threat. Thereafter, his parents became increasingly concerned for his well-being, and after many discussions in their 'kitchen council', they decided that he should leave the mill. The four shillings Robert was now earning was less important to his parents than his health, and they concluded that he should learn a new, and healthier, trade. It was agreed that he should follow in his step-brother's footsteps and join William at Jacky Birch's smithy in Ilkley, six miles away in Wharfedale. Jacky, the former master blacksmith at West House had moved to Ilkley several years before, and when Samuel Collyer asked him to take on Robert as another apprentice, he readily agreed "for old time's sake, an' wi' nae footing to pay". The 'footing' was money claimed by a master from a new apprentice when he commenced the apprenticeship. In this way, young Robert Collyer came to leave the family home. It was August 1838, and he was just fourteen years old.

---

the premises, and assess fines. Sally Mitchell, ed., *Victorian Britain: an Encyclopedia* (London: St. James Press, 1988), 282

[28] Thomas Day's book '*The History of Sanford and Merton*' was a popular book with both American and British children throughout the 19th century and passed through several editions. It was originally published in three volumes in 1783, 1786 and 1789.

[29] Conway, *Harper's Magazine* (May 1874): 826.

4 : The Ilkley smithy

The day for Robert's departure from West House arrived. His father had arranged that Robert's brother, William, would be home for the weekend and that the two of them should walk over to Ilkley on the Sunday afternoon. The family ate Sunday dinner in an atmosphere of strained jollity. His younger brothers and sisters teased Robert; the parents said that this was a great opportunity and the best thing for him; and William made reassuring remarks about the smithy and the Birch household. But, with the meal over and the two sons ready for their walk over the moors, the emotion overflowed, and his sisters and mother sobbed their farewells. Meanwhile, the brothers John and Thomas, viewed it all as a great adventure and carried on with their banter. Samuel decided to walk part of the way with them, so the three set off. Robert turned at the end of the row of cottages to look once more at his mother. She stood in the doorway, his sisters huddled against her skirts and the brothers standing a little way apart. They waved, and with a forlorn wave back, Robert turned and walked, with head bowed, out of the village.

The three did not talk for some time. They strode out across Blubberhouses Bridge and turned up the Otley Road. Up the long drag of Shepherd Hill they came alongside each other and Samuel put his arm around Robert's shoulders. He repeated the much-rehearsed arguments of why they had decided Robert should leave the mill, how the smithy offered employment for life and how he was to benefit from living in a place like Ilkley. The father told him, not altogether convincingly, that they would be able to see each other quite often, emphasizing that Ilkley was only six miles away, but Robert already knew that

William's visits were infrequent. They walked on, turned right at Timble Lane End cross-roads, along the lane past Sourby Farm and out onto the moor beyond. At the high-point of Ellarcarr Pike, Samuel gave Robert a last, long hug. He shook William's hand and said his goodbyes, his voice breaking with emotion. Quickly turning his back on the boys, Samuel strode off downhill, back to the Washburn valley.

Thereafter Robert found the going easier. There was a good path, the `Catholic Gate', heading almost due west across Denton Moor. For centuries the path had been the main link between the outlying villages of Washburndale and the Catholic chapel at Middleton Lodge above Ilkley.[1] On special feast days in pre-Reformation days, it was the scene of a general pilgrimage of Dalesfolk making their way to Mass. The path crossed a long tree-less stretch of heather and peat bogs flecked with wind-tossed cotton grass. They followed it for some miles. To their left and ahead, the view opened out and Wharfedale beckoned them on. The valley was a mosaic of green pastures and darker woodland and towering above, on the far side, the rocky outcrops and heather of Ilkley Moor, brown and purple in the afternoon sunlight. Robert felt a quickening of the pulse as he anticipated his new beginnings. They walked on, now losing height, and came off the open moor down into a gully, 'Fairy Dell', which led to a series of field-paths. Going past Moor Houses Farm, they took the lane down Hunger Hill, then cut through the woods, and went over Ilkley Bridge.

Although Ilkley was only a village in 1838, it was certainly a large affair as far as young Robert was concerned.[2] The number of houses, the shops, the inns, and the people strolling around in their 'Sunday best', seemed like a new world. Nevertheless, it was the horses that impressed him most. West House had its working horses at the mill, and those that pulled the owner's barouche, but here were horses aplenty. A coach and four had just pulled up outside the Rose and Crown hotel, the terminus for the coach service from Leeds, and a line of wagonettes and drags waited close by to take the passengers to their final

---

[1] Alfred J. Brown, *Broad Acres: A Yorkshire miscellany* (London: Country Life Ltd, 1948), 47. Over the long period of Catholic suppression in England (1558-1829), Myddelton Lodge was the only place where Catholic Mass was celebrated in Mid-Wharfedale and Nidderdale.

[2] Although of great antiquity — it was originally the site of a Roman fort, Ilkley remained small. In the 1841 census there were only 778 inhabitants. The population grew markedly during the Victorian era thanks to Ilkley's reputation as an inland spa and a desirable place to live, and by 1901 had reached 7455.

destinations .[3] Several horses were tied to a rail by the side of the Wheatsheaf Inn, while yet more made their way up and down Brook Street; some old and tired pulling humble dog-carts, while handsome thoroughbreds strutted in front of elegant broughams.[4] Robert could see lots of work for a good farrier.

They walked into Eastgate, the entrance to Otley Road. William stopped, and pointed to a low building ahead and on the left. "That", he indicated, "is the smithy." Robert did not respond but he felt disappointed. The building itself was dilapidated. Outside lay a collection of old wheel hoops, troughs filled with oily water, an old anvil, a grindstone, broken ploughs and other farm implements. It being Sunday, the smithy doors were closed. William took Robert round the side of the smithy to Birch's house at the back. William knocked to announce their arrival, and a plump, smiling woman came to the door. Mrs Birch greeted Robert with a warm embrace (she had been brought up in West House and knew the Collyer family well) and her welcome continued as they entered the house .[5] Rising from an afternoon nap in his fireside chair, Jacky Birch swayed towards Robert and extended his right hand. He attempted some words of welcome, but very few emerged, and he soon slumped back into his chair. Mrs. Birch told Robert "not to mind 'im, 'e's fuzzled" (the worse for drink), and asked William to take Robert up to their bedroom. He led him into a dark, low-ceilinged room at the back of the house. It was sparsely furnished with two narrow beds, a battered chest of drawers and a washstand with a plain, cream-colored bowl and a cracked mirror. Robert unpacked his few possessions, a couple of 'best' shirts, some well-worn underclothes, three pairs of heavy woolen socks, a colored kerchief and four of his treasured books [6].

---

[3] The Leeds coach at this time was the 'British Queen' (1835-1841) which ran from the Rose and Crown, Leeds, to the Inn of the same name in Ilkley. Tom Bradley, *The Old Coaching Days in Yorkshire* (Otley, Yorkshire: Smith Settle, 1988), 212.

[4] Arguably Ilkley's oldest inn, the Wheatsheaf takes its name from one of the badges of the Middelton family, Lords of the Manor of Middleton and Stubham, and subsequently of Ilkley.

[5] Robert Collyer was almost 'family'; not only did his father work with Jacky Birch at West House mill, but Birch married Frances (Franky) Robinson, daughter of Thomas Robinson, the blacksmith at the toll-bar down Otley Hill, and sister of Michael, manager of the factory. 'News from Dr. Collyer', *Wharfedale and Airedale Observer,* April 30, 1909.

[6] Weekday shirts were provided as part of the apprenticeship contract. Collyer was 'bound' to the smithy until he was twenty one, and for his part, Birch agreed to give training, house-room and food, shirts and leather aprons.

Later there was supper around the kitchen table when Robert met Sam and William, two lodgers who shared the next room, and Mary, the household servant[7]. They lingered around the table after the meal exchanging stories over tankards of ale. Robert went to bed earlier than the others but only slept fitfully. The weeping faces of his mother and sisters interrupted his sleep, and he heard again the faltering farewells of his father.

William rose early and Robert was unusually ready to leave his bed. A wash in cold water cleared the last vestiges of sleep from their faces. Bowls of hot, salty porridge greeted them downstairs, and then it was work. The first job each day was to light the fire in the forge. The cinders and clinker were cleared from the two fire-pots in the elevated hearth and thrown into the ash-pit.[8] On most mornings, a few hot embers could be stirred into life with the bellows, but on Monday mornings the fire was completely cold, and had to be re-started with paper, kindling and coal. Three tools were essential to maintaining the fire, a pointed poker to clear the air passages from the bellows nozzle underneath, a small rake to pull coal from the margins into the fire, and a watering can with a sprinkler to dampen the fire around its edges. William set about familiarizing Robert with the other tools of the trade, innumerable pairs of tongs for handling hot metal, each with its special characteristics, and pliers and pincers for holding cold work. There were various hammers, ranging from one to sixteen pounds in weight, with rounded or flattened heads suited to different jobs, and punches of varying diameter with which holes could be 'drifted' through the metal prior to riveting. He told Robert never to hit the anvil directly with a hammer; it was liable to bounce straight back and hit him. William was full of such good advice and seemed to enjoy having a new pupil. Master Birch, on the other hand, was a skilled worker but a reluctant teacher. His main aim in life was to get through the work as fast as possible so as to maximize the time available for supping ale. Thus, if necessary, Jacky Birch could shoe all four feet on up to ten horses in a day, but impart little of the farriers' craft to Robert, save that which he could see for himself. Robert's job consisted of working the bellows, leading and holding horses, fetching and

---

[7] It appears that the house had room for two apprentices and a couple of lodgers. In the 1841 census the occupants are listed as John and Frances Birch, William Wells, Robert Collyer, Mary Dolphin (Female servant), Samuel Jagger (Cloth weaver) and William Tipling (Wood turner).

[8] The hearth was about 5 feet square — large enough to take a hoop for a wheel, but generally the fire was kept much smaller than this.

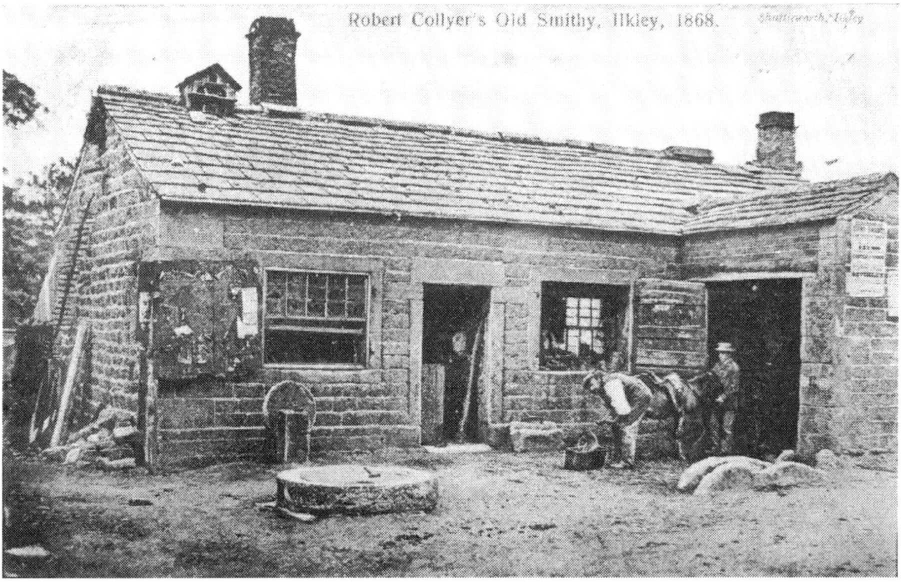

A picture postcard showing 'Robert Collyer's Old Smithy, Ilkley, 1868'. He had departed for America 18 years before. The card was published in Ilkley in 1906 by which time Collyer had become a local celebrity, and the smithy long since demolished.

carrying shoes and nails, and serving as the butt for Birch's complaints and invective. Even handling the horses was a trial for a lad conditioned to factory work. When Master Birch was good and ready, Robert had to lead the correct horse either from the smithy's own rail, or from that outside the Wheatsheaf or the stables at the Rose and Crown so that it could be shod while the owner enjoyed refreshment inside. At other times, helpful owners like John Ellis from Holling Hall, stayed with their horses and helped to steady them. Needless to say, they were not always steady. It seemed to Robert that the last horse of the day was often the most fractious. Usually calm words and reassuring stroking of their neck and flanks calmed them down but as a last resort, a cart-rope was placed round the horse's neck fastened at each side and around the fetlocks of the back legs. William and Robert (or the owner) would have to pull at either side, drawing in the fetlocks so that the animal came down, whereupon Jacky would set about the shoeing.[9] Meanwhile, the waiting farmers exchanged

[9] Details from Marie Hartley and Joan Ingilby, *Life and Tradition in the Yorkshire Dales* (London: J. M. Dent & Sons Ltd, 1968), 85.

gossip, talk of the weather or prices at the auction. Most farmers wore the traditional knee-length linen smocks with large flat collars, a neck scarf and a wide-brimmed hat, and their trousers (only visible when they reached for their pockets) were tucked into long side-fastening leather boots. By contrast, the men at the smithy wore the shirts, waistcoats and trousers favored by industrial workers.

Those first few months were a torment for Robert. He considered himself of little use in the forge, was unknown to anyone outside it, and he was desperately homesick. It was a period that presaged Collyer's life-long emotional difficulties. The pain of separation from 'home' was to become a leitmotif through his life in America, and the episode provides the first indication of his vulnerability to depression.

The one person who could relieve Robert's feelings of melancholy was Mary, the servant girl. Although only 12 years older than Robert she was able to exert a steadying and supportive influence on him. She talked, comforted and, in private moments, she enclosed him in a warm, affectionate embrace that was totally innocent and devoid of sensuality. Thanks to her attentions, the gloom gradually lifted. Robert found himself increasingly in tune with the rhythms of work and the household. He began to enjoy the meals; they were substantial and wholesome, and there was usually a babble of conversation around the table. Home-brewed ale washed down the food, quenched the thirst of the forge, and loosened the more reticent tongues. There was rarely enough, however, to quench Master Birch's thirst. After supper, he usually adjourned to the Wheatsheaf Inn where the ale, and the dubious charms of the barmaid Nancy Wharton, held equal attraction. Jacky Birch and his cronies gathered there most evenings, holding forth in their `Pint-Pot Parliament', until the debate degenerated into inebriated ramblings, and the landlord, Tom Barnes, suggested that they should all go home.

After a few months at the smithy, Robert became more confident in the various tasks he had to undertake - not that some of them required much experience. One of his principal jobs was to operate the bellows, a task that was tiring on the arm but tedious on the brain. He decided to mix work with pleasure and began to read books in the forge. Robert could be seen standing by the hearth, bellows handle in his right hand, book in his left, completely oblivious to the showers of sparks that occasionally flew around him. He spent most evenings reading by the light of a tallow candle in his room, and even took to reading at mealtimes. On a fine Sunday afternoon (after morning service at the Parish Church), he would take a book for company on solitary walks on the hills surrounding the village. Ilkley Moor was a magnet for Robert, constantly drawing him to its heather-clad slopes.

Young Collyer reading while working the bellows. An engraving by C.S. Reinhart. Harpers New Monthly Magazine, May 1874.

Robert would cross the footbridge over the village stream as it passed in front of the smithy on its way to join the Wharfe, and walk alongside it up Brook Street. On his right, the stream flowed in a gully whose banks were clothed in yellow meadow rue, lady's smock and ragged robin. On the far bank lay the carriageway and, beyond that, a jumbled row of heather-thatched cottages. At its head, the street opened out; more old thatches lay ahead and to the left, while along to the right ran Green Lane (later called The Grove). The path skirted around the lower of two ancient corn-mills and headed up by a tumbling stream, passing the white-wash of Mrs. Downes's house and the upper mill, to join Wells Road above the mill-dam. Higher up, Robert would leave Wells Road and take a steep path upwards towards White Wells, the old bath-house, and the source of Ilkley's reputation as a watering-place or 'spaw'.[10]

Robert usually headed for the wooded knoll just above White Wells, sat on the raised plank of wood that served as a bench, and briefly surveyed the majesty of Wharfedale laid out below. Soon, however, he would become completely absorbed in his book.[11] The words he read and re-read became so familiar to him that they began to enter his vocabulary. On occasions, the newly acquired words were so out of tune with the broad dialect of his upbringing that they produced a wry smile or even a rebuke from those seated around Master Birch's table.

The trials of Robert's first year in Ilkley were relieved by an occasional visit home. The visits were necessarily brief as the round trip had to be completed on a Sunday, his only non-working day. Unfortunately, in the summer of 1839 Samuel Collyer decided to leave West House mill. He could see that its future was problematic and thought that he should get out before it closed down[12]. He moved with the family to Leeds and soon afterwards secured employment in a machine works.[13] However, the new family home in Beeston, Leeds, was twenty miles from Ilkley, too far to walk there and back in a day, and too expensive a journey by coach. The visits to his family could only take place at

---

[10] The word 'spa', rendered in Yorkshire dialect as 'spaw', derives from the health resort of Spa in the Belgian Ardennes and came to be applied to any mineral-containing natural spring whose water was drunk for its 'health-giving' properties. As far as the water at White Wells was concerned this was a misnomer for it contained no dissolved minerals on which to base its medical usefulness.

[11] Collyer tells us that; "On a day I can still recall, a still November day, when a mist lay on the holmes (riverside meadows) and the yellow sunshine touched the crags on the moor, Cooper came to me with 'The Last of the Mohicans', and almost persuaded me to become an Indian. I was later led to read Scott's Waverley novels by a religious book that denounced them as immoral". Holmes, *Life and Letters,* 1: 71.

[12] This gloomy prognosis was correct as far as flax production was concerned, the flax mill closing in 1844.

[13] Peter Fairbairn and Company in Wellington Street, Leeds

holiday times, Christmas and Easter, and Robert felt increasingly isolated. He became even more absorbed in his books, at least they offered escape and adventure for his vivid imagination. There was one Christmas when he could not go home, "for some forgotten reason, and found solace in a borrowed copy of Washington Irving's Sketch Book."[14] Robert saved the few pennies he earned through 'tips' and the like, and bought cheap-editions or second-hand books; but still he could not keep pace with his voracious appetite for reading. To re-read books was worthwhile, but frustrating, for he constantly strove to broaden his knowledge and his appreciation of literature. This frustration ended when he was befriended by John Dobson. Dobson was an enigmatic character; a second-generation wool-comber with a passion for 'Scotch metaphysics' and a large collection of books. Although ten years older than Robert he became a close companion and, in time, a 'friend that sticketh closer than a brother.' Collyer was to write later, "(he) was beyond all comparison the best-read man and of the finest culture among the native men of the town. John Dobson — let me write his name *for loves sake* — was my whole college of professors. There was no library where we could borrow books, so *he* must buy them out of his scant wages; for I had no money. This he would gladly do, bringing them to me with shining eyes."[15] Dobson encouraged Robert to join his Young Men's Reading Group, which he did. However, the group consisted of only two others at that time; John Hobson — a schoolmaster who was in his thirties[16], and Ben Whitley — a 'mechanic' (and odd-job man) in his forties. A few years later they

---

[14] Washington Irving's *Sketchbook,* published in 1820 under the pen-name of Geoffrey Crayon, was hugely popular both in England and the United States and contained the tale of 'Rip van Winkle' and the 'Legend of Sleepy Hollow', stories set in New York during the time of Dutch control.

[15] Collyer, *Some Memories,* 25. Collyer's relationship with Dobson is open to differing interpretation. Dobson was a life-long bachelor who enjoyed the company of younger men. Perhaps words written by Collyer about his visit to Yorkshire in 1865 are enlightening, "Presently I must go to Ilkley and there for the first time in my manhood I kissed a man, my dear old friend John Dobson, who had done more for me in loving care and counsel, ... than any or perhaps all the men I had known through those years so momentous to a youth." Collyer, *Some Memories,* 170.

[16] "They read aloud, and in turns. Any holiday they had was passed in the fields, reading, and the parson got only the dismal Sundays, the bright ones being passed in a larger temple. I can hear now one of us saying, "Now, Bob, thee tak' a turn". John Dobson quoted in Moncure D. Conway, *Ilkley* (Harpers New Monthly Magazine, May 1874), 824.

were joined by Thomas Smith, a horse lad at Low Austby farm, destined to become the schoolmaster at Bradley, a village near Keighley.

John Dobson at his books. From Collyer and Turner, 'Ilkley Ancient and Modern'

The group warmly welcomed the much younger Robert, and the four met frequently to read books together.[17] "When he first came to Ilkley", remembered Dobson, "he was about thirteen years of age. As he grew, I very soon perceived that he was an unusually clever boy, and used to follow him about, though I was older. He didn't talk so very much, nor did I ever notice so much his humor and love of fun; he was grave and sober. When he got older I used to notice that he had a remarkable way of saying things. If there was anything much talked about in the village — any controversy between Catholic and Protestants — he used to put the whole thing in a few words. He saw through and through it in a moment. And sometimes ... I remember thinking that I didn't know where it would end. He seemed to me rather too big for this place."[18]

---

[17] Report of an interview with John Dobson in Conway, *Ilkley*, 824.

[18] Some indication of the depth of Collyer's interest in literary criticism is given in two letters written to John Dobson when the latter was on one of his tours of Scotland

The reading group was not the sum of Robert's circle of friends. He became friendly with Christopher Hudson, who shared Robert's literary interests, but he also enjoyed a drink with the laborers he knew from the forge.[19] He met the horse-lads from Low Austby and two of the farm-hands from Holling Hall in the Wheatsheaf, and Ned Hudson at The Fleece Inn in Addingham . Collyer also makes mention of Mary Ann Smith 'who lived across from the forge' among his Ilkley friends, but there is no indication of a romantic attachment. Without doubt the firmest friend during the early years in Ilkley was his half-brother, William, a companion who all too soon was taken from him.

Towards the end of 1841 it became apparent that William was becoming progressively more breathless and more easily tired when working in the forge. He had been coughing blood for some time but had not admitted this either to Robert or his parents. He took a tonic mixture containing iron, arsenic and quinine, and cod-liver oil that he purchased from the local apothecary, John Showsmith, but with no effect. Christmas at home in Leeds was a dismal affair. William had lost weight and was obviously a sick man. His parents had seen too many mill-workers with consumption not to recognize the disease now afflicting their son. Reluctantly they saw him return to Ilkley. Master Birch put him on lighter duties, and Mrs Birch tried to build him up with nourishing meat broths and arrowroot, but it was to no avail. Over the next few months, William steadily deteriorated. By April all hope of recovery was lost, and he gradually slipped into a coma, oblivious to the concern of those around him. He died on May 29, 1842, his fatal tuberculosis a macabre legacy from West House Mill. William Wells was buried in an unmarked grave on the north side of All Saints parish church in Ilkley.[20]

At the smithy, the gap left by William's untimely death was filled by another apprentice, John Williams, and Robert found himself sharing the farriers' craft

---

and reproduced in Moncure Conway's brief biography (Conway, *Ilkley,* 827). "In the earliest letters, which are dated from Ilkley in 1845 there is evidence of a very careful reading of the reviews, chiefly the *Edinburgh* and the *North British.*"

[19] The horse-lads were Thomas Smith, and Robert Metcalfe, while John and William Hardisty worked at Hollin Hall Farm. *Wharfedale and Airedale Observer,* Sept 16, 1910.

[20] In 1833 a special minute is entered in the parish accounts ordering the sexton to use his best endeavors to persuade the relatives of deceased persons to bury the corpse on the north side of the church. There was a long-standing prejudice throughout Yorkshire against using this part of a graveyard, but it appears to have persisted longer in Ilkley than elsewhere. William Wells, aged 23, was buried on June 2, 1842. The officiating minister was Rev John Hutchinson, in *Ilkley Parish Church Burial Register.*

with the novice. They spent most of the day working together and Robert began to enjoy John's company. The feeling was obviously a mutual one, because within a few weeks of his arrival at the Ilkley smithy, John had invited Robert home to visit his mother. John's home was close to Bolton Bridge, about five miles upriver from Ilkley. Hannah Williams lived in a cottage nestling against the western end of the bridge that carried the Harrogate-Skipton turnpike over the Wharfe. Robert was made very welcome, and he was to repeat the Sunday excursion on many subsequent occasions. Not only did he appreciate the warmth of their hospitality, but the cottage itself, built in the sixteenth century and called 'Ferryhouse', fascinated him. The house had originally been a priory chapel belonging to the Bolton estate and, before the building of the bridge, people would gather there to await the ferry crossing, no doubt offering up a prayer for their safe passage. Indeed, the traveler was reminded to do just that by an inscription on one of the wooden cross-beams opposite the entrance, "Thou that passes by this way: one ave maria here you say".[21]

During his late teens, a combination of Mrs. Birch's nourishment and Mr. Birch's heavy demands had conspired with nature to change Robert from a puny factory-hand into a strapping, muscular farrier.[22] One old man, a regular visitor to the smithy, came in to warm his hands and was moved to remark, "How thou dost grow to be sewer (sure); if thaa doesn't stop soin (soon) we shall hey to put a stiddy (anvil) on thee heead."[23] Robert had also learnt most of the skills of the farrier and blacksmith. He became adept at making horseshoes. Starting with a red-hot iron bar, he beat it flat on the surface of the anvil, re-heated it and hammered it into a curve around the anvil's 'pike-end'. He then pierced it with a punch, hammering a series of holes that would take the nails. Holding the work in his tongs he then plunged the hot iron into the water trough to 'slake' it and then lifted it onto a hook on the wall with other shoes. Most shoes were made ahead of time and hung in groups, according to size. Final shaping, to fit the shoe accurately onto the hoof, was carried out at the time of shoeing. Robert would put on a split leather apron that allowed him

---

[21] After Samuel Collyer's death, Robert Collyer introduced his mother to Hannah Williams and they too became good friends. She continued to visit Ferryhouse after Robert's emigration. (see William Smith ed., 'Robert Collyer, the poet preacher' in *Old Yorkshire* (London: Longmans, Green & Co., 1881), 239. The house, at the western end of the old Bolton Bridge, still stands today.

[22] "Master Birch kept a good table.... The food was simple and rough, but it was wholesome, plentiful and had some variety." Holmes, *Life and Letters,* 1: 61.

[23] Holmes, *Life and Letters,* 1: 62.

to stand astride the horse's fetlock, which was then jammed between his knees. After removing the old shoe, the hoof was rasped and trimmed with a paring knife and the 'made to measure' shoe held in place while the nails were partly hammered in. Robert was careful to point the nails outwards and upwards to avoid the sensitive part of the hoof. The shoeing hammer had a claw-end that he would use to 'clinch' (bend over) the protruding heads of the nails to hold the shoe firmly in place.[24]

Robert became equally adept at hooping a wheel, although this was always a two-man job and Master Birch usually took the lead. The cartwrights would bring the wooden wheels to the smithy to have the iron 'tires' fitted and on a busy day four to six wheels could be hooped.[25] Any more than six would be, according to Master Birch, 'a killer' of a day.

After one such hectic day, Birch and the apprentices went straight from work to the Wheatsheaf Inn where the Master bought a large jug of ale for all to share. The group were sitting around the table under the tap-room window when the barmaid, Nancy, came across to introduce a gentleman, a Mr. Hamer Stansfeld of Headingley, Leeds. He told them that he was responsible for building the Hydropathic Hotel that was taking shape on land above the neighboring hamlet of Wheatley. He was looking for 'a good and ancient name' for the building.[26] Stansfeld particularly wished to know the name of the upland field on which the Hydro stood, but none of the group could help. It was Nancy who chipped into the discussion with 'Bean Ridding', a name she'd heard her father use when he worked on the Bolling brother's farm in Wheatley. Some weeks later it emerged that Stansfeld and his partners had actually adopted this name but felt that some adjustment of the spelling to 'Ben Rhydding' gave it a more romantic tone.[27]

---

24 Details from Marie Hartley and Joan Ingilby, *Making Ironwork* (Skipton, Yorkshire: Dalesman Publishing Ltd.,1997).

25 Ilkley had two cartwrights at this time, Bill Fozzard had a shop in Eastgate just along from the smithy, and there was a second at the top of Brook Street.

26 Wheatley was a hamlet situated a mile to the east of Ilkley. Following the building of a railway station to serve Ben Rhydding Hydro, the village grew and the name Wheatley gradually gave way to the name Ben Rhydding.

27 The origin of the name as 'Bean Ridding' is disputed but, in a letter to *Notes and Queries* (February 9, 1867; vol XI; p 114), a 'C.H.' of Leeds writes, 'I happened one day to be in conversation with one of the most active of the founders.....We wanted, of course, some name; and looking into our deeds, we found that the field on which we had erected our establishment was conveyed to us as the Bean Ridding; and we just struck

The jugs of ale quickly washed away the toil of the day. The apprentices left for their supper, but Master Birch would not be dislodged; he preferred to stay on and drink with his cronies, a preference that would lead to his downfall.

out the *a* in the first word, and metamorphosed the second by changing *i* into *hy,* and so we made Ben Rhydding.' Ben Rhydding was the first and best-known of the Ilkley Hydropathic Hotels; building commenced in 1843 and the hotel opened in 1844. The subject is extensively reviewed in Mike Dixon, *Ilkley — History and Guide* (Stroud, Gloucester: The History Press, 2002), 77-99.

5: More deaths

Early in July 1844, Robert received a letter from his sister Maria in Leeds. The letter explained that his father Samuel had died suddenly while at work. The news came as a complete shock to Robert. He carried the image of his father as the strong and healthy provider for the family. Now he was dead of a heart attack at the age of forty-seven. Robert joined the grieving family in Leeds - his mother, sisters and brothers, as they laid his body to rest in St. Peter's churchyard.

Although Robert often neglected church in favor of a meeting with his book-reading friends or a visit to Hannah William's cottage at Bolton Bridge, the death of his father prompted more regular attendance. Sometimes it seemed as though the old stone walls themselves spoke to him more eloquently than the preacher, but he rarely failed to gain some comfort from his visits.

Robert had finished his apprenticeship with Jacky Birch on his twenty-first birthday in December 1844 and became an independent craftsman. He continued, however, to help Birch on the bigger jobs. One such job was the installation of a new heater in the parish church. The occasion was remembered by Collyer as one that demonstrated Birch's dislike of hard work, and his craftiness. 'Jacky spied the Parson coming, and said, "Noo, than, let's all be liftin an' grainin (groaning) as 'e comes in, an' than we can happen git summat oot on him ta drink".[1] Jacky Birch, however, was shortly to be judged by a higher authority than the vicar.

It was June 2, 1846. The day started much as usual. Edward Dobson, the junior apprentice, arrived at 6.30am to get the fire going before the others arrived at 7am. Jacky Birch was the last to arrive. He appeared to be his usual self, grumbling about the work and grunting out the order of jobs for the morning. He wearily set about his first task. He began to lift a heavy cartwheel on to the stone tyring-platform – a job usually requiring the combined efforts of two of the apprentices – but as he took the full weight, he let out a stifled shout and sank to the ground. He landed heavily on his knees and slumped forward so that he lay face-down in the dirt of the smithy yard. Robert and John Williams rushed to him and, grabbing him under the armpits, dragged his limp body into the smithy. Meanwhile, Edward ran through to the house to fetch Mrs Birch. By the time she arrived, her husband had blood pouring out of his mouth. His chest heaved convulsively, and more blood flowed from his mouth down his shirt and apron. His breathing became irregular. He coughed as each indrawing of breath met the blood pooling in his throat. His breathing stopped abruptly. His face turned a dusky blue and his head slumped forward, and a last gush of blood flowed from his sagging mouth. Mrs. Birch began wailing; an inconsolable outpouring of horror and grief that was to continue for much of the day.

Birch was buried in All Saints churchyard on June 8. He was fifty-eight years old. The small group of relatives and friends who had earlier listened to the old Vicar's words, re-assembled in the Wheatsheaf Hotel next door. There they toasted the name of Jacky Birch, and commiserated with his poor widow who, nevertheless, had to pay for their hospitality - money she could ill afford.

Over the next few weeks, Robert learnt some important lessons. Jacky Birch had indicated that if anything happened to him he wanted Robert to take over as manager of the smithy. However, the owner, William Middleton, Lord of the Manor, had other ideas. He considered Robert too young for this position and appointed his own blacksmith, Samson Speight, as Birch's successor.[2] Before long, however, Speight discovered Robert's worth and acknowledged him as his 'right-hand man'. He offered Robert 18 shillings a week and made him manager in all but name. Robert ran the smithy on Speight's behalf and

[1] Moncure D. Conway, *Ilkley* (New York, Harpers New Monthly Magazine, May 1874), 824.

[2] The name is variously spelt Samson or Sampson in different sources.

ran it so well that he was soon given a further two shillings a week pay rise. Robert was well pleased with his promotion. Over these same weeks, however, the fate of Mrs Birch caused him some distress.

The Wheat Sheaf Hotel was next door to Ilkley Parish Church (All Saints) and was much used for funeral teas. It was demolished in 1959. The chimney of the town's original gasworks is seen on the right. From a lantern-slide, courtesy of Alex Cockshott.

Like many working men, Jacky Birch had lived from hand-to-mouth. Although as a skilled worker he had received a good income, his only investments lay in the pockets of the Ilkley publicans. His drinking had not only killed him, but it had rendered his widow a pauper. She had to leave the tied house at the smithy and would have faced the Workhouse but for the charity of her sister and husband with whom she took up residence. [3]. Robert

[3] In this account Birch died from a massive hemorrhage (hematemesis) from ruptured varicose veins in his gullet (esophageal varices) consequent upon alcoholic

resolved always to set aside 'something for a rainy day'. Many rainy days lay ahead but for the present there was only sunshine, and books.

Through his friendship with the Parratt brothers, Joe and Ben, Robert became acquainted with a retired gentleman who lodged at their house in Church Street. The man's sight was affected by cataracts and his reading days were over. When he learnt of Robert's love of books, the old man offered him 1s 6d a week to sit, read and talk with him after the day's work in the smithy or at the weekend. In a letter to John Dobson, who was away on one of his 'explorations' of Scotland, Robert wrote, "I read him (the old gentleman) the essay on ecclesiastical miracles, and the first half of Carlyle, and he was famously pleased with them both. He was better able to appreciate the first, perhaps, than me, for he has travelled through Italy and France in company with the revivalist Caughey. He has been engaged this morning giving me from memory specimens of Caughey's sermons and conversations". Dobson had apparently sent down from Scotland an article on Australia for Robert to read. Collyer writes, "It is a noble exposure of the wrongs and oppressions of those sons of the soil, and a clever defence of their right to the land which gave them birth. Poor degraded children of the wilds! The time will come, but not, perhaps, till your race has passed away from the earth, when Britain will blush to read, and wish it was blotted out from the page of history, that fire-water and the musket were made to do the work of civilization for the aborigines of her colonies, and that state-trickery and chicane should interfere to hurt the interests of men over whom they have no right but that of might."[4] Such was the correspondence between a simple blacksmith and an itinerant wool comber!

---

cirrhosis of the liver. This corresponds to Collyer's brief account of his death; "I attended to him; and then one morning as I was lifting him, great gouts of blood came jetting out of his chest, and in a few moments he was dead." (John Haynes Holmes, *The Life and Letters of Robert Collyer* (New York, Dodd, Mead and Co., 1: 79)

[4] written on 22 February1846 (a Sunday) and reproduced in Conway, *Ilkley*, 827.

6: Marriage and Methodism

In May 1846, Robert was attending morning service at the Parish Church when he noticed a young woman who was new to the church. She was sitting with Mrs Parratt in the pew directly across the center aisle from his seat. She wore a pretty straw bonnet and a tight-fitting brocade dress. He fixed her with a steady gaze and willed her to take her eyes off the preacher and look in his direction. Some minutes passed before her eyes started to wander. She first looked at the pews ahead of Robert and worked her way back through the rows until she had turned full-face towards him. Robert was so fixed upon her, it was inevitable that their eyes should meet. In that moment, she looked down towards her lap, but immediately returned to confront Robert's stare. Robert detected a look of assurance and he felt a perceptible impulse that produced a shiver of excitement. Her eyes moved back to focus on the preacher, and he followed suit, but the feeling stayed with him.

At the end of the service, Robert approached Mrs Parratt eager for an introduction to her companion. She proved to be her younger sister, Harriet Watson, whose family home was in Bingley but who now lived with the Parratts in Church Street. She made and sold straw-bonnets. After an exchange of pleasantries, Robert expressed the hope that she would be at church next Sunday and that, perhaps, they could go for a short walk after the service. Harriet smiled and nodded in acknowledgement.

Although Harriet Watson was by no means the first young woman to stir his emotions, Robert found himself counting the hours up to the next Sunday morning. There had been several girls with whom he had kept company, but in each case these romances lasted only a short time. The previous year during the May Day celebrations, he had met Alice Bolton, a niece of the well-known

Ilkley family, the Beanlands, and developed 'an intense attachment', only for it to prove another short-lived affair. Certainly, he had never felt such an overwhelming attraction as Harriet Watson now held for him.

The next Sunday's church service seemed interminable as Robert nervously awaited the rendezvous. Outside the entrance, Robert paid his respects to both Mrs Parratt and Harriet, and escorted them along Church Street. Then bidding farewell to the older sister, he sauntered on with Harriet into Bridge Lane. Robert found her conversation playful and humorous. They lingered at the bridge and spent some moments gazing into the fast-flowing waters of the Wharfe. He felt completely at ease as they exchanged stories and discovered mutual friends and interests. They strolled back to the Parratts' cottage, and parted with a promise to go for a longer walk the next Sunday.

So it was that after a few more summer Sundays, the twenty-one years old Harriet and twenty-three years old Robert considered themselves a courting couple, they were 'going out'. Before long they were also going in! The weather was poor, especially it seemed on Sunday evenings, their preferred time for meeting, and when faced with another wet walk, Robert invited Harriet round to the smithy-house. By using the back steps that gave access to the upper story, they could enter the house and reach his room undetected. This tryst became the regular pattern of their Sunday meetings.

Thus, the summer Sundays passed, with an exchange of knowing glances across the pews at the morning service, and the evenings spent at the smithy house[1]. The outcome was predictable; by November, Harriet knew she was pregnant. They waited to see if she would 'hold on to it', but by March her pregnant state had become clear to see, certainly to Robert. Loose dresses were the general fashion, and these hid her condition for some time longer, but the couple decided it was high time they got married. Harriet informed her parents of her pregnancy and her intention to marry the father. Accordingly, Robert was summoned over to Bingley to meet Mr. and Mrs. Watson, and the wedding arrangements were made. Harriet and Robert married on May 25th, 1847 at

---

[1] Collyer does not, of course, give intimate details of his courtship. On the contrary, he reports that "We were both busy week-days, and so we took Sunday evenings. I counted thirteen Sundays in succession on which it rained, and we had to court under an umbrella." (Holmes, *Life and Letters*, 1:76). Understandably, there is no explanation of how Harriet came to be seven months pregnant at the time of the marriage if all their courting was conducted under an umbrella. The present account offers a plausible version.

Bingley Parish Church in the presence of a few family members and two of Robert's close friends, Thomas Stevenson and John Walker. After the wedding, Harriet stayed with her parents. The child, a boy whom they called Samuel, was born at Ann Street, Bingley, on July 13.[2]

After Harriet's confinement, she and Robert moved back to Ilkley, into a small cottage on the north side of Church Street. Young Samuel grew apace, Harriet resumed her bonnet-making and Robert supervised the working of the smithy — their married life was happy and harmonious. Autumn moved into winter and the days were filled with a contented round of housework and smithy-work, childcare and chores, while the evenings were times for fireside talk, hopes and plans.

When the weather (and funds) allowed, Grandma Collyer would pay an occasional visit. She travelled from Leeds by coach and stayed for two or three days to be with her first, and much loved, grandchild. Months passed, and Wharfedale became vibrant with the noises and colors of Spring. In June, Harriet told Robert that she was pregnant again. This time the news was a subject of unqualified delight and they looked forward to adding to their family. Through June and July, Harriet endured weeks of sickness, but thereafter kept reasonably well until Christmas time. They had gone over to Bingley for Christmas Day and it became clear to her mother that Harriet, now in advanced pregnancy, was a sick woman. Her skin was pale and sallow, and her whole body tired and weak. They decided that Harriet and little Samuel should stay in Bingley for the last few weeks of her pregnancy. When Robert returned the following weekend, he was alarmed by Harriet's condition; she was breathless just sitting in a chair, and her ankles were swollen. He asked her father, Elisha, to call for a doctor. Later that day the elderly family doctor appeared. After completing his examination of Harriet, he recommended complete bed-rest and prescribed a blood-tonic.

When Robert next visited, Harriet seemed a little better and he went back to Ilkley reassured that all would be well. The next two weeks passed

---

[2] It is possible that to cover the embarrassingly short interval between marriage and childbirth, Collyer claimed that he was married in 1846. Certainly, Collyer's biographer, John Haynes Holmes, gives the marriage date as June 1846 and the child's birth date as July 5, 1847 (Holmes, *Life and letters,* 1: 75). Both dates are incorrect; copies of the Marriage and Birth Certificates in the author's possession show that they were married on May 25, 1847 (Registration District of Bradford: Marriage Entry No. 331) and Samuel was born on July 13, 1847 (Registration District of Keighley: Birth Entry No. 271).

uneventfully, but as the time for the delivery approached she became jaundiced. More alarmingly she began to have 'fits' in which her limbs would flail around in jerky, involuntary movements. The doctor prescribed chloral as a sedative, and Harriet would spend much of the day asleep. On January 30, the contractions started. Harriet was weak and distressed, and cried out for Robert to be present. Elisha Watson took the morning coach over to Ilkley to fetch him. When Robert arrived, he found a neighborhood midwife in attendance. He waited anxiously in the kitchen while Mrs Watson and the midwife scurried up and down stairs with bed-linen, towels and bowls of warm water. He was called upstairs. Mrs Watson stood holding the baby, a girl, cradled in her arms. Harriet lay still, and unresponsive. The efforts to expel her baby had finally tipped her into unconsciousness. Robert took hold of her clammy hand. He watched her intently, praying for some response, but none came. The doctor was called again. He offered sympathy but little else; it was a case of waiting and watching. Hours passed; her breathing became more labored.

Over the next day, the jaundice deepened. Robert remained at her bedside, occasionally slumping forward to rest his head on the bed, but he did not sleep. From time to time, Mrs Watson tried to give the baby some milk from a bottle, but the sickly child took in very little. Harriet was slipping away. Her breathing became irregular and intermittent. Robert listened intently from one breath to the next. The intervals increased. He watched her chest and strained to hear the slow indrawing through her open, parched mouth, but the breaths became shallow and faint. Finally, there was no movement of her chest, no whisper of air, just an awful silence. Choking with tears, he turned to her bewildered parents. Harriet was dead.

Three days later, baby Jane - a name chosen for a girl-child many weeks before, also died. Robert had their bodies transferred to the cottage in Ilkley, and on February 4, Harriet with her child clutched in her frozen arms, was laid to rest in All Saints churchyard, in the grave that already contained the moldering remains of Robert's half-brother, William Wells.[3]

Harriet's death plunged Robert into despair. He decided to vacate the cottage in Church Street immediately; any return there would have heightened his sense of loss. Sarah Parratt offered to clear out Harriet's clothes, a task he

---

[3] The Ilkley Parish Church Burial Register records that Harriet: Wife of Robert Collier (sic) aged twenty-five years, and Jane Collier - five days, were buried in one grave on February 4, 1849. The Rev John Snowdon officiated.

could not even contemplate, and Thomas Stevenson offered him a room. The Stevensons occupied a house next door to the smithy, and Thomas's wife, Lucy, would help to look after young Samuel.

Grave of Collyer's half-brother William Wells, Collyer's wife Harriet and their baby daughter Jane, situated on the north side of All Saints Church, Ilkley. The headstone was erected many years after Harriet's death hence she is described as 'wife of Rev. Robert Collyer of Chicago, America'. (Author's collection)

Over the next few weeks Robert withdrew deep into himself. Collyer wrote in his memoirs; "my life was dark in the shadows of death, for which I found no help in books and I must find help in God. I did not consult with flesh and blood, not even with my dear friend and good helper John (Dobson). The whole experience seemed too sacred. The secret lay between God and my own soul."[4]

In response to some prompting, possibly at the suggestion of John Dobson, Robert started to attend the Wesleyan Methodist Chapel situated at the edge of the village on the Addingham Road.[5] While this was a new experience, he found himself among old friends. Methodism appealed to a section of society largely alienated by the Church of England. The Methodists' emphasis on individual salvation gave a new sense of dignity to the underprivileged. Hence, Robert took his seat in the pew alongside laborers, wool combers, farm-workers and the like, the artisans and their womenfolk. This was the church of the 'below stairs', the maidservants, the cooks, the coachmen and the gardeners, while their masters and mistresses genuflected at All Saints, the Church of England. Although a regular churchgoer, Robert had never considered himself 'religious', but through the Wesleyans he caught something of the spiritual revival that was then sweeping the northern counties.[6] In particular, the hymn singing lifted this note of revival up 'to the very throne of God'. Sung with enthusiasm and conviction, the chapel rang with 'resounding joy' in marked contrast to the stilted psalm-singing of the Anglicans. The great hymns of Charles Wesley seemed to speak directly to Robert's condition.

The turning point for Robert came during an evening service at the Addingham Chapel conducted by a local (lay) preacher called Henry Flesher Bland. Although Bland was only five years older than Robert, he already had a reputation as an orator. His sermon 'took a wondrous hold' on Robert, and 'at last the light came.' Collyer later acknowledged that, 'By heaven's grace, I underwent a good old-fashioned conversion.' The Ilkley Methodists took him on probation and put him in old Jim Delves's class for 'proper instruction', and

---

[4] Collyer, *Some Memories*, 28.

[5] Methodism was first established in mid-Wharfedale in Addingham with the formation of a Society in 1748 and the building of a Meeting House in 1778. A Society was formed in Ilkley in 1777 encouraged by George Hudson of Middleton, a friend of John Wesley. Addingham became head of a 'circuit' in 1808.

[6] Frederick S. Popham, *A History of Christianity in Yorkshire* (Wallington, Surrey: The Religious Education Press, 1954), 133.

in a few weeks they received 'the ardent and regenerated young man into the full communion of the church.'[7]

These events had three important consequences for Robert Collyer. The first change, albeit a gradual one, was the lightening of his mood and outlook. His deep depression lifted, at least partially; his life took on new purpose and some of his former enthusiasm returned. Secondly, he became personally aware of the positive power of a conversion experience. Years later he wrote; 'this change of heart, this conversion, this new birth, is the most essential human experience of which I have any knowledge, and of all men in the world it is most essential to the man who is called to be an apostle.'[8] Thirdly, Robert discovered his powers of oratory.

Long before his conversion he had practiced public speaking, but his only listeners had been sheep! During his frequent wanderings over the moors, he had found himself declaiming to the open air. 'Something would set me thinking and talking back, as we say, with no audience but the moor sheep that were all about me, and they would look up in wonder as to what it all meant, and then say, Baaa.'[9] His listeners among the Methodists proved to be more appreciative.

One evening, Jim Delves was absent from his class, and Tom Smith, another member, urged Robert to lead that night. He was anxious, and protested, but Smith was persistent.

"Nah, lad," he said, "tha mun lead t'class to-neet; tha can do't if tha tries." The decision to try was a momentous one. He found that the words came readily, and his listeners heard a fervent message that came straight from the heart. Some months later, the Rev. Murray, the Superintendent Minister of the Addingham 'circuit' of Methodist Chapels, approached Robert about taking a service. The Minister told him that the Local Preachers Meeting had unanimously decided to invite him into their number. "What do you think of

---

[7] Quotations from Holmes, *Life and Letters,* 1: 82. In the Methodist church every member was allocated to a 'class' under the care of a senior member of the fellowship — the class leader. In 1849 Ilkley church had only 22 members divided into two classes; one (with 15 members) led by James Delves and the other class of 7 members led by Samuel Walker. Both leaders worked as wool-combers. *Addingham Circuit Schedule Book,* 1840-1856. West Yorkshire Archive Service.

[8] Robert Collyer, *Clear Grit: a collection of Lectures, Addresses and Poems* (Boston: American Unitarian Association, 1913), 177.

[9] Holmes, *Life and Letters,* 1: 84.

it?" he asked. Robert replied that if they thought he should be given the chance, then he was ready.

His first chance came in Addingham, where he was 'planned' to conduct an afternoon service.[10] He liked the idea of an afternoon, the servants had free time on a Sunday after dinner, and that could boost the numbers. However, when he got there he found only a handful of listeners. He had spent a lot of time on his sermon which, like many he had heard, was in three parts. Two parts were of his own devising, but the middle part was taken directly from the writings of 'a good Scotch divine' called McCheyne. He knew that it was frowned upon to read the sermon verbatim, so he committed as much as he could to memory and only took a few notes into the pulpit. The service passed off, and Robert started for home well-pleased that he had his first full sermon under his belt. Part-way home, however, he suddenly realized that he had completely forgotten the middle, and arguably the best, part of his address. Sometime later, he met Flesher Bland, who unknown to Robert, had been sitting behind a screen in the Addingham Chapel to monitor his preaching. Bland told him that as a first attempt it was a worthy sermon but the jump from first to third part had him puzzled![11]

Thereafter Robert was ordained as a local preacher and had a regular place on the plan. Every Sunday he went trudging up the dale or across the moors to meet some little group of Methodists and lead them in a service of worship. Sometimes he would attend a small chapel but for other services a cottage or a farm-kitchen would suffice. The Addingham circuit was an extensive one. In addition to the main church in Addingham there were Methodist 'societies' at Aden (or Eden, a farm-house), Addingham Moorside (again, a farm house meeting), Beamsley, Burnsall, Cononley, Cross Hills, Draughton, Ickornshaw, Ilkley, Kildwick, Langbar, Silsden, Silsden Moor, and Sutton.[12] Local preachers were needed at all these locations, and for Robert this could mean, for example, a 24-mile round-trip on foot to conduct a service at Burnsall.[13]

Collyer recalled with affection an early service at a farm in Addingham Moorside that for many years had been a Quaker, and then a Methodist,

---

[10] On two Sundays each month there was a service at 1.30pm. Every Sunday there were services at 10.30am and 6pm.

[11] Holmes, *Life and Letters,* 1: 87.

[12] *Addingham Circuit Schedule Book 1840-1856*. West Yorkshire Archive Service.

[13] Collyer, *Some Memories,* 38.

meeting place.[14] 'It was June. I am aware of the fragrance of the wild uplands stealing through the open lattice on bars of sunshine, to mingle with the pungent snap of the peat fire on the hearth which gives forth the essence of the moorlands for a thousand years. And I still mind how heavy my heart was that afternoon. I had been trying all the week to find a sermon in a parable; but there was no pulse to answer, no vision. Still there I was, the preacher, and they were simple-hearted folk up there, eager and hungry for the word of life, and ready to come in with the grand Amens. The big farm kitchen was full and they sang with a will; and where in all the world will you hear such singing with a will as in Yorkshire and Lancashire! Then I must pray. I cannot make a prayer. I felt that day the prayer was making me. Then the time came for the sermon. Some stammering words came to my lips, and then some more, while gleams of light began to play about my parable. And their eyes began to shine, while now and then the great Amens came in as a chorus from the chests of men who had talked to each other in the teeth of the winds up there from the times of the Saxons and Danes. And now after all these years I feel sure it was given me that day what I should say.' 'So the service ended, and the good man of the house came, laid his hands on me, and said very tenderly; "My lad, the Lord has called thee to preach the gospel. The Lord bless thee and make thee faithful in the truth." And all the people said Amen, while I have always said that this was my true ordination.'[15]

His 'ordination' over, one of the farmers, Mr Thackwray, invited him to stay for tea, and what a tea it proved to be. Thick slices of ham lay across the plate, partly hidden by pickled onions, beetroot and hard-boiled eggs, and there was crusty bread and butter to be washed down with mugs of strong tea. The farmhouse tea was the usual reward for the itinerant local preacher and in most instances proved to be a very satisfactory 'fee'.[16]

---

[14] The farm house, Upper Gate Croft, was licensed as a Quaker preaching house in 1689. Subsequently, Methodist services were held there for many years only being discontinued in the 1950's. William Lemmon, *Methodism in Addingham* (privately published, 1983).

[15] Collyer, *Some Memories,* 33.

[16] Five farmers took turns at hosting the preacher at Addingham Moorside where the service commenced at 1.30pm and finished at a convenient time for afternoon tea. In addition to J. Thackwray, the other farmers who 'received the Preachers' were J. Pickard, W. Greenwood, J. Lancaster, M. Grunwell and R. Lambert. The Wesleyan Plan of the Addingham Circuit 1850. Author's collection.

A few weeks later Robert had his first appointment at his 'home' chapel, an evening service in Ilkley. Although he had grown greatly in confidence, he faced this service with unusual nervousness. After all, he now had to preach for his friends, young men and women with whom he had shared so much of his growing into adulthood, and he didn't want to let himself down. He worked long and hard at his sermon - drafting, refining, rehearsing, until the big day arrived, and he felt that he was entering the Ilkley pulpit with a worthy message for his peers and elders. He conducted the service without a hitch, and left the chapel feeling that he had made a good impression on all his listeners. A glow of self-satisfaction was still warming his mind on his way to the forge next morning. The old village cobbler called out to him from where he was hammering away underneath his porch; "I say, lad, come 'ere, I ha' summat to say to ye. I heard thaa preach last night." There was a broad grin on his face.

"Did ye, though?", returned Robert, proudly.

"I did, and I think thoult ne'er mak a preacher as long as thaa lives, Bob." Robert was stunned by this, for the cobbler was the village oracle. The latter saw how sorely he had hurt him, and kind-heartedly added;

"Now, doant mistake me, Bob. Thou wants to reason too much. Thaa may'st lecture; but thaa can never be a preacher!"[17] Fortunately, he didn't let this hurtful, but well-meant rebuff put him off preaching.

Although by the summer of 1849 the Methodist church held Robert's allegiance, he was about to leave his most durable legacy in Ilkley to the parish church. As part of Rev Snowdon's improvements, the churchyard was to have a new wall built around it and new railings and gates were required. Robert, as Master of the smithy, was called upon to undertake the job. He was initially nervous about making the gates, after all they would be a very public demonstration of his work and he did not welcome the scrutiny. Robert considered himself primarily a farrier and recognized his limitations as a metal-worker; "I think I was never a very good blacksmith, not nearly as good as my father; for to do anything supremely well you must give your whole mind to it, yes, and your heart, and these for me were given to the books".[18] Nevertheless, he took on the work 'with no proper tools or skill', and passed the making of the railings over to Samson Speight. Robert spent hours, cutting the rods, hammering the ends to create the decorative finials, drifting the holes

[17] William Smith, *A Yorkshireman's trip to the United States and Canada* (London: Longmans, Green and Co., 1892) 43

[18] Collyer, *Some Memories*, 39.

in the cross-bars, making the hinges and locking mechanism, and, finally, riveting them in place.

Gates and lamp-holder at All Saints Church, Ilkley, made by Robert Collyer in 1849. Photograph taken by the author in 1990.

However, Robert did not carry out this work as an act of Christian charity. He presented the parish with a bill for £7—10 shillings, while Speight charged 25 shillings and eight pence for his work on the railings.[19] When the gates were hung, Collyer considered them 'as homely as a barn door', but what they lacked

[19] from Harry Speight, *Upper Wharfedale* (London: Elliot Stock, 1900), 206

in artistry they made up in strength, for with only modest renovation, the gates are still there over 170 years later.[20]

Thus, towards the end of 1849 Robert had firmly established himself in day-to-day control of the smithy. He had also established himself in the Methodist church and had acquired a reputation as a gifted and natural speaker. Increasingly he was sought after as a preacher, and his continuing appetite for reading provided both the inspiration for many of his sermons, and the anecdotes and illustrations that enhanced them. It was no doubt widely assumed that Robert would continue as the Ilkley blacksmith and a local preacher for many years to come, but by the summer of 1850 he was living in America.

---

[20] The gates were renovated in October 1993.

7: Emigration

By the end of 1849 Robert had made up his mind to emigrate. In coming to terms with the death of his young wife, he discovered that the roots he had put down in Ilkley were only shallow. He was still a young man, just turned twenty-six, yet he was already a father and a widower. During the months of depression that followed Harriet's death, his thoughts turned increasingly towards making a new start in a new country. In some respects, this was unfinished family business; his parents had decided to go to America soon after Robert's birth, but the economic slump of 1823-24 meant that they could not afford the fares. The arrival of more children and their continuing hardship frustrated any further hopes of emigration, but they would often sit by the fireside and discuss their 'dead or dying hope'[1]. The receipt of a letter from Tom Ross, one of Samuel's former work-mates who had emigrated to America, invariably led to talk of 'what might have been' and these discussions planted a seed in Robert's mind that was beginning to germinate. However, his decision was not merely that of a son trying to fulfil the thwarted ambitions of his parents. He had many reasons of his own for a new start in America.

Economic factors were at the forefront of his thinking. Even as Master at the smithy, he had to work long and hard to earn one pound per week. Not that Robert had extravagant financial goals. "My whole ambition," Collyer wrote, "was to make my way as a blacksmith. But I wanted a place where I could have a little home of my own, with books to read, and the chance to educate my

[1] Robert Collyer, *Some Memories* (Boston: American Unitarian Association, 1908), 41.

children."[2] But there were other motives shaping Robert's thinking, "I did not want to be a cipher in a monarchy, but a citizen in a republic. I had no vote[3]; I wanted one, and also to learn how to use it honestly and well. I had to bow and cringe before men who had rank and title. I hated to do it."[4]

Revolution and social reform were in the air in many European countries, but the aristocracy and holders of capital had an iron grip on the conditions of the worker in England. Nevertheless, such was the level of despair and frustration among the disillusioned and disenfranchised working class that some authors predicted imminent revolution or civil war. The Chartist movement had raised a flicker of optimism but the abject failure of the reform-seeking petition to have any influence on an intransigent Parliament, weighed heavily on Robert[5]. He read the gloomy predictions of William Cobbett who claimed that England "has become the land of domestic misery and of foreign impotence and contempt" but preferred to read more practical works that would help him in the process of emigration.[6] He purchased cheap editions of guides for emigrants and pored over their contents.[7] However, he needed no advice regarding his destination. His mind was made up, he was going to America.

When it was known that Robert was going to emigrate, a gentleman of some standing approached him; "You will go to Canada of course, and I will give you letters to friends in Montreal or in Australia, if you choose to go there." When Robert confirmed that he was off to America, the man assumed that he

---

[2] John Haynes Holmes, *The Life and Letters of Robert Collyer* (New York: Dodd Mead and Company, 1917) 1:96.

[3] The entitlement to vote in the 1840's was tied to the ownership of property, or a tenancy over £10 per annum. Collyer did not qualify – along with about 80% of the adult male population of England.

[4] Holmes, *Life and Letters,* 1: 97

[5] The Chartist movement stems from a Charter drawn up in 1838 that sought, among other changes, universal male suffrage, a secret ballot, and the removal of property qualifications for Members of Parliament. After riots in 1839 were cruelly suppressed, the Chartists adopted a non-violent approach. Their third petition, bearing 1.5 million signatures, was presented to Parliament in April 1848 but the interests of capital prevailed, and the movement was stifled. See Andrew N. Wilson, *The Victorians* (London: Arrow Books, 2003) 113-120.

[6] William Cobbett, *Rural Rides, 1830* (London: Penguin Classics, 2001)

[7] Charlotte Erickson, *Invisible Immigrants* (Ithaca and London: Cornell University Press, 1972, Note 77), 491.

must have friends there and was taken aback when Robert confessed; "I don't know a soul."[8] Collyer related how he walked some miles to visit a relative of Harriet's who had been to America three times to seek his fortune and who could give him valuable advice. Robert asked him if the Americans were well disposed towards the English. "No," he answered, "they are nayther. Wha' they'll tak the varry teeth out o' yer head if ye don't keep yer moath shut!" As the chap had lost some of his front teeth, Robert didn't find this statement particularly encouraging.[9]

Robert began his final preparations for emigration, but as he did so his thoughts began to turn to taking a new wife. His loneliness, the needs of his motherless child and the prospect of having a companion and home-maker in the new country, led him to contemplate marriage. It appears that Robert had not paid too much attention to the writings of Cobbett. In his *Emigrant's Guide (1829)*, Cobbett advises that married men thinking of emigrating will need; 'that quality which enables a man to overcome the scruples, the remonstrances, and the wailings of his wife. Women, and especially Englishwomen, transplant very badly.'[10]

Early in 1850 Robert became friendly with Ann Longbottom, a young woman he met when a group from the Young Peoples' Fellowship at Eastbrook Chapel in Bradford came over to Ilkley for an excursion.[11] He was drawn to her happy disposition and ready smile and they began to see each other at weekends. Within a month of their first meeting, Robert had proposed to her. Having already made up his mind to emigrate, he offered to go out to America on his own, find work and make a home for her to come to, but she would have none of it. They would be married, and she must go with him.[12]

Robert had not expected this response and had to arrange the marriage before his departure. The earliest opportunity fell only five days before the date they were due to sail to America and they were married at the Eastbrook

---

[8] Collyer, *Some Memories,* 42.

[9] Collyer, *Some Memories,* 43.

[10] Quoted in Richard Ingrams, *The Life and Adventures of William Cobbett* (London, Harper Collins, 2005), 145

[11] Eastbrook Wesleyan Chapel was erected in 1825 to replace the Kirkgate Chapel in the centre of Bradford which the congregation had outgrown. The chapel was demolished in 1899 and replaced by the new Eastbrook Chapel (later Eastbrook Hall) which was opened in 1904.

[12] Holmes, *Life and Letters,* 1: 100.

Chapel on Tuesday, April 9, 1850.[13] After the simple ceremony, the couple and a few close friends walked to North Parade for a modest tea generously provided by Ann's employers of many years' standing, Mr. and Mrs. Thomas Cropley[14]. From there the couple took a train to Leeds, the first stop on their way to Liverpool, and made their way to his mother's house in Beeston. It was there that the newly-weds spent their wedding night. Robert and Ann spent that first night separately, Ann in a bedroom shared with her new-found sisters, Martha and Maria, and Robert downstairs on a couch.

Early the next morning, they said their tearful farewells to the family including Collyer's son, Samuel; he was to stay in the care of his grandmother while he and Ann established themselves in America. The parting from his mother was the most emotional and distressing event that Robert had yet faced. With a final wave from the hired cab, he and Ann headed for Wellington Station in the center of Leeds. Waiting for them at the station was John Dobson. John had come over from Ilkley to say farewell. Reaching the platform for the Liverpool train, they noticed a woman, her eyes red with crying, being comforted by an anxious young man. Robert guessed that they could be fellow emigrants. John inquired on the Collyers' behalf, and found that to be the case - she and her husband, a shoemaker from Leeds, were also set to sail for America. "After a few minutes' conversation," Collyer recalled, "we resolved to make a league together.... at which they seemed mightily pleased; so was I."[15]

Belching smoke and steam, the train left Leeds punctually at 6am. After stopping at Sowerby Bridge and then Hebden Bridge, the train passed through a series of long tunnels before emerging from the Pennines and made a further stop at Littleborough[16]. Now they were in Lancashire, and for Collyer and his

---

[13] In *Life and Letters,* 1: 100, Holmes gives the name of Collyer's wife as Ann Armitage; this is not correct. On a certified copy of the Marriage Certificate in the author's possession (Bradford Union 1850/101) the name is Ann Longbottom resident of North Parade, Bradford, where she is a Domestic Servant. Her father is John Longbottom, a stonemason.

[14] Ann is listed as a servant at the house of Thomas and Elizabeth Cropley in North Parade in the 1841 Census.

[15] Many details of the journey are taken from a letter quoted in Moncure D. Conway, *Ilkley* (New York: Harpers New Monthly Magazine. May 1874), 827

[16] The Littleborough (Summit) tunnel was the first trans-Pennine tunnel to be completed and took 3.5 years to complete. The completed line between Leeds and

bride they were in new territory. Collyer related in a subsequent letter to John Dobson, "It was a fine morning and we enjoyed the ride amazingly. I don't know how many tunnels we went through, but I should think six or seven, one a most awful length. The only large town we saw was Rochdale. We got to Liverpool about half past eleven o'clock."

In 1850, over 281,000 people emigrated from the British Isles and two-thirds of them left from Liverpool. The great majority (233,000) went to America, and of these, most came from Ireland - their sea-passages starting at Dublin, Cork, or Belfast, followed by transfer to the North Atlantic ships in Liverpool. Most of the emigrant ships sailing out of Liverpool were American owned and many were 'packet' ships, so-called because they carried the North Atlantic mails and ran to a regular timetable. The American captains were a much better class of men than British masters; they were almost always part-owners of their ships which the British were not, and the character of the captain was an important consideration for those companies that insured passenger ships. Many of the British captains had reputations as bullies and tyrants, and their crewmen were little more than thugs. For most passengers, the conditions on board any of the North Atlantic ships were appalling. Even one of the well-built American packets; "may have looked like a palace in dock, or at least the captain's cabin and the cabin passengers' saloon may have looked like pieces of a palace, but by the time anything up to a thousand emigrants had been packed into steerage she began to look like a slaver."[17]

'Steerage' referred to the accommodation given over to the poorest class of migrant. The author Robert Louis Stevenson, who made an Atlantic crossing in a second-class cabin but spent much time visiting steerage, described how; "to descend on an empty stomach into Steerage No. 1, was an adventure that required some nerve. The stench was atrocious; each respiration in the throat tasted like some horrible kind of cheese; and the squalid aspect of the place was aggravated by so many people worming themselves into their clothes in the twilight of the bunks."[18] During a storm the misery was compounded by the lack of access to the main deck. The hatches might be battened down for a week or more but usually only after a few heavy seas had poured in and soaked

---

Manchester was opened in March 1841. Jack Simmons, *The Victorian Railway* (London: Thames and Hudson, 1995), 22.

[17] Terry Coleman, *Passage to America: A history of emigrants from Great Britain and Ireland to America in the mid-nineteenth century* (London: Pimlico edition, 1992), 92.

[18] Robert Louis Stevenson, *Essays of Travel: The Amateur Emigrant* (London: Chatto & Windus, 1909), 44

bedding and clothing alike. These would remain damp and reeking for the remainder of the voyage.[19]

To minimize the spread of disease and, if possible, prevent its introduction into the crowded breeding-grounds of steerage, all passengers had to undergo a medical inspection before boarding the ship. A medical practitioner appointed by the Emigration Officer had to certify that each passenger was free from contagious disease and for this duty was paid £1 for every hundred passengers inspected. However, the numbers involved and the necessity to process them rapidly meant that this examination was, to say the least, cursory. Only the most advanced cases of disease, or people with gross infirmities were picked out by this charade, which only served to appease the emigration authorities and line the pockets of the medical officers. All passengers would have to allow two or three days in Liverpool prior to sailing to purchase their ticket, undergo the 'medical', and buy the food and other requirements for their passage.

Aware of the problems and pitfalls of emigration from his reading, Robert Collyer made several important decisions before his departure for Liverpool. He had identified one of the few honest shipping brokers with whom to arrange his passage, and he wrote ahead and reserved berths on an American sailing ship, the *Roscius*. Importantly, he knew that the additional cost of a berth in a second-class cabin would be money well spent. He had been given the address of a reputable boarding house, and he knew that no matter what the circumstances he must not accept any service or advice from a 'runner' whose sole intent was to sell tickets, and gain commission, for the worst kind of emigrant ships, or to 'look after' the passengers' luggage which may not be returned to its owner it before the sailing. Thus, Robert anticipated that the three days that he and Ann had to spend in Liverpool would be busy, but not fraught with the dangers and risks of deception that was the lot of most emigrants.

Sometime before the train reached Lime Street Station, Robert and Ann had fallen into conversation with another pair of emigrants who were bound for the *Roscius*, Mr. and Mrs. John Whitely, who together with their other new-found Leeds friends made a party of six. Collyer wrote in a letter home; "Plenty of men wanted to take our luggage, but we let them talk until they were tired; left the women to watch it while we went to seek lodgings. Here we were at fault. The man (Whitely) had an address, but it was at least two miles off; I had

[19] Melvin Maddocks, *The Atlantic Crossing* (Amsterdam: Time-Life Books, 1981), 145.

one, but it was most difficult to find; so we agreed we would ask someone about one. We went into what seemed a respectable shop, and the mistress told us to go to a certain house in the next street. We went; knocked at the door of a most forbidding place. The knock was answered by a dirty, bare-legged girl. Mr. Whitely being pushed forward as spokesman, asked if she had lodgings. The mistress came and took him in to look at them. He stayed perhaps three minutes, and it would have made anybody laugh to see the disgust on his face, and the effort he made to hide it from the mistress. I was forced to turn away. 'Where do you put the luggage?' says he. 'Down there' pointing to a hole below, with a door to the street. 'Will it go in?' says he to me. 'Oh yes, if it was here,' said I. So, we turned away, saying if we decided to come we should be there directly. Of course, we did not go, but set off for our friend's distant place. About half-way we stumbled upon a temperance hotel; I proposed we should try there. We went in, engaged lodgings, and I must say that, though they were not so tidy as we have been used to at home, they were good enough. If we wanted anything to eat, we got it pretty reasonable. We had a good public room, never annoyed with company. We had a sofa and all the comforts they could give us, a single bedded room for the married people, and the charge was a shilling a bed, that is 6d each. They were perfectly honorable in their contact, charged us nothing for our luggage, and wished to advise us, I believe, for the best. We got a cart for our boxes, for which we paid 1s-6d; that was 6d each. I had sent three hundred-weight by Pickfords; found it, but let it stay till we went on board. We got dinner, and went to look after our passage; paid our fares, and by that time it was night and we were tired."[20] So, in a single-bed, in a small dismal room in a Liverpool lodging-house, Robert and his wife of two days made love for the first time. Their tiredness, and the strangeness of their surroundings, made this an awkward and difficult experience.

They got up early next morning and after bread and a bowl of porridge, set off for the Medical Inspection. Although it was only 8.30 am as they neared the docks, their progress was hindered by a mob of runners and street-hawkers, the latter laden with articles, both useful and useless, but all of inferior standard and at hugely inflated prices. Robert and Ann literally threaded their way through the mounds of bedding; the poles hung with cooking utensils and cans for the daily water ration; the trays of bacon, herrings and salt-beef; and the stalls stacked with bottles of whisky and brandy and pouches of tobacco. They

[20] Moncure D. Conway, *Ilkley* (New York: Harpers New Monthly Magazine, May 1874), 828.

finally reached Waterloo Road and found the end of the queue for the 'Doctors' Shop'. Although the inspections did not start until 10 am, the queue was already two or three hundred strong. They took their places, resigned to a long wait. Once the door of the inspection building opened, they found that people shuffled forward reasonably quickly, and a constant trickle of passengers emerged from the exit door.

'The Medical Inspection' from Illustrated London News, July 6 1850.

After a couple of hours in the queue, Robert and Ann entered the building and finally reached the tables of the two Medical Officers on duty. It was then that they realized how the government doctors managed to deal with up to 1000 passengers a day. Without drawing breath, the doctor asked Robert; "What's your name? Are you well? Hold out your tongue; all right," and while stamping Robert's passage docket, began to address the next person in the queue.

Emerging with their precious stamped tickets, the couple were now ready for embarkation. However, no passenger was allowed on board a ship until 24 hours before sailing, so they had to fill the rest of the day and spend another night in the lodgings. They decided that they would look at their ship, but first there was dinner. Robert and Ann reached Tithebarn Street. At every ten steps there were spirit vaults, some already filled with seamen, the doorways sheltering disheveled women with young figures and old faces. Placards advertised beds for the night. The walls of the houses were covered with notices posted by the brokers promoting ships to the United States and Canada, and advertisements for suspect medical products, new clothing in the American style, and inducements to all seamen disgusted with the merchant service to accept a bounty and join the Royal Navy. Apparently, very few took up the offer.[21] After half an hour's walking, Robert and Ann decided that satisfying their hunger was more pressing than maintaining their standards of hygiene and, at the next eating place they came to, they bought two bowls of lob scouse - a stew made from neck of lamb or some other cheap meat, barley and root vegetables, served with chunks of coarse bread.[22]

Feeling refreshed, they walked back to the docks. They found blackboards on which were chalked the locations of the various ships and walked alongside the tall, impressive warehouses on the one hand and a forest of masts and spars on the other. Eventually they found the *Roscius* in the northern basin of the Waterloo Dock, flying the blue and white flag of the 'Dramatic Line'[23].

The Dramatic Line was the creation of a flamboyant New York shipping magnate, Edward Knight Collins. Echoing his own larger-than-life character, Collins named his ships after theatrical figures. The first, *Shakespeare,* was followed by sister ships *Garrick, Sheridan* and *Siddons.* The last to be built was the *Roscius*, named for a Roman comic actor, launched in 1838. The *Roscius* was the first New York packet to exceed 1,000 tons and cost more than $100,000, an enormous amount of money in 1838. It also boasted several innovations; Collins moved the passenger cabins from below deck, where they were subject to nauseating bilge odors, to a long deck-house on the main-deck stretching

---

[21] Coleman, *Passage to America,* 66.

[22] The former popularity of 'lob scouse' is the likely explanation for Liverpudlians being called 'Scousers'.

[23] The S.S. *Roscius* was built in 1838 by Messrs Brown and Bell of New York. When built, Roscius could out-sail any of her competitors and made the crossing from Liverpool to New York in an average of 26 days. The *Roscius* was sold in 1852 and then did service with the Pelican Line between New York and Mobile. She later returned to the Transatlantic route and sank with the loss of all on board on 26 August 1860 on her westward passage from Liverpool to New York.

from the stern almost to the mainmast. Thus, the cabins got more air and light, but without making the ship top-heavy or harming her behavior or safety.[24]

The ship towered over Robert and Ann standing on the dock-side, and it was not difficult to believe that when she was built she was the largest clipper in the world. Robert remembered the glowing testimonial he had read about 'this most remarkable ship' in one of the guidebooks. She offered passenger accommodation of superb quality with her cabins finished in the world's most expensive woods. Her mainmast extended to a height of 160 feet above her brilliantly white decking, above which she could carry a vast expanse of equally white canvas. She had been 'built to go,' and go she had. On her first three trips westward, *Roscius* logged an average of 26 days, two full days better than the other packets in the line.[25]

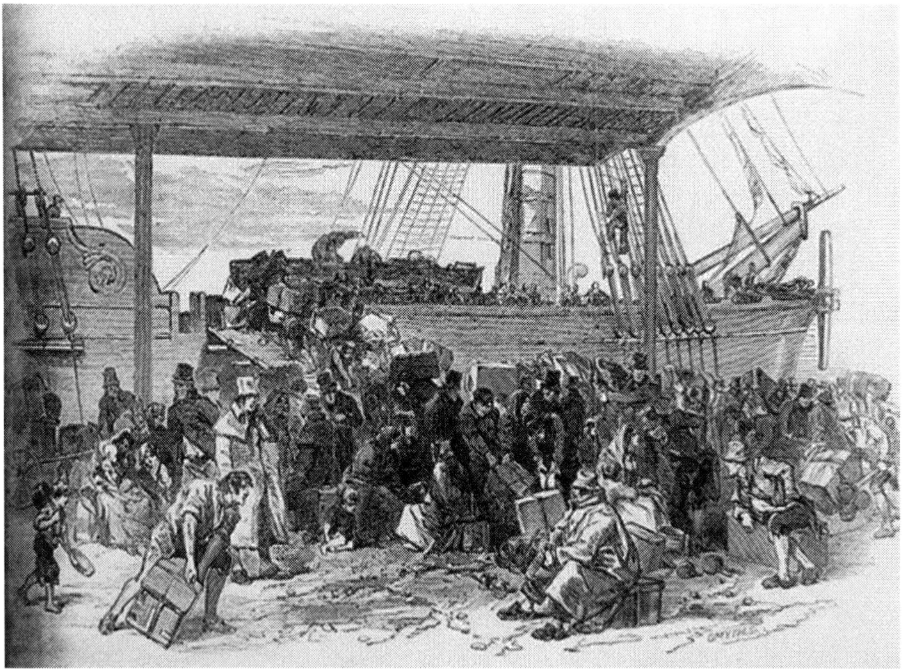

'The Embarkation, Waterloo Docks, Liverpool'. From the Illustrated London News, July 6, 1850.

[24] Stephen Fox, *Transatlantic: Samuel Cunard, Isambard Brunel and the Great Atlantic Steamships* (New York: Harper Collins, 2003), 6.

[25] Warren Armstrong, *The Collins Story* (London: Robert Hale Ltd., 1957), 47.

Robert and Ann gazed for some time at the dockers and crew-members carrying goods up the ship's gangway and the bustle of activity on the main deck, then turned to walk back to their lodgings, well satisfied with what they had seen. After another night of fitful sleep and a more leisurely breakfast, they packed their bags and headed back to the dock, this time to embark for America.

The Collyer's first port of call was the Pickford's depot where they identified their luggage and supervised its transfer to the ship. They then returned to the *Roscius.* After climbing the steep gangway, they stepped on to the main deck. They somewhat nervously announced their names to the second mate and, in the company of a steward, were led down a narrow companion-way into the section given over to the second cabins. Collyer later recounted; "All the difference between second cabin and steerage is that one is at one end of the ship, and the other at the other; they are both on a level, but there is rather more air in the second cabin, and a little more light – not enough to read by except in some particular places. We got a berth at one of the places where it was pretty airy; got our luggage there, but a man who had possession cursed and swore, and would not budge an inch; so I went back to the office, got the manager down, and he gave us our choice either to turn the man out, or to have another place in the cabins on the main deck. We gladly took the (other) place, paying 10 shillings extra, and got two very nice people from Worcestershire (and their baby) to join us. It is a good job for us; we are far better off than in the second cabin, albeit it is a queer place, about six foot square and seven or eight feet high, for four people and a baby." The additional headroom and the extra light in their new cabin adjacent to the staterooms greatly alleviated the sense of claustrophobic gloom that prevailed in the 'tween decks', even in the second-class cabins.[26]

Robert returned to his cabin and, after describing the scenes in steerage to his companions, eventually fell asleep with the sounds of continuing revelry in his ears. Apart from two short periods when the baby cried and awoke them, that first night in port was the best that they would have for the next four weeks.

[26] The height of the 'tween decks on the Roscius was 6 feet 6 inches which was regarded as being 'ample for the comfort of steerage passengers'.

'The departure'. Illustrated London News, July 6 1850.

8: Passage to America

The day of departure, Saturday April 13, 1850, started bright and fine. Filled with excitement and expectancy, Robert and Ann went up on deck to watch the final preparations. As the sailing time approached, the dockside swarmed with activity. Donkey-carts laden with goods drew up to the gangway as another party of emigrants struggled on board with all their worldly possessions contained in a motley collection of trunks, boxes and carpet-bags, or simply tied into mis-shaped bundles. It was surprising how little time these passengers allowed for embarkation. Robert watched, as with frantic gestures to the porters, to the crewmen and to each other, newly arrived passengers tried to penetrate the press of people at the foot of the gangway. He was even more amazed when the gangway was removed with dozens of would-be passengers still on the dockside. Obviously, the ship was to be towed out of the dock at the scheduled time whether or not they were on board.

The *Roscius* slipped its moorings and a steam tug hauled the ship towards the dock gates. At that point the ship stopped for several minutes, and Robert and Ann watched with increasing incredulity as men, women and children clambered up rigging slung over the ship's side and, pitching their belongings onto the deck, tumbled after them. Crewmen roughly grabbed at the arms of the passengers and bundled them up and over the ship's side like so many sacks of old clothes. Ann gasped as one poor woman lost her grip and fell into the water of the dock. Fortunately, after much shrieking and thrashing about, two men in a small boat, who followed the ship for this eventuality, hauled her out of the water. In addition to the milling crowd of frantic passengers and porters, the dockside was thronged with spectators. Most were relatives about to wave a tearful farewell, but others were simply curious sightseers. As the tug finally pulled the great ship out of the dock, everyone (apart from some abandoned passengers) waved fluttering handkerchiefs or raised their hats and cheered. The waving continued until the ship was well out into the Mersey where a small overcrowded tender pulled alongside, and another group of emigrants and a confused mass of luggage were hauled up. Their embarkation was achieved at considerable personal danger for they had to climb from the bobbing, swaying tender onto the ship-side rigging. For some this would be the most dangerous part of their voyage.

The tug continued to tow the *Roscius* down river. During this period of slow and sedate progress, two further preliminaries to sailing were conducted, the search for stowaways and the roll-call. The passengers were summoned to the poop-deck, whereupon the search party comprising the First Mate, the Clerk from the ship's passenger brokers and four crewmen, set off to look for stowaways. Armed with a hooded lantern, crowbars, hammers and poles tipped with sharp nails, they poked into dark recesses and piles of bed-clothes and levered open suspicious crates or barrels. Sometimes these searches ended tragically; on occasion, a stowaway has been found suffocated after hiding in a barrel which some accomplice had sealed too tightly.

The search for stowaways. Illustrated London News, June 6 1850.

The cabin passengers were spared the irritation and ignominy of the roll-call, but Robert and Ann decided to watch the proceedings anyway. One of the mates presided, and the ship's doctor was in attendance. The roll call served two purposes; it verified the passenger list and allowed a second medical inspection on behalf of the Captain and owners. In addition to a poll tax of one dollar 50 cents per passenger, the City of New York fined the owners 75 dollars for each helpless or deformed person brought in. Thus the medical officer's task was to weed out any obviously diseased individuals that had evaded the dockside inspection or any poor cripple who could not give security that he had friends to take care of him on arrival in America. The mate called out each passenger's name and he or she had to show a valid ticket. Those without a ticket, or without the funds to pay for one, together with any captured stowaways, would be put on the tug and returned to Liverpool. Although on this occasion the roll-call passed off without incident, this was by no means always the case. One crew-member told Robert that; "sometimes a woman who had included on her ticket an infant at the breast, may be seen when her name is called, panting under the weight of a boy of eight or nine held to her bosom. Sometimes a youth of nineteen, strong and big as a man, has been entered as under twelve to qualify for half fare. Sometimes a man, with a wife and eight or ten children, who may have paid a deposit for his passage money, attempts to evade paying the balance by pleading he has not a farthing left in the world; and trusting that the ship will rather take him out to New York for the sum already paid, than incur the trouble of putting him on shore again with his family."[1] After two hours, the roll-call, and the search for stowaways, were complete and all 435 of the ship's passengers had been accounted for.[2]

About five miles or so down river, the *Roscius* cast off the tow rope, the tug drew it in and then veered off, back to port. This was the signal for a series of barked orders from the officers. Men toiled at the capstan, hauled on ropes and blocks, or clambered up the rigging. Great sheets of canvas unfurled and, catching the breeze, swelled into arcs of white and cream that snatched at the tethering ropes and strained on the spars and cross trees. Robert felt the ship

[1] 'The tide of emigration to the United States and the British Colonies', (London: Illustrated London News, 1850) Saturday 6 July. https://viewsofthefamine.wordpress.com/illustrated-london-news/the-tide-of-emigration-to-the-united-states-and-to-the-british-colonies/

[2] The number is representative and is taken from the log of the similarly-sized sister ship, the *Garrick,* sailing from Liverpool to New York on July 3, 1854. The detailed breakdown of the emigrants on this voyage was Irish 324, English 86, Scotch (sic) 14, other countries 11. From 'Maury's Sailing Directions' quoted in Basil Lubbock, *The Western Ocean Packets* (Glasgow: Brown, Son & Ferguson Ltd., 1956) 118

heave as the wind powered it through the increasing swell at the mouth of the river. Staring back at the receding coastline, he reached for Ann's hand. He looked at her and saw the tears welling up in her eyes. Robert put a reassuring arm around her and for several minutes held her tightly against him.

'The roll-call on deck'. Illustrated London News, July 6 1850.

The fine weather of Saturday gave way to a day of cloud and intermittent rain on the Sunday. Between the showers, an impromptu church service was held on the main deck. Collyer relates; "On the Sunday morning, Church prayers were read by a Methodist local preacher from the neighborhood of London. The matter was brought about by a Churchman from Limerick, in Ireland, who brought a splendid prayer-book out for the purpose. Mr. Whitely and I proposed a hymn or two, and carried our point. The man who read prayers in the morning preached at night. After we went to bed there was the most dangerous piece of navigation we have had all the way, a strong wind setting for the coast of Ireland, a rough sea, a narrow channel. The sea was rough next morning and a poor fellow who could not sleep went on deck about four o'clock. A sailor mistook him for the preacher, and giving him an oath, told him it was all through his preaching that the wind had risen."[3]

[3] Collyer was lucky to experience only one relatively minor storm on his crossing. One of the worst winters in the history of the packets was that of 1852-3. Leaving

Over the next few days, the passengers settled into the ship's routine. 'I am here at the door of my berth,' Collyer wrote, 'and within two yards of me are a crowd of Irish clamoring for the 'tay and sugar' they are giving them from the stores. At my feet is the hatchway leading to the steerage and second cabin. Up and down they go all the day long, sometimes getting down very well, very often slipping at the second or third step and tumbling to the bottom, with the bacon, or rice, or 'praties' (potatoes) or 'tay', or clap-cake, or stirabout, or anything else, tumbling about their ears, while screams and laughter and Irish brogue stream up from below in glorious confusion. My writing-desk is my knee, and my head goes with the ship, and she is going about eight knots'.[4]

The Dramatic Line clipper 'Roscius'.

Sociable and inquisitive, Collyer became acquainted with the officers. He was particularly impressed by the Captain. "Our Captain is as fine-looking a

Liverpool on 17 December 1852, the *Roscius* encountered a violent storm on the 1 January; "during a strong gale from the NNW........ it was found that four of the crew had been washed overboard, the mate had one of his arms broken and one of the crew his leg smashed, besides several of the others severely injured." from Lubbock, *Western Ocean Packets,* 98

[4] quoted in Moncure D. Conway, *Ilkley* (New York, Harpers New Monthly Magazine. May 1874), 827

man as you will find in a county," Collyer wrote," about five feet eleven, built in a mould of perfect strength, and withal a perfect gentleman."[5] The Captain admitted to Robert that he was embarrassed about the state of the ship. While the owner, Edward Collins, had spared no expense to get the finest possible materials and workmanship for the *Roscius,* he was not so keenly interested in the rigging. Because of this his ships had a bad reputation for losing spars and canvas[6]. Furthermore, although only twelve years old, the ship had been poorly maintained and suffered badly from wear and tear. They were not many days out of Liverpool, when Robert concluded that the ship should have been named the *Atrocious* rather than the *Roscius.*[7] He wrote; "The first mate was also an American; the second mate is an Irishman; the third mate a Welshman, with a voice like a trumpet, and a stock of oaths and curses that would beat the whole Castle-yard (the worst dwellings in Ilkley) and all their allies. The crew, twenty-six, a German, a few English, two or three Irish, one a fine foreigner (I think Spanish), the rest Yankees, far more intelligent than you would suppose."[8]

Collyer had plenty of time to study the crew and he was a keen observer of their duties. The ship's company included a carpenter, a cook who prepared meals for the crew and cabin passengers, a boatswain (who oversaw general maintenance), two stewards to look after the cabins, and a few ship's boys who acted as general dogs'-bodies for the three mates and had to learn the skills of sailing from the seamen. The latter were classified as 'able' or 'ordinary' according to their experience. The ordinary seamen did all the tedious work of hauling on ropes, climbing aloft to furl and reef the sails as ordered, and took a turn at the wheel. Robert recognized that the able seamen were masters of many crafts. They not only had to be skilled in the workings of the many sails, spars and ropes, but also turn their hands to making hooks and rings for the

---

[5] The American captain, Asa Eldridge, had succeeded John Collins, the first captain of the *Roscius.* When the *Roscius* was sold in 1852, he transferred to the *Pacific,* a Collins Line ship which had briefly (1850-1) held the Blue Riband for the fastest eastward Transatlantic crossing. Eldridge was lost with all on board when the *Pacific* went down some time after leaving Liverpool on 26 June 1856.

[6] Frank C. Bowen, *A century of Atlantic travel 1830-1930* (London: Sampson Low, Marston & Co., 1930), 20.

[7] John Haynes Holmes, *The Life and Letters of Robert Collyer,* (New York: Dodd Mead and Company, 1917), 1: 104.

[8] quoted in Conway, *Ilkley,* 828

blocks, weave rope yarn into mats and fenders, and sew rings and collars of hempen lace about the shrouds to secure them in place.

The crew was divided into two watches each under the command of one of the mates, and each with a variety of duties to perform. Day and night, a seaman stood at the helm, keeping the ship set on a course set by the captain. In stormy weather, when the vessel pitched and yawed, two men might be needed to hold the wheel steady and both were in danger of being swept overboard by waves that washed over the stern. At least one seaman had to stand at the bow to keep a constant eye out for signs of changes in the weather, other ships, icebergs or land. Although the lookout's job was pleasant enough in fair weather, it had to be done in rain, snow and blistering sun alike. Robert came to admire the seamen's calm efficiency and acceptance of discipline. They certainly lived up to his expectations of the well-drilled packet crews that he had read about, qualities that had persuaded him to sail on an American ship rather than a cheaper British alternative.[9]

Even on-board ship, church services were not without their doctrinal disputes. Collyer writes; "The young Methodist and the leading Churchman got across (each other) in the first week. He (the Methodist) would read prayers no more. The Churchman was in a fix. He thought the Methodist was ordained, and of course he durst not read the absolution himself; so he asked him as a special favor to read that bit for him. He complied. I went to the Service the second Sunday, and when I saw it I was sick; so were some more. I spoke out after about it, and he would read no more for him. Mr Whitely let it out that I was a local preacher, so I was requested to conduct a service on the Wednesday following. The place was well filled. Next day hearts and hands clustered round me in numbers. Before Sunday we had leave to hold a meeting on deck, and the young man conducted it. The (Catholic) Church had prayers below (in steerage). At night our young Methodist man claimed 'the below' as our right. He and they were at daggers drawn in a minute. Such a stir! He wanted me to preach. I would not listen to it till matters were settled. I went to the parties, exerted all my tact, and brought things about."[10]

The days ran into weeks and the voyage seemed to be never ending. Robert and Ann passed the time in reading; eating the second-class, second-rate meals; walks on deck for air and exercise, and prayer meetings. Fortunately, neither

---

[9] details of the crew's activities are taken from Maddocks, *Atlantic Crossing*, 92.

[10] Conway, *Ilkley*, 829

of them suffered from the sea-sickness that plagued their traveling companions, and the weather was kind, too kind for a speedy crossing.

Eventually, on Sunday 12 May, twenty-nine days after setting sail from Liverpool, they saw land. The coast of Long Island came into sight at 10:12am and they spent the rest of the day and much of Monday sailing on a south-westerly course with the Island on the starboard side. Gradually, over to the left, the coast of New Jersey came into view. The sighting of the Sandy Hook Lightship, just off the Jersey coast, was the signal for the Captain to send up flares to summon a pilot. The twenty-five mile stretch from Sandy Hook to the East River piers in New York was a treacherous water-way of shifting sand-banks and strong currents, and it was obligatory for all ships to take on a local pilot. At the sight of the flares, four or five pilot schooners raced towards the *Roscius* as the packet captain usually gave the job to the first pilot on hand. The fee was between $25 and $55, depending on the size of the ship[11]. Once the pilot was on board, the *Roscius* began a slow crawl into the harbor — the pilot's reputation rested on his safety record not on speed — besides which the ship had to anchor for some hours in the quarantine area opposite Staten Island.

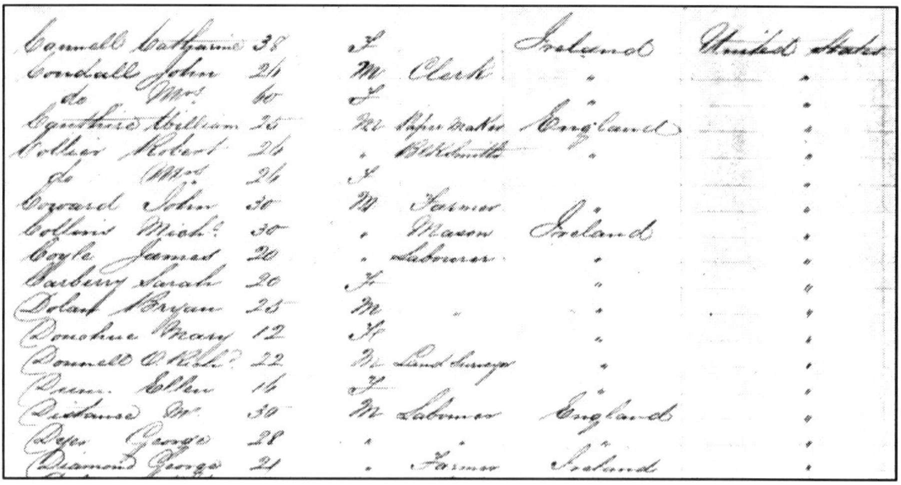

"Robert Collier (sic) age 26, Blksmith, and Mrs Collier, age 26" arrived on the Roscius on 13 May 1850. Detail from New York, Passenger and Crew Lists 1820-1957.

[11] Maddocks, *Atlantic Crossing*, 136

At this point two customs-house officers came on board, soon followed by the doctor. All passengers had to be examined and if any sick were discovered they were sent to the hospital on the Island[12] and the ship quarantined for thirty days. However, the examination was not much more thorough than that carried out in Liverpool. The passengers, by now all out on the deck, were herded onto the poop-deck and the rear part of the main deck. A rope was then tied across the deck leaving a small space at one end through which each passenger had to walk, one at a time, under the gaze of the health officer. Some of the emigrants were questioned as they passed his scrutiny, but all must have given satisfactory answers because no one was detained and the ship was given a clean bill of health. They sailed on into the Upper Bay. Amid mounting excitement, the ship approached the docks. Small skiffs carried hawsers to the quay, and once they were secured, a dozen crew-members at the capstan wound in the heavy rope. The great ship pivoted around the corner of the dock and finally came to rest against the wooden piles of the wharf. It was six o'clock on Monday, May 13. Robert and Ann looked down on the bustling South Street quay of New York, relieved and thankful that they would soon be on dry land.

'Roscius' (on right) in New York harbor with the Cunard Line ship S.S. Asia on left.

[12] The hospital was situated at Tompkinsville, near the north-east point of Staten Island, and just north of the narrows where the Verrazano Bridge now joins Brooklyn and the Island.

While they waited to disembark, Robert heard shouting in a Yorkshire accent coming up from the dockside. The voice belonged to a tavern-keeper who was touting for business. Robert knew that New York was equally as bad as Liverpool for its tricksters and runners, but the familiar accent reassured him, and he decided that they should take up the Yorkshireman's offer of accommodation. Most of their luggage would not be available until after Customs clearance on Wednesday and so, descending to the quay with their ship-board baggage, Robert and Ann followed their host to the tavern. Swaying a little as they tried to regain their land-legs, they crossed over South Street and headed for the Old Slip.

Robert was immediately impressed by the size of the buildings and the numerous windows. In England, the imposition of a Window Tax meant that most buildings were designed with a limited number of small windows to minimize the financial burden[13]. The lower parts of the buildings were literally covered in advertisements and notices, extolling the virtues of a host of goods and services in highly exaggerated terms. The most mundane of articles were described in poetry and prose, or embellished with testimonials, all praising them for their unique and unrivalled properties. The surprising thing was that these universally acclaimed items could be bought for only ten or twenty-five cents! After walking a couple of blocks, they turned into Water Street. The tavern was down an alley-way near the intersection with Pine Street.

Fortunately, Robert's confidence in the Yorkshire-man was not misplaced. They enjoyed a simple but wholesome meal, eating their first fresh vegetables and un-salted meat in four weeks. During the night, however, Ann felt acutely sick. Perhaps the change of food had upset her stomach, perhaps it was 'nerves'. Whatever the cause, Robert needed to get some medicine. In the morning, his host suggested he walk up Cedar Street to Broadway where, opposite the City Hall Park, he would find a drug-store where he could get medicine.

Broadway lived up to its name; in contrast to the narrower streets Robert had already walked through, here was a wide thoroughfare flanked by broad sidewalks and lined by high buildings. The smooth paving stones, polished every day by a hundred thousand shoes, shimmered in the morning sunshine. Robert strode purposefully up the sunny side of the street towards the Park. At

---

[13] In the early 19th century houses in England with 7 to 9 windows had to pay two shillings, and from 10 to 19 windows, four shillings. After 1825 houses with less than eight windows were exempt, and the tax was abolished completely in 1851.

each street corner, the din of youngsters hawking newspapers competed with the noise of horse-drawn carriages, hackney cabs and wagons clattering past. The smart dress on view greatly impressed him. Men in sharp suits hurried past while occasionally ladies in colorful dresses paused to survey a shop window display or exchange greetings with some acquaintance[14]. Robert found the drug-store and told the man in charge what he needed. The man addressed Collyer in an inquisitive, but friendly, fashion. "Had I just landed? Where was I from? What was my business? And I answered him, but thought the while that this may be the way we lose our teeth. I must see what he charges. "How much, sir?" I said. And he answered: "Not a cent. Glad to do it. Come in again and let me know how you are getting along if you stay in New York." This was my first lesson: the first thing I bought in this new world I must not pay for."[15] Robert did not, however, intend staying in New York; his chosen destination was Philadelphia.

Robert and Ann departed the tavern on Wednesday morning. The bill came to two dollars. A dollar a day for the two of them for board and lodging struck Robert as very reasonable, but with only twenty dollars to his name, he knew that he would have to get to Philadelphia as cheaply as possible and find a job as quickly as he could. Robert had determined that the cheapest route was a combination of ferry to South Amboy and train and river steamer to Philadelphia. In the early afternoon, they walked down to the wharf where the *Roscius* was moored, hired a hand-cart and collected their luggage. Fortunately, they were only a short distance from the pier where the ferry departed, just beyond the busy Wall Street pier. They pushed the cart along South Street, and reaching the pier, unloaded their luggage, resisting all the while the noisy offers of help from ever-eager runners. Using two of the larger trunks as seats, Robert and Ann waited excitedly for the ferry to appear.

The ferry journey took them south past Staten Island to the coast of New Jersey at South Amboy. A train belonging to the Camden and Amboy Railway stood awaiting the arrival of the ferry, but it took two hours to transfer all the passengers' luggage from ship to train. In the meantime, Robert and Ann walked to a nearby house serving refreshments where they enjoyed tea, bread, butter, smoked ham, cheese and fancy cakes, all for 20 cents. The train left at

[14] These first impressions of New York are based on Charles Dickens (1842), *American Notes for General Circulation* (London: Penguin Books, 1985), 127-144, and Arnold Schrier and Joyce Story, *A Russian looks at America: The journey of Aleksandr Borisovich Lakier in 1857* (Chicago: Chicago University Press, 1979), 65.

[15] Collyer, *Some Memories,* 44.

6pm and headed through wild country towards the Delaware River. Here and there, a white-painted shanty peeped out of the woods, while elsewhere the line traversed bogs and white sand.[16] The train stopped frequently at a succession of small towns and villages[17] but very few passengers got out or got on, everyone appeared to be heading for Philadelphia. They arrived at Bordentown, the rail terminus on the Delaware, at eleven o'clock and left the train. Everyone headed for the steamer waiting at a nearby jetty, and the boat departed as soon as the passengers and their luggage were aboard. Robert and Ann were exhausted. They snatched a few hours' sleep, lying together among the other passengers, 'hand over head, on the floor, benches, and tables – Dutch, Germans, Yankees, Irish, and English – all together.' At first light, the immigrants were out on the deck, excitedly watching the passing scene. Collyer claimed that; 'I never enjoyed a ride as much as that down the Delaware.'[18] It was a ride that took them into the opening chapter of their American adventure.

---

[16] Conway, *Ilkley*, 830

[17] The intervening stations were Browns, Spotswood, Jamesburg, Cranberry, Hightstown, Windsor, and Yardville.

[18] Conway, 830

9: First impressions

Excited and apprehensive, Robert and Ann stepped down onto the Delaware quay and made for one of the dockside depots where they left their heavy luggage. The great city of Philadelphia beckoned[1]. They headed for an inn that their host in New York had told them was cheap, conveniently situated and above all, run by a fellow Yorkshireman. With the name written on a slip of paper, and the wit to ask directions, they soon found their intended accommodation at the junction of Dock Street and Walnut Street. The inn was of an antique variety, its fabric tired and dilapidated, but they found the rooms clean and tidy. Robert booked a room for two nights, hoping that they would not have to stay longer.

Collyer's choice of Philadelphia as his ultimate destination in America had no rationale. In later life he confessed that he just liked the sound of the name, the 'city of brotherly love'.[2] Fortunately, his first impressions were positive. The city held an atmosphere of order and civility. Its regular grid of broad streets lined by well-kept houses and fine buildings, had an air of constancy and

---

[1] Philadelphia was established by the English Quaker William Penn. King Charles II of England gave the land comprising Pennsylvania to Penn in settlement of a debt. Penn's 'free colony for all mankind' or his 'Holy Experiment,' as it was more generally known, was founded in 1682 as a haven for those seeking religious freedom. In the nineteenth century, Philadelphia became the point of entry for many immigrants from the British Isles and elsewhere.

[2] John Haynes Holmes, *The Life and Letters of Robert Collyer* (New York: Dodd Mead and Company, 1917), 1:
108.

orderliness. An earlier and much more illustrious visitor, Charles Dickens, found the city so regular that after walking for an hour he claimed that he would have given the world for a crooked street. Dickens also felt; 'the collar of his coat stiffen and the brim of his hat widen under the city's Quakerly influence'.[3] Collyer was aware that the city was home to a great many Quakers, presumably living in the 'brotherly love' advocated by its founder William Penn[4]. Nevertheless, their number and the peculiar manner of their dress surprised the wide-eyed immigrants from England. Men with broad-brimmed black felt hats and strangely-cut frock coats, and women with billowing grey dresses and large hooded bonnets, were frequent sights on the city streets. In contrast to the animated expressions of the New Yorkers, the predominant face in Philadelphia was one of inner tranquility or, perhaps, just one lost in serious thoughts. Their first walk through the city streets had revealed a prosperous and bustling place that gave them promise of employment. The day ended with their hopes high.

The next morning, Friday 17 May, Robert went out to buy a newspaper. He returned to the inn with a copy of *The Public Ledger* and immediately began to scrutinize the Situations Vacant columns. With evident excitement in his voice he read aloud, "Wanted, a blacksmith. Apply to No. 5 Commerce Street." Robert added; "This is it, manna from heaven," and rushed off to find Commerce Street.

Number 5 proved to be an Agents' Office where the manager seemed sufficiently satisfied by Collyer's previous experience as a blacksmith to offer him the job. However, the job was not in Philadelphia as he had anticipated, but at a forge in a place called Shoemakertown, about ten miles north of the city. He told Robert to report there the next day. After ascertaining the precise whereabouts of the forge, he left the office and quickly made his way back to the inn to share the good news with Ann. Meanwhile she had been searching the Ledger for job opportunities for herself. This had not yielded anything

---

[3] Charles Dickens (1842), *American Notes for General Circulation* (Reprinted in Penguin Classics, London: Penguin Books, 1985), 145, 344

[4] William Penn and a surveyor, Thomas Holme, laid out the plan of the city of Philadelphia in 1682. A year later he described the city in a prospectus sent to the committee of the Free Society of Traders in London, commenting on the great 'checker-board' layout of eight streets from river to river, and twenty streets (beside Broad Street) across the city, each fifty feet wide. In John T. Faris, *Old Roads out of Philadelphia* (Philadelphia: J. B. Lippincott Co., 1917), 14

suitable, but she had found a notice advertising an `Intelligence Office' for immigrants. Once Robert had finished his breathless account of the happenings at 5 Commerce Street, she brought this to his attention. The address given for the Intelligence Office was nearby, 'next to the tavern, Front Street and Market', so they headed there straight away. Robert and Ann were surprised to discover that a Reverend gentleman, a Mr Thomason, ran the Office. Thomason, they soon learnt, had recently retired on health grounds from the Presbyterian ministry in New Orleans and now managed this office to give assistance to the many unemployed and bewildered immigrants entering Philadelphia. He must have seen some particular qualities in Ann for, after a short discussion, he offered her a temporary position in his own household helping his wife with sewing and housework. Given that the post would provide Ann with at least short-term accommodation as well as a small wage, the offer was eagerly accepted. Thus, within a single day, the new immigrants were both in employment. America was fulfilling its promise as the land of opportunity.[5]

Early next morning, dressed in working clothes and carrying a battered carpet-bag, Robert set off to walk to the Shoemakertown forge. Ann would settle the bill at the tavern and depart for the Thomasons' place. They arranged to meet again the next Sunday. Picking up the start of the York Road[6] near Front and Arch Street, Robert fell into a purposeful stride and headed out of the city. It was a glorious May morning. The sky was an intense blue and the sun lit the fields and woods with a clarity that made Robert's eyes dance across the rolling Pennsylvania countryside. At the Rising Sun tavern, the road forked. The Germantown road went off to the left, while Robert continued on the Old York Road to the right. A little further on, Robert was passed by a carriage-and-pair that abruptly pulled up ahead of him. As he drew alongside, the gentleman at the reins asked Robert where he was headed; "A place called Shoemakertown, sir," Collyer answered. "I am going that way," the gentleman replied, "Get in and have a ride this hot day."

---

[5] Robert Collyer, *Some Memories* (Boston: American Unitarian Association, 1908), 45-47.

[6] The (Old) York Road connected Philadelphia to New York. The route-way gradually developed from local roads, some laid on Indian trails, connecting the intervening settlements. The road out of Philadelphia was ordered in 1683 and the entire Pennsylvania section had been roughly graded by 1725, while the whole of the road across New Jersey opened for vehicular traffic in 1759. James and Margaret Cawley, *Along the Old York Road* (New Jersey: Rutgers University Press, 1965), 5.

So, for the first time in his twenty-six years, Collyer was invited to share a carriage with a gentleman. After discovering that Robert was a recently-arrived immigrant going to his first day at work, the man enquired sympathetically about Robert's intentions. Robert told him of his hopes but not his fears, and the man responded encouragingly that he was sure to prosper. The gentleman was well acquainted with the Shoemakertown forge as he had an interest in a similar enterprise, a shovel factory at Milltown which, he explained, was another village in Cheltenham township[7]. He told Robert that several mills had been built in this area to take advantage of water-power from the Tookany Creek[8], and that some had gone over to the manufacture of metal goods - forks, shovels, nails, axes and the like. The forge at Shoemakertown made hammers.

The journey passed quickly, and they were soon at the toll-house at the junction with Church Road. The gentleman apologized that he could not take Robert to the forge that lay a mile away to the east, and, clasping his hand, wished him good fortune. Robert never saw the man again, but he left an enduring impression of kindness and openness typical of so many he was to meet in his adopted country.

Robert resumed his walk. Church Road ran alongside the Tookany Creek as it flowed eastwards in its meandering course towards the Delaware. He passed the Myer's Fork Factory[9] and then, as instructed, took the next lane to the right. Just around the corner he came to a small garden with lilacs in full bloom foaming over its low fence. He could not resist gathering them in his arms and burying his face in the blossoms. The heady fragrance triggered

---

[7] Cheltenham township was a tract of land purchased by 15 English Quakers. Two of these first purchasers came from Cheltenham in Gloucestershire, hence the name. The land was traversed by the Tookany Creek and several water-powered mills were established on it. Small communities developed around these mills and in 1850 the villages comprised Milltown (in 1863 became Cheltenham Village), Shoemakertown, Ashbourne, Edge Hill and Harmer Hill.

[8] The Tookany Creek flows for about 8 miles through Cheltenham township before entering the outskirts of Philadelphia as the *Tacony* Creek. It enters the Delaware at Bridesburg. William J. Buck, *Cheltenham Township,* in Theodore W. Bean, ed., *History of Montgomery County, Pennsylvania* (Philadelphia: Everts & Peck, 1884), 803

[9] This also started life as a grist mill built in 1706 on Leech's Run, a tributary of the Tookany Creek. In 1848 it was purchased by Jacob Myers who re-tooled it to make farm implements including heavy and light forks. Elaine W. Rothschild, *A History of Cheltenham Township* (Cheltenham: Cheltenham Township Historical Commission, 1976), 26.

memories of gardens thousands of miles away, and his eyes filled with tears. Just then a woman emerged from the cottage. He thought to himself that he would hear the rough side of the woman's tongue as she enquired what he was doing with her lilacs. But no, she asked him in the cheeriest of voices if he would like some. Robert answered that he would be glad to have one. Whereupon she cut a whole bouquet of blossoms and handed it to him with a pleasant word and a smile. He walked on with the blooms tucked between the handles of his bag and soon arrived at the Tacony Edge Tool and Hammer Factory.

Hammond's Factory, Shoemakerville. (Old York Road Historical Society)

Robert had been told that the factory owner, a Mr Charles Hammond, lived next to the factory in a small stone house known as the Carpenter House. It was here that Robert had to report. After introducing himself and announcing that the Philadelphia office had offered him a job, Robert had to convince Mr Hammond that he was the right choice. The owner was rather disconcerted to discover that he had been a farrier rather than a maker of tools, but Robert assured him that he was adaptable. Mr Hammond led him into the Lower Forge Shop and introduced the foreman, Joel Tompkins, who wasted no time in putting Robert in a leather apron and showing him how to make a claw-hammer.

Tompkins was a straightforward man who immediately put Robert at ease. Besides showing Robert the correct way to make a hammer-head, he was full of sound advice on many topics. Importantly, he found Robert somewhere to stay. Tompkins lived close by the forge, and just a few houses away John Clark and his wife had a room to let. At the end of the afternoon, Robert called at the house and was able to settle the arrangement. He would move into their spare room straight away, with the intention of Ann joining him after a few weeks employment in Philadelphia. In this way they hoped to start their lives together on a sound financial footing.

The Clarks' took Robert under their wing. They looked after Robert on the Sunday, the day being spent in conversation, walking around the neighborhood and sharing in the family meal. Work started at 7am on the Monday. To begin with, more of his hammer-heads were rejected than passed forward for shafting, but Robert knew he would soon be turning out perfect heads every time. The more hammers he produced the higher his wage, and 'piece-work puts a man on his mettle'[10]. By the end of that first working week, 1pm on Saturday, almost all his hammer-heads passed inspection. He had settled into work, and into living with the Clarks.

As soon as work was finished, he grabbed his coat and bag and headed off for the York Road and Philadelphia. On this occasion there was no lift from a passing gentleman, but the ten miles passed quickly. He had a spring in his step as he warmed to the prospect of seeing Ann once more. He found the Thomason residence, but the reunion was not as he expected. Ann was sick, and Mrs Thomason had turned nurse. On only her second day in the house, Ann was taken ill with a fever, probably an illness acquired on the *Roscius*. Collyer relates; 'It was of a bad type. There were I think four children in the home. There would be peril (for them) if she was kept there, and the right thing to do would be to send their charge to hospital. I think this never entered into their minds. Mrs Thomason isolated her in a sweet, bright room in the house, called in their own doctor, took care of her with no nurse to help, and said I must be their guest, and come there until my wife was well able to join me, and we could start our home in good fashion'[11].

Robert stayed at the Thomasons' house over the next several weekends. During the week, Mrs Thomason nursed Ann back to health, while Robert mastered the making of hammers. At the end of each week his wage increased

---

[10] The men were paid by the dozen hammer heads completed.

[11] Collyer, *Some Memories*, 46

in line with the greater number of hammers he was producing. Robert realized that he had passed muster as a hammer maker when he was allocated one of the eight small forges in the Hammer Forge Shop. In his first month in the forge he earned twice as much as he was paid as foreman at Ilkley, but he also acknowledged that 'he worked twice as hard as he ever thought of working in the old country smithy of his homeland'.

Robert spent some of his weekend visits to Philadelphia wandering around the city streets. It was not long before he was drawn into a bookshop, although he had vowed not to spend any of his hard-earned money on books, not for a while anyway! Engaging the bookseller in conversation, Robert discovered that he was both a Methodist and a local preacher. He showed the man, Thomas Stokes, a letter he had brought with him from Mr Murray, the Secretary to the Local Preachers in the Addingham Circuit in Yorkshire, which attested to Robert's experience as a preacher. Mr Stokes read the letter and immediately extended the right hand of fellowship. He invited Robert to attend his church on the following Sunday. This Robert duly did and was presented to the minister, who was also glad to read his letter and welcome him. There was a prayer meeting after the regular service, and Collyer was asked to 'make a prayer'. As Robert and his new-found friend walked away from the church, Stokes said; "I feel sure that was a good prayer, but we did not understand the half of what you said. I suppose you spoke in the Yorkshire dialect. You will have to speak as we do here in America if you are to be a local preacher". Collyer had never thought about this. Indeed, he rather prided himself on his good English and it certainly was not broad Yorkshire, but Thomas Stokes did not know that. No matter if Collyer thought it was good English, it was not good American. Yet he was eager to return to preaching. Collyer writes; 'Here was another panic. If I must learn the new tongue and forget the old before the people could hear me, rectify the aspirates, change the accents, alter the vowels, and all the rest, when could I begin to be heard at all?'[12] The answer would be after several months of adjustment and frustration.

Towards the end of June, with Robert established in well-paid work and Ann fully recovered, they decided that Ann should move to Shoemakertown[13].

---

[12] Collyer, *Some Memories*, 56

[13] Shoemakertown got its name from the old corn-grist mill at its centre that for several generations had been in the Shoemaker family. In 1846 the mill was put up for sale and was purchased by an employee, Charles Bosler, a man who some years later would become a good friend to the Collyers, (William J. Buck, *Cheltenham Township*, 1884, 807). Shoemakertown was later re-named Ogontz after the famous Girls' School

When they were ready to go, Robert offered to repay the Thomasons for the medical expenses, food and hospitality that had been given over the past six weeks. "For this we pleaded," Collyer wrote; "but they would not hear us for a moment. Not a penny should we pay them: much more they said. And then the dear old man laid his hands on us and gave us his sweet benediction. The measure was full. This was the answer to the cousin's caution touching the greedy and selfish Americans", and their teeth were safe![14]

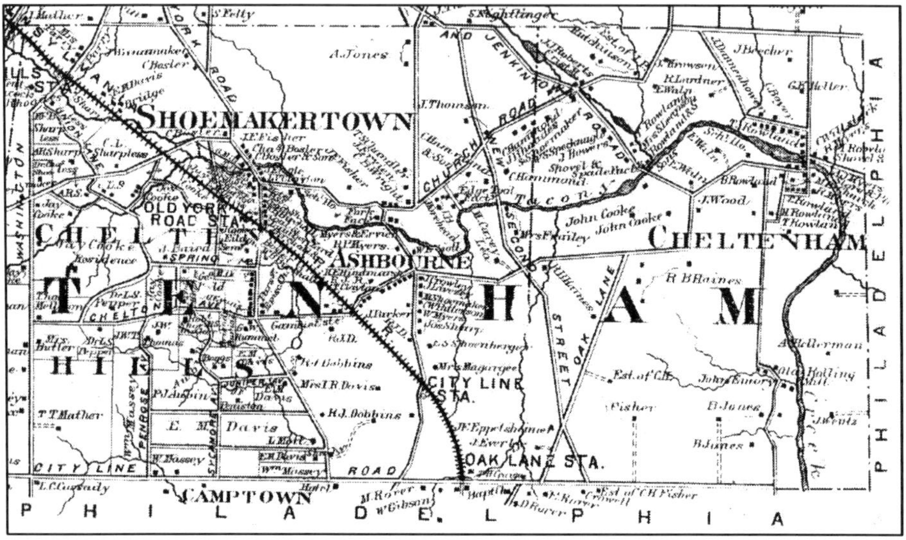

Detail from an atlas of 1871 showing the position of Ashbourne, Cheltenham and Shoemakertown just north of Philadelphia's City Line and their relation to the Old York Road and the railroad.[15]

Just half a mile south-east of Shoemakertown, lay the village of Ashbourne, named after the town in Derbyshire, England. Ashbourne had its origin around an old corn-grist water-mill, built sometime before 1750. In Collyer's time it was no more than a hamlet.[16] The land 'section' belonging to Ashbourne

situated there between 1883 and 1916, but it is now an indistinguishable part of the Elkins Park district in the northern suburbs of Philadelphia.

[14] Collyer, *Some Memories*, 47

[15] From the Abington and Cheltenham page of the *Atlas of the County of Montgomery and the State of Pennsylvania* (Philadelphia, G.M. Hopkins & Co. 1871).

[16] Ashbourne remained a hamlet until 1856. In that year the construction of the North Pennsylvania Railroad linking the village to Philadelphia encouraged its rapid

bordered Shoemakertown and reached northwards to the Tookany. In the early eighteen hundreds, a fulling-mill existed at this northern limit, which later went over to the production of forks and shovels. In 1843 Charles Hammond purchased the property and established his claw-hammer factory. A few years later, a son, Charles Jr, joined the partnership. They extended the factory and enlarged the range of products. In the 1850's when Collyer worked there, the factory employed 60-70 men.[17] It was in the shadow of this factory that the Collyers' had their first place together, a rented room in John and Eliza Clarks' house.

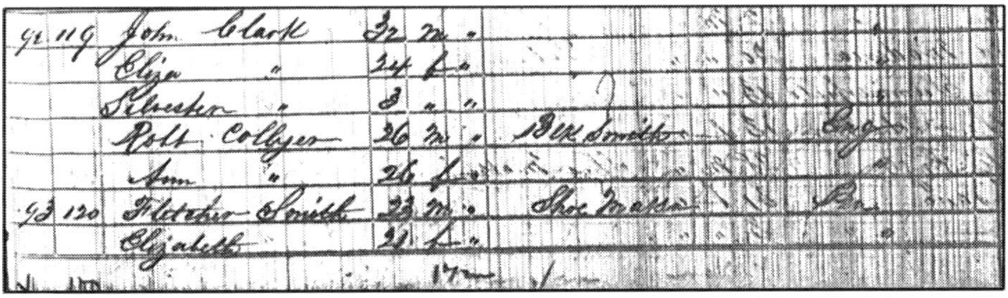

92	119	John Clark	32	m		
		Eliza "	24	f		
		Silvester "	3	"		
		Robt Collyer	26	m	Blk Smith	Eng
		Ann "	26	f		
93	120	Fletcher Smith	23	m	Shoe Maker	Pa
		Elizabeth	21	f		

Extract from the Cheltenham Township census giving details of the Clark household on 2 September 1850 (page 354)

No sooner had Ann moved in with Robert, than their financial stability disappeared. In July, the factory owners decided that the old boiler at the forge had to be replaced. Steam power was used to drive the fans that blew the fires at the forge, so with no boiler there was no work. The factory hands were laid off for three weeks without notice and without pay. Unlike many of the other workers, Robert had no reserves, so he must find work. He managed to get two weeks work on a neighboring farm making hay. When the hay was in, Robert approached Mr Hammond hoping that there might be some casual work helping with the boiler installation. Mr Hammond thought for a few moments and told him that the only work he could offer was unlikely to be suitable, he would have to carry bricks for the bricklayers. 'Suitability' did not come into it; Robert grabbed at the chance. He worked a full week and earned six dollars, but it was a hard week. He had to carry the bricks through a jagged hole in a

growth and by 1880 it had 65 houses, a store, a post-office (1876) and church. The old grist-mill was converted into the railway station.

[17] Rothschild, *History of Cheltenham Township*, 28.

wall and at the end of the week there were many new bumps on his head. Nevertheless, he and Ann had managed. The new boiler was commissioned on schedule, and work resumed at the forge, but another matter now came to the fore, Ann was pregnant.

Although life with the Clarks and their small boy, Silvester, was reasonably harmonious, Robert and Ann could not countenance staying there with a baby. Robert set about finding a house to rent. It was several weeks before he found somewhere, but by the beginning of October, they were able to move. The house was about a mile from the forge in a quiet lane on the edge of Shoemakertown.[18] It was to be their home for the next nine years.

Collyer rented the nearer half of this house in Mill Road. (Photograph from John C. Mellor)

[18] The house in Mill Road was built sometime between 1790 and 1810 and was originally two houses ('twin' or semi-detached). About 50 years ago these were converted into a single house, No. 7707. *Personal communication* — John C. Mellor, 2004

10: Church and Children

The day after they moved into their new home, the woman next door came calling with a bowl full of stewed tomatoes. "I wonder if you know how good 'tomatusses' are?" she asked. "We have more than we can use, and I thought you would not feel offended if I should bring some in." They were certainly not offended.[1]

The Collyers learnt that most of their neighbors were of German stock, some third or fourth generation in America. They found that there were a good many 'Friends' also, but they were not very friendly. 'Their soul was like a star that dwelt apart, with the exception of one old lady well into her nineties who came over painfully on her crutch to greet us.' Another neighbor, old Michael, was of good German stock - hard-working and taciturn but with a lively twinkle in his grey-blue eyes.

"Did you ever see George Washington?" Robert asked him one day.

"Yes indeed I did," he answered, "and it were this way. We lived in Germantown when I were a boy, and one day I saw General Washington coming along our lane[2]. So I waited until he come near to where I were standing, and then I took off my cap and made the best bow I could muster,

---

[1] Robert Collyer, *Some Memories* (Boston: American Unitarian Association, 1908), 49.

[2] This is entirely possible. In 1793 when the Yellow Fever epidemic was at its height in the then U.S. capital, Philadelphia, George Washington and his cabinet retreated to Germantown where they stayed in the house of a Colonel Franks. The following year Washington and his wife returned to the Franks' house for a vacation.

and he looked down at me a-smiling, patted me on my head, and said, 'fine lump of a Dutch boy.' Me ? a Dutch boy! What do you think of that?"[3]

On another occasion, Robert discovered that the same old man had attended school at Milestown, about a mile down the York Road from Shoemakertown.[4] Robert had read that Alexander Wilson, the eminent ornithologist, had once been a school-teacher in Milestown.

"Did you ever have a teacher called Wilson?" Collyer asked.

"I did," Old Michael answered promptly.

"And do you remember anything you would call queer about him?"

"Yes, out of school hours he were always poking among the bushes after birds and bird's nests."

"Well, he poked to good effect. He went on to produce a grand book about American birds."

Old Michael was delighted to learn that his former master had made good.[5]

Christmas came and went in a frugal celebration blighted by homesickness, but January was filled with renewed optimism as Ann neared the end of her pregnancy. A daughter Emma was born on 11 February 1851. Robert was delighted; 'Children are as welcome as the flowers in May,' he wrote, 'I felt that in all human probability I should always be able to feed them and clothe them and keep them warm, and give them the education befitting the children of a poor man.'[6] Nevertheless, they put off a decision regarding Samuel, still with

---

[3] Collyer, *Some memories,* 50.

[4] Milestown was named for Thomas Miles, a Revolutionary colonel. It was situated around the junction of the Old York Road and Oak Lane just inside the northern city limit of Philadelphia. At this time Oak Lane connected Milestown to Milltown (Cheltenham Village). In 1855 the North Penn Railroad opened a station across the city line from Milestown in Montgomery County. The suburb that developed around it became Oak Lane and the name Milestown gradually disappeared. William B. Campbell, *Old Towns and Districts of Philadelphia. Philadelphia History IV* (Philadelphia: City History Society, 1942) 5: 126.

[5] Alexander Wilson was born in 1766 in Paisley, Scotland, and emigrated to America at the age of 28. His *American Ornithology,* a nine-volume work, established his reputation as a major figure in ornithology both in America and internationally. He is remembered by a statue in Paisley and, more fittingly, by birds named in his honor, Wilson's Warbler, Wilson's Phalarope and Wilson's Storm-Petrel. see http://www.electricscotland.com/history/other/alexander_wilson.htm

[6] John Haynes Holmes, *The Life and Letters of Robert Collyer* (New York: Dodd Mead and Company, 1917), 1: 113.

his grandmother in Leeds. They read of the boy's progress in letters from Robert's sister, Maria, but Ann did not feel able to cope with him just yet. Anyway, how was he to be brought over to America? They were in no position to afford another trans-Atlantic journey.

Robert and Ann became members of the Methodist church at Milestown, the one nearest to their home in Shoemakertown.[7] Robert also contacted the Superintendent Minister of the circuit, the Rev. John L. Taft, and showed him the letter of introduction.[8] Although Taft seemed impressed by the effusive testimonial from Yorkshire, Robert formed the distinct impression that Taft was suspicious of a man who spoke such a strange language and yet claimed to be English. "You want to preach, do you?" said Taft, after a lengthy pause. "Well, I guess we may someday give you an opportunity." The interview was finished. Robert could tell that the chance to preach would be a long time coming if he waited for Taft to put him on the preaching plan. He must make his own opportunity.

Robert had noticed that Taft was inclined to ask one of the local preachers to take the service when he was tired or had a very small congregation. After months waiting for an opening, and with his mind full of something to say, Robert decided to go over to a service at Harmer Hill where Taft was preaching. The services were held in a small school-room.[9] It was high summer. The weather was stiflingly hot, and it occurred to Robert that Taft might be glad to be relieved of the sermon. Collyer recalls 'There was a little congregation gathered, looking resigned, as they had to, because they were going to hear the Rev. Taft. I stepped up toward the altar and he looked at me an instant, and said: "Would you like to preach here now?"

"Yes," I said, "I would, very much."

---

[7] later the Oak Lane Methodist Episcopal Church, 70th Avenue and Old York Road. A newspaper cutting published in 1906 including a photograph of the church, together with a notice of a service commemorating the centenary of the birth of Robert Collyer held on Sunday December 9th 1923, are in the Campbell Collection of the Historical Society of Pennsylvania, 17: 80-81.

[8] The Milestown ministers during the period of Collyer's residence in Shoemakertown were; 1850-51, John L Taft; 1851-53, James L Huston; 1853-55, Stephen Townsend; 1855-57, Gasaway (sic) Oram; 1857-59, James B Ayars; 1859, John W Arthur, from *Oak Lane Methodist Episcopal Church 1831-1931. Centennial anniversary services with historical sketch* (Privately published, 1931), 10.

[9] The Harmer Hill Methodist Church opened soon after Collyer's first visit, in 1851. The village of Harmer Hill later became known as Glenside, its present name.

"Go right on," said Taft.

So Collyer started. He had no notes, but he had a rich store ready to share. He forgot all about his dialect, and so it seemed did the small group of listeners. The farmer's kitchen on the Wharfedale moor side and the small schoolhouse at Harmer Hill became one. He had a Pentecostal feeling that he was speaking to each one in their own tongue, and there was a burning desire in him that lit up the plain room. He sat down covered in perspiration. After the final benediction, Taft gave him a strong grip of the hand, and said, "Brother, you shall have all the work you want to do."

Milestown Methodist Church, north side and rear view, taken in 1895 immediately prior to its demolition. The church was built in 1834 on the Old York Road. The vestibule extension on the north side was added in 1880. (Old York Road Historical Society)

Now the door was open. Robert was given appointments at all four churches in the circuit and was soon as busy with preaching as he had been in Yorkshire.[10] As time went by, he learnt a new way of speaking; he slowed his

10 Collyer refers to four churches in the Milestown circuit. It later comprised six churches; Milestown itself, Olney, Harmer Hill, Jarrettown, Rising Sun and Milltown.

speech and began to acquire the American idiom, although he never entirely lost his Yorkshire 'burrs'. He never, however, adopted the monotonous delivery that characterized some of the Americans he met. His speech retained its native vigor and his forceful delivery made him a natural orator. He became a welcome speaker at the village churches along the York Road. One old man confessed to Collyer in later years that he had not understood him for a long time, "But I felt good, so I always came to hear you."[11]

He became increasingly effective as a preacher, not simply because his language became easier to understand but through an expanding fund of experience and anecdote and his maturing qualities of human understanding and sympathy. He had a natural gift of speech which was allied to personal charm and infectious good spirits. His sermons were rich in common sense and strong convictions. While he took a homely interest in the tasks of daily living, he also had an inspired vision of things spiritual. His preaching belied the poverty of his formal education and brought his listeners new insights and inspiration. He seemed to speak directly to the hopes, the insecurities and the deep concerns of his listeners.

Collyer's powers of oratory were not only appreciated by the simple country folk and artisans of his neighborhood, but he also exerted the same charm on more sophisticated listeners. A contemporary observer wrote; 'I was about 13 years old and my father, who was a Methodist minister, would frequently mount me on an old white horse to ride over to the factory and get Brother Collyer to preach on the following Sunday. I would probably have supposed Collyer to be of the usual run of local preachers but for the fact that a manufacturer's son of the neighborhood, who had just come out of Dickinson College, told me confidentially that Collyer was a remarkable man, and the only man he cared to hear preach in the Methodist pulpit.[12] I recollect that the last day I went over to get Mr. Collyer I arrived on the ancient white horse at the dinner hour, when he was lying down on the grass with thirty or forty other workmen, all with their dinner-kettles, and he had a book propped up in the grass from which he read while he took his meal. His strong English face, with a smile upon it, welcomed me, and he always accepted the preaching invitations. In his preaching he did not shout, nor roar, nor hold the people

---

From Carrie V. Speck Copp, *Some Historic Facts of Cheltenham Township* (Jenkintown, Pennsylvania: Old York Road Historical Society Bulletin, 1944), 8: 3-11.

[11] Holmes, *Life and Letters,* 1: 134

[12] Dickinson College was a private educational institution in Carlisle, Pennsylvania, founded in 1783.

over red-hot stoves, and tell them that in seven minutes by the watch, unless they experienced a change of heart, they would be no better than so much roast pork.... He preached with feeling but traced human nature along through its pains and daily troubles, taking them to stopping places of relief and inward exultation as doubt after doubt disappeared and man became reconciled to life and grief.'[13]

Meanwhile, matters did not go nearly as well for Ann. As Robert became more and more Americanized, and as his reading took him onto higher planes of learning, so the distance between him and Ann became greater, or so it seemed to Ann. Her simple ways and homely conversation seemed a world away from the increasing esteem enjoyed by her husband. Naturally, Robert spoke to her in the old tongue and he did not flaunt his learning or new-found standing in the community, but Ann felt a gap between them. Robert was tender towards her; he was always caring and considerate; but she was aware that their relationship was one of companionship and familiarity rather than true bonding of mind and feelings. She became lonely. Her Yorkshire dialect was a barrier to new friendships; her Germanic neighbors were kind but kept their distance. The folk at church found her 'strange' and diffident. She felt isolated, yet Robert was largely unaware of her predicament. He had his work, his reading and his preaching. She had very little. There was baby Emma, but there was no family and no friends to support her, only a husband with his head in a book and his mind full of ideas.

A second daughter, Agnes, arrived. Unfortunately, the baby was sickly from birth and died after a few weeks of feeble life. Ann fell into a depression and was unwell for several months. She felt somehow responsible for the child's death; an irrational notion, but she thought that her milk might have been insufficient or even tainted. Besides the grief and guilt, there were other anxieties. She had put on a lot of weight in her two pregnancies. She had long felt unworthy, now she felt ungainly.

Towards the end of 1853, Robert decided that his son Samuel should join the family. He might have thought that having a healthy boy around the house would lighten the mood and help Ann's condition. On the other hand, the decision might have been entirely a matter of expediency. Robert learnt that one of his work-mates at the factory, a man called Gallagher, was visiting his home in Scotland in December and returning at the beginning of February 1854.

---

[13] The author of this account is not identified. It is reproduced in Holmes, *Life and Letters,* 1: 135

Gallagher agreed that if Samuel could be brought to Liverpool, then he would return to America on a Liverpool-Philadelphia ship bringing the boy with him, ostensibly as his son. The cost to Robert would thus be minimal. After an exchange of letters with Maria, the arrangements were made. Maria and her husband John, travelled with Samuel, now aged six, over to Liverpool and met up with Gallagher. No doubt with many misgivings and much sorrow, they handed him over into the stranger's care. Samuel and Gallagher sailed to Philadelphia on the S.S. City of Glasgow, in a second-class cabin shared with six other passengers.[14] Sixteen days later, Robert and Samuel were re-united at the quayside in Philadelphia after almost four years of separation. Just a few weeks later Robert read with horror that the City of Glasgow had sunk in mid-ocean with the loss of all 480 passengers and crew on her return sailing from Philadelphia to Liverpool.

Inman Line steamship 'City of Glasgow', built in 1850 and lost in 1854. From National Maritime Museum, London, via Wikimedia Commons.

Whatever the motives behind Samuel's reunion with his father, his arrival in the household signaled the beginning of Ann's recovery. The presence of a

---

[14] The S.S. *City of Glasgow* was built for David Tod, who intended to run a regular service from Glasgow to New York. The ship was launched in 1850. However, after a few successful crossings the ship was bought by William Inman for his Liverpool-Philadelphia service which commenced on 11th December 1850. The ship carried 52 first class passengers in two-berth cabins, and 85 second-class in 4 or 8 berth cabins, while the steerage could take up to 400 passengers in the usual 'open-plan' arrangement.

boisterous six-year old boy and the sound of another happy Yorkshire voice in the home had a tonic effect on Ann. For his part, Samuel took well to his step-mother and responded lovingly to her kindnesses. Her health and spirits improved. Ann became pregnant again. She gave birth to twin girls, Amy and Alice, but they only survived for a day.[15] Once more, the home was plunged into sadness. Ann's spirits were only fully restored after the birth of a healthy baby, Harriet Norman, on 14 June 1857.

As his family grew, so Robert grew in knowledge and public standing; the self-educated blacksmith and local preacher began to respond to a new calling, that of political activist and community leader.

---

[15] Agnes, Amy and Alice were buried in the cemetery at Milestown Church (now Oak Lane cemetery).

11: The Abolitionist

Collyer's insatiable appetite for reading continued unabated. There was no spare moment when he did not read. He read at the factory while the iron was in the fire, he read while he ate his meals, he read in the evenings and in the early morning. Ann was frequently moved to say, "I cannot get you to talk as other husbands do. Look up and let me hear your voice."[1]

Robert brought about 20 books with him from Yorkshire, and Bunyan, Burns, Goldsmith and Shakespeare were read and re-read. His vow to Ann that he would not spend money on books was broken shortly after it was made, although his spending was to remain very modest for several years. One of his early purchases had a profound effect on him. He saw a copy of Charlotte Bronte's *Jane Eyre* on a bookstall and bought it for twenty-five cents. 'I began to read it at once,' he says, 'and when I got fairly into it, I felt as if I was borne away on invisible wings right into the old nest. I saw the hills and moors once again, standing out against the northern skies, heard the old tongue again, and was folded back into the old life, could hear the bells ringing in the steeples and the voices singing in the churches, and watch the light play on the faces at the fireside. I knew every spot when I came to them one by one, as I knew the cottage where my mother was sitting thinking about her boy who had wandered away and was lost to her loving old heart and eyes in this strange

---

[1] John Haynes Holmes, *The Life and Letters of Robert Collyer,* (New York: Dodd Mead and Company, 1917), 1: 127.

new world over the sea'.[2] The book provoked a period of intense homesickness and again this brought Robert low for a while. These early years in America were suffused with a yearning to see the old country, and his ailing mother. But this was impossible – Robert could neither afford the fare nor the time away from paid employment.

On a later occasion a book purchase presented Robert with a dilemma. He found a bound collection of *Littell's Living Age* magazine on sale and couldn't resist buying this tome of 752 pages for just less than a dollar. Having bought the book, he dare not walk in the house with it. He hid it under a currant bush until the morning and got up early to smuggle the thing into the house. It was some days later when Ann saw him reading it. "Where did you get that book?" she enquired. "Why, I have had this book some time," Robert answered. In a way this was true. He had owned the book for a whole week. Ann smiled, but said no more. He was forgiven; she was good at forgiving.

Within a year of starting his preaching ministry in the Milestown circuit, an old farmer who was driving his wagon and a team of horses into the city stopped by to ask Robert a favor. "Could you come over one Sunday to preach at our church at Hatboro. We've heard about you, and we're eager to hear you for ourselves." Robert accepted without hesitation. The farmer made no mention of transport although Hatboro was a good six miles away, nor was there an indication of a fee. That was not at all unusual. In eight years of preaching in and around the Milestown circuit he received only 'one almanac, several pecks of apples, a heterogeneous assortment of household necessaries, no end of teas and suppers, and ten dollars in money for three sermons to the Baptists.' Nor was the six-mile walk a hardship. He walked everywhere and maintained the long-acquired skill of reading while he walked. So, he went over to Hatboro, to the Lehman Methodist Church, and found a good congregation waiting to hear his words. Once in the pulpit, however, he opened the ragged Bible only to find that the page containing the key passage that formed the text for his sermon was missing. He went through with the service but with more than a touch of anger in his heart. At the end, he was warmly thanked by the old farmer who asked him to come again. Collyer

[2] Holmes, *Life and Letters*, 1: 138.

replied; "I shall gladly come again when I'm free, and after you've got a new Bible."[3]

On a second visit to Hatboro, his farmer host apologized for the ragged bible, now replaced, and explained why the Hatboro church was so poor. It was built with money donated by a Mr. Joseph Lehman and his wife who had also endowed the church with an income approaching three hundred dollars a year. Far from acting as a blessing, the endowment was a bane. The guaranteed income discouraged the members from giving their own money, despite many being well-to-do farmers, and the church suffered a chronic lack of funds. Once again, Robert was offered no fee, but on this occasion he gained a rich reward. When the farmer learnt that Robert had a passion for books, he told him about the Union Library in Hatboro and declared, "I shall be glad if you will use my ticket, with no cost to yourself, sir." Robert gladly accepted.

The Union Library of Hatboro c. 1905 (Old York Road Historical Society)

Free use of the library proved to be a God-send for a poor man obsessed with reading. Collyer called it 'a spring of living water.' The Union Library was

[3] The Lehman Methodist Church was the first church built in Hatboro. It was built in 1836 by Deborah and Joseph Lehman in memory of their son. See http://www.pitrone.com/church.html

almost one hundred years old and had only recently moved into a splendid new building.[4] It boasted an extensive collection of American and European literature, and Robert was able to borrow books at will. To his store of the great English writers he now added Hawthorne, Longfellow and Harriet Beecher Stowe. Working feverishly at the forge, he would get ahead of his target and finish work early to visit the library. Making light of the twelve-mile round trip, Robert carried his precious supply back to Shoemakertown, reading as he walked.[5] The bibliophile did not remain content with membership of one library. After the opening of the rail link to Philadelphia in 1856, Robert became a borrower at the Mercantile Library in the city.

Although Collyer's thirst for knowledge was now largely satisfied by a ready supply of books, he continued to drink at other springs. He enjoyed discussion and debate with fellow workmen during the breaks from work, and with members of his Class at the Milestown church.[6] Arising out of these discussions came the notion of establishing a Lyceum in Shoemakertown, a meeting place that would serve as a venue for lectures and debates.

The Lyceum movement was an interesting phenomenon.[7] In America the movement began through the efforts of Josiah Holbrook who formed the first village Lyceum in 1826 at Millbury, Massachusetts. He aimed to provide a forum for community education and self-improvement. Soon Lyceums were established throughout New England. An article published in 1829 declared; 'Wherever these Lyceums have been established, they have been found to

---

[4] In August 1755, four men of Hatboro called a meeting at the Crooked Billet Tavern to discuss the formation of a library. Thirty-eight citizens signed the 'Instrument of Partnership' that brought the Union Library Company into existence. In 1848, Nathan Holt, bequeathed $5,000 to the Library. Three thousand dollars was used to purchase land and build a permanent library building, and the Greek Revival style building was completed in 1850. The library continues to operate under the original charter. see http://www.pitrone.com/library.html

[5] Edward W. Hocker, 'What the Union Library did for a blacksmith', Hatboro, PA: *Public Spirit* (newspaper), 1931), 5 February.

[6] From the time of the founder, John Wesley, Methodist congregations or 'Societies' were subdivided into 'Classes' that met on a weekly basis for teaching and mutual support.

[7] The name 'Lyceum' derives from a gymnasium and grove of trees next to the Temple of Apollo Lyceus in Athens, where Aristotle taught. Aristotle's teaching was characterized by informality and conversation. The Lyceum movement emphasized self-education through lectures and discussion.

improve the condition of the people, by introducing subjects of useful knowledge, instead of the ordinary frivolous topics of conversation, by giving a proper direction to amusements, by creating a taste for reading and thus introducing the public libraries.'[8]

Collyer and his associates were probably inspired by a Lyceum further up the York Road at Jenkins Town (later Jenkintown). The activities at Jenkins Town Lyceum consisted principally of lectures, recitations and debates. Subjects discussed were usually of a moral or literary nature, and partisan political issues of the day were largely avoided. The members seem to have learned this lesson from an early experience that led to a complete schism in the Lyceum. In the first year of its existence a serious division of opinion caused by the anti-slavery issue led to a dissenting faction walking out and establishing a new group. Nevertheless, the lecture program continued to include such potentially controversial topics as Capital Punishment, Women's Rights, Follies of Fashionable Life, Education of Children and Philosophy of Death.[9]

The Shoemakertown Lyceum started in a small way in the winter of 1854, holding their meetings in the village schoolhouse. Men from the forge and young farmers made up the group that, unlike the wary approach of the Jenkins Town members, met to discuss 'questions of moment' hopefully without fear or reproach. The hope was not sustained. A furious argument followed a talk on human evolution 'by a gentleman from the city'.[10] Collyer writes; 'We were not prepared to admit the question, only to condemn the whole heresy from alpha to omega. The creation of this world in six days, the story of the making of man, and the woman from his rib, and the Fall, and what followed, - he whistled these down the wind. These things were myths he said, or poems or what not. Man had not fallen, but had won his way from the monad (a single-celled micro-organism) to the eminence on which he stood.

---

[8] *Freedom's Journal*, (New York), January 24, 1829, see http://www.assumption.edu/ahc/Lyceum%20Site/DEFINI~1.HTM

[9] The Lyceum was formed in 1838 and moved into its own building a year later. Abram Clemmer, *The Jenkins Town Lyceum* (Jenkintown, PA: Old York Road Historical Society Bulletin, 1952), 16: 3

[10] These were pre-Darwinian days; the *Origin of Species* was not published until 1859. The speaker may have had no other authority than he had read *The Vestiges of the Natural History of Creation* published anonymously in 1844. Loren Eiseley, *Darwin's Century: Evolution and the men who discovered it* (London: Gollancz, 1959), 132.

Well, I for one was amazed.'[11] This was the first meeting of the Lyceum to arouse strong passions and condemnation, but it was certainly not the last. In 1855 a Lyceum meeting provided the spark that ignited a fire within Robert Collyer; the meeting was on the subject of Abolition.

In the 1850's the word 'Abolition' meant only one thing, the abolition of slavery. It was a word avoided in the Methodist pulpit, and Collyer had been forced to obey an unwritten rule that slavery was not to be mentioned. He complied with great difficulty. Collyer was instinctively an Abolitionist. He had early memories of his own father going without sugar in his tea for many years and giving the money he saved to help free the slaves in the West Indies.[12] Little wonder that Robert grew up with a deep loathing of slavery. When he joined the Methodist Church in Pennsylvania, however, 'he found a religion that must uphold a system of caste as marked as that of Hindustan. No colored man was allowed at the sacrament until all else were served. No child, colored ever so little, ever sat on the same seat (as white children) in Sunday School, nor a grown person in church. ..... No prayer (was) ever uttered on behalf of the slave.'[13]

When the Shoemakertown Lyceum was addressed by an Abolitionist speaker, Mr. Edward Davis, Collyer found himself in a dilemma. Conditioned by five years of silence on the subject in the Milestown pulpits, he found himself advocating a laissez-faire policy when his natural inclinations leaned towards support for the Abolitionist cause. The ensuing exchanges became so heated that it was decided to continue the debate at another meeting. For this second meeting, held in Philadelphia, Davis decided to bring along another Abolitionist speaker to add strength to his side of the argument. The speaker was his mother-in-law, Lucretia Mott.

Collyer, like many before him, came under the spell of Lucretia Mott at that Lyceum meeting. He found her a compelling speaker whose arguments were so eloquently delivered that he was completely won over. "I fight henceforth under this banner," he declared. At the time of this address, Mott was aged

---

[11] Collyer, *Some memories*, 67.

[12] The great majority of British slaves were in the West Indies working on the sugar plantations and Collyer's father was taking part in a national movement in his boycott of sugar. Ignited by several pamphlets on the issue, the sugar boycott burst into life in response to the U.K. Parliament's rejection of the slavery abolition bill in 1791. see Adam Hochschild, *Bury the Chains: The British struggle to abolish slavery*, (London: Macmillan, 2005), 193

[13] Holmes, *Life and Letters*, 1:143

sixty-two. She was a small, fragile-looking woman in a simple, plain grey dress with a lace cap over her silver hair. Her features were delicate and, though wrinkled, her face had a beauty that owed as much to inner radiance as to its outward appearance. Her dark eyes flashed with intelligence and strength. At the Lyceum meeting she spoke extemporaneously, as was her usual practice. Mott frequently spoke to large audiences without any notes, in a day when women seldom addressed public gatherings. As with all great orators her listeners felt that she spoke directly to their hearts and invited their personal response.

Lucretia Mott was born in 1793 into a Quaker family on the island of Nantucket, off Massachusetts. She went with a sister to a private boarding school in New York State and, at the age of fifteen, was taken onto the staff as a teaching assistant. James Mott, her future husband, also taught at the school. When she moved to Philadelphia with her parents, James Mott followed and entered business with her father. Shortly afterwards Lucretia, aged , and James, aged twenty-three, were married. Thereafter Lucretia had children and worked hard in the home and in self-education. At the Friends' Meeting she displayed a precocious talent for public speaking and leadership, and at the age of twenty-five she became a Quaker 'minister'.[14] Thus began a career that was never far from the public limelight, or from controversy.

Lucretia Mott: Quaker, abolitionist, women's rights activist, and social reformer. (Courtesy Friends Historical Library of Swarthmore College.)

[14] Margaret H. Bacon, *Valiant Friend: The life of Lucretia Mott* (New York, Walker and Co. 1980), 37. While the meetings of the Society of Friends (Quakers) are usually constituted without a minister, Bacon writes, 'In January 1821 she (Mott) was formally recognized as a minister, a tribute rarely paid to a young woman still in her twenties.'

Mott's first battle was over the liberalization of her religion. She was attracted by the views of Elias Hicks, and as a so-called Hicksite Quaker, she became the target of opprobrium from the predominantly orthodox membership of the Philadelphia Meetings. Nevertheless, she stuck to her principles and was in the van of a 'free' religious movement that had much in common with Unitarianism.

Lucretia Mott came to wider public attention, however, through her espousal of Women's Rights. Mott's early experience of public life soon demonstrated that as a woman she was denied the same rights as her husband. At some conferences they attended, women delegates were not invited onto the platform and could not address the meeting. Women could not hold office in many organizations, and it was widely assumed (by men) that in intellect and knowledge they were invariably inferior to the male. Besides, men claimed, their temperament and emotionalism were ill-suited to public debate. For a young woman of Lucretia's intelligence these strictures aroused a smoldering and indignant anger. She set out to challenge the prevailing attitudes and embarked on a life-long crusade for Women's Rights. In 1848, with the help of Elizabeth Cady Stanton and others, Lucretia organized the first Woman's Rights Convention at Seneca Falls in up-state New York. The women hit upon the idea of re-drafting the Declaration of Independence as an embodiment of their grievances. Their so-called Declaration of Sentiments held a hitherto suppressed challenge to the status quo, 'We hold these truths to be self-evident: that all men *and women* are created equal'. It emphasized the prevailing subjugation of women, drawing attention to 'the repeated injuries and usurpations on the part of man toward woman' and their 'absolute tyranny over her.' The women were pleased with their statement and the success of the meeting, but they were totally unprepared for the storm of criticism and ridicule that followed. Almost every newspaper in the country carried an editorial attacking the notion of equal rights. The *New York Herald* treated it as a huge joke and predicted that 'Miss Lucretia Mott' would soon be running for President! The paper referred to her as a modern Lucretia Borgia, 'full of old maid-ish crochets and socialist violations of Christian dignity.'[15] History has come to a kinder and more serious verdict on this meeting and on Lucretia Mott's overall role as a pioneer of Women's Rights.

The third, and arguably most passionate, of Lucretia Mott's causes was the slavery issue. She first became active in the abolitionist cause in the eighteen-

[15] Bacon, *Valiant Friend,* 126.

twenties. In 1830, following a visit by a young radical journalist, William Lloyd Garrison, both Lucretia and James adopted this issue with a will. When James became a founder member of the American Anti-Slavery Society, Lucretia, not to be outdone, established the Philadelphia Female Antislavery Society. The Motts spent a large amount of their own money supporting the work of the movement and sponsoring sympathetic newspapers and magazines. They both lectured, either together or separately, at meetings throughout New England, including numerous Lyceum appearances. For Lucretia, one of these happened to be at Shoemakertown where a young blacksmith hung on her every word. This blacksmith was to become a disciple, a friend and, two years later, a near neighbor.

Collyer's recruitment to the abolitionist cause soon led to some personal difficulties. He joined the local Abolitionist society and attended meetings in Philadelphia where he furthered his growing friendship with Lucretia Mott. His links with the Abolitionists, however, alarmed his friends and fellow Methodists. Some rebuked him in a kind way, others were plainly hostile. To most Methodists, the Abolitionists were infidels of the worst brand. The general attitude was that he 'was touching pitch and must be defiled.'[16] Collyer was unmoved. He decided to take his opposition to slavery into the political arena.

Collyer chose to become politically active in 1856, the year of a Presidential election. There were three candidates, James Buchanan, a Democrat from Pennsylvania; Millard Fillmore, a former Whig nominated by the 'American' party; and John Fremont, an ex-Democrat running on the newly organized Republican ticket.[17] The Democratic Party journal in Philadelphia, the *Pennsylvanian,* asserted that Negroes were so dangerous that slavery was needed as a form of race control. To free the Negroes would jeopardize the peace, safety and prosperity of Southern whites; a war of races would

---

[16] Collyer, *Some memories,* 71. Although Collyer does not attribute this quotation, it is taken from Shakespeare's *Much ado about nothing, Act III, Scene iii,* 'they that touch pitch will be defiled.'

[17] Fremont achieved wide public acclaim for his adventures in exploring the 'Oregon Trail'. In 1850 he became a Senator for the state. Fremont's 1856 Presidential campaign was abolitionist but he also tried to gain wider support by denouncing polygamy. See Jon Krakauer, *Under the Banner of Heaven* (New York: Anchor Books, 2004), 6.

inevitably break out, disastrous to the Negroes.[18] In making this claim they were simply echoing the majority view among white Philadelphians. In contrast, the Republicans aimed at abolishing slavery but were also vigorous Unionists and argued against those Abolitionists who wanted a break up of the Union to free the North from any responsibility for slavery. Despite the Republicans' clear statement regarding the maintenance of the Union, the Democrats played on peoples' fears of secession and argued that abolitionism and a breakup of the Union were the greatest issues in the election. Naturally as a fervent abolitionist, Robert threw in his lot with the Republicans, and lent his support to the Fremont campaign.

One evening Robert attended a Fremont meeting at Norristown, the Montgomery County seat. The Unitarian minister and committed abolitionist Moncure Conway was also at the meeting. He recalled in his autobiography that, 'Filled with enthusiasm I attended a Fremont meeting at Norristown. The chief speaker was Senator Hale, and there I first heard the voice of Robert Collyer. The great hearted Yorkshireman was clamoured for by his fellow working-men at the meeting, but being unknown to the chairman, it was after some delay that he was brought to the platform. He came up shyly, being still in the iron-works' dress, but no garb could disguise his noble presence, and the enthusiasm excited by his speech was the great event of the evening'.[19]

The November election confirmed the popularity of anti-abolitionist and anti-Negro sentiments in Philadelphia. The Democrats won 53% of the votes, and another 36% preferred Fillmore to Fremont; the latter winning only 11% of the votes. The Democrat Buchanan became President by winning the electoral votes of practically all the slave-states, as well as a few of the free ones.[20]

Later that month, Collyer, realizing that many Methodists considered his abolitionist stance to be a heresy, tendered his resignation as a preacher but the

---

[18] William Dusinberre, *Civil War issues in Philadelphia 1856-1865* (Philadelphia: University of Philadelphia Press, 1965), 27.

[19] Moncure D. Conway, *Autobiography: Memories and Experiences of Moncure D. Conway* (New York: Cassell and Company, New York, 1904), 1: 210. Conway (1832-1907) was a Methodist minister in Virginia who in 1854-6 became pastor of a Unitarian Church in Washington, D.C., but his anti-slavery views brought about his dismissal from this post. He moved to Cincinnati and became increasingly involved in publishing. During the Civil War he lectured in England on behalf of the Northern cause, and remained in London for 20 years as Minister at the Unitarian Chapel in Finsbury. He returned to the United States in 1884 and thereafter devoted himself to literary work.

[20] Dusinberre, *Civil War issues,* 42

Local Preachers' meeting refused to accept it. They knew that Robert was much loved by their congregations. Despite their distrust of his liberal views, they would not let him go. Collyer was moved by this loyalty for, on his part, he held a deep affection for his Methodist brothers and sisters. He also felt an increasing loyalty to his adopted country, and, at a simple ceremony in Philadelphia, Robert and Ann pledged their allegiance to America.[21] They stood with hands on heart before the flag and made their oath. In return they were welcomed as Citizens of the United States. Robert and Ann Collyer were henceforth 'Americans'.

In mid-March 1857, James and Lucretia Mott moved from their house on Arch Street, Philadelphia, to a renovated farmhouse on the Old York Road just a short distance from Shoemakertown. Rather unimaginatively, they called the house '*Roadside*'. It was situated on the edge of an extensive area of farmland that James Mott, in partnership with his son-in-law, Edward Davis, had purchased in 1851. In the intervening years the Mott family had used the farm as a summer retreat from the oppressive heat of Philadelphia.[22]

Now occupied by a staunchly anti-slavery family and standing on the main route from Philadelphia to New York, *Roadside* was an ideal stopping place for fugitive slaves as they made their way north. Their arrival on the Motts' doorstep was not simply fortuitous. The fugitives were guided from one safe-house to the next along a network stretching from the southern slave-states up into Canada, the so-called 'Underground Railroad'. The Motts' house in Philadelphia had been a 'station' for several years, but *Roadside* had a better situation and, being more isolated, was more suited to this illegal traffic. Had law enforcement officers felt it expedient to expose the underground railroad, they could easily have done so, but they appear to have turned a blind-eye to the traffic unless directly confronted by fugitives. The authorities only needed to read the facts reported in the *National Anti-Slavery Standard.* This paper described in 1857 each of the forty-seven fugitive slaves recently forwarded to Canada. Stations on the railroad were not publicly identified but were often located at the houses of prominent abolitionists. The Mott house was an

---

[21] P. William Filby and Mary K. Meyer (eds), *Passenger and Immigration Lists Index: Volume 1 A-G* (Detroit, Michigan: Gale Research Co., 1981) 355.

[22] *Roadside* was Lucretia Mott's home from 1857 until her death in 1880. After 1912 the house was demolished as part of the development that is now Latham Park. Elaine W. Rothschild, *A History of Cheltenham Township,* (Cheltenham, Cheltenham Township Historical Commission, 1976), 36.

obvious refuge. From 1853 to 1860 about 1100 fugitive slaves passed through Philadelphia.[23]

'Roadside', the residence of Lucretia Mott on the west side of Old York Road. The house was demolished in 1911 (Old York Road Historical Society).

Roadside was only a mile from Collyer's house, and he became a frequent caller on Lucretia Mott. The relationship between the sophisticated Quaker lady and the intelligent but humble blacksmith is an intriguing one. A woman of great personal charm, Lucretia, was mentor and inspiration to a succession of less-advantaged young men and women who shared her ideals. Through the spring and summer of 1857, Robert spent hours at *Roadside,* but his affection and interest was not solely directed towards Lucretia. He also had a deep respect for James Mott. Collyer later wrote; 'When I first knew them they had lived together more than forty years, and I thought then as I think now, that it was about the most perfect wedded life to be found on earth. They were both of a most beautiful presence, both of the sunniest spirit, both free to take their own way as such fine souls always are, and yet their life was so perfectly one that neither of them led or followed the other. James Mott would open his heart

[23] from Dusinberre, *Civil War issues,* 53.

to those he loved, and touch you with wonder at the depth and beauty of his thought.'[24] Nevertheless, it was with Lucretia that he spent his hours at *Roadside*. She had the skills of conversation, and the spirit of conversion. She had the intellect, the quick-wit and the deep well of biblical understanding that gave her discussions with Robert their special appeal. Thirsty for knowledge and understanding, he repeatedly returned to that well. Robert had plenty of time for conversation in the autumn of '57. He was out of work.

On August 24, 1857, the New York branch of the Ohio Life Insurance and Trust Company reported that the entire capital of their Trust's head office had been embezzled. Immediately New York bankers put severe restrictions on even the most routine transactions. A widespread loss of confidence led to depositors demanding payment in gold from the banks, and to compound the problem a huge shipment of gold to the eastern banks was lost at sea. The steamship *SS Central America* carrying gold worth millions of dollars from the San Francisco Mint went down in a hurricane while sailing from Panama to New York.[25] This sent a shock wave through the financial community. On October 3 there was a huge increase in withdrawals from the banks, many of which collapsed. Although the East coast was hardest hit, with bank closures in New York, Philadelphia, Baltimore and elsewhere, bank failures also stretched into the mid-West. The climax came on 13 October when banking was suspended in New York, and throughout New England. Unemployment rose, property prices fell, manufactured goods piled up in warehouses, the railroads defaulted on their debts, and land schemes, many dependent on railroad construction, also failed.[26]

It was in mid-October that the forge closed. The fires went out and were not re-lit until the spring of 1858. The situation in the Collyer home, as in thousands of homes throughout the country, was desperate. There were three children to feed and clothe, and Ann suffered from poor health. In the preceding years they had managed to save a little money and would have had more but for Robert being laid off on two occasions, one with a broken arm, and another

---

[24] Holmes, *Life and Letters,* 1: 157

[25] The steamship had on board 581 persons (many carrying great personal wealth) and over $1 million in commercial gold. She also carried a secret shipment of 15 tons of federal gold intended for the eastern banks. The boat went down in a hurricane about 200 miles off the coast of South Carolina on 12 September 1857. Of the 478 people set adrift only 53 were later rescued by passing ships.
http://memory.loc.gov/ammem/today/aug24.html

[26] from http://urbanography.com/1857/

time for a splinter of steel in his eye. Certainly, the savings would not see them through the winter, so Robert had to find work where he could. He did not care what the job was, as long as it was honest, 'for a dollar a day meant independence, while to fold your hands meant beggary.' [27] He began by helping to dig a well, and then had a spell breaking stones on the turnpike, but these jobs were intermittent and poorly paid. In between jobs, he worked around the house and helped with the children and was grateful to Mrs. Mott for gifts of food and clothing.

Fortunately, Lucretia was not his only source of help. Robert was making some purchases at the village store when Albert Engle, the proprietor said, "You mustn't scrimp your family for anything we have in our store. The work will start up again, and I know you'll pay me when you're able." Likewise, Charles Bosler, the miller, went to see him and said; "Come to my mill for all the flour and meal you need. I can trust you." Finally, the owner of the Collyers' house, George Heller, followed suit and deferred all payments of rent until Robert was back at work. In March 1858 the fires were lit again, the hammers rang on the anvils, and debts were paid off, but Collyer never forgot these acts of kindness.[28]

[27] Holmes, *Life and Letters,* 1:120.

[28] In October 1896, Collyer returned to Shoemakertown to give the oration at the funeral of Albert Engle. "I told the large gathering present the story of my acquaintance and intimacy for 46 years with the departed one, and spoke of him as the good husband, the good father, the good citizen, the good friend, and the good merchant, and said to them that I would pledge my confidence that Albert Engle did not possess one unclean dollar when he died". Holmes, *Life and Letters,* 1: 120

12: The road to Unitarianism

After seven years of preaching in the Milestown circuit, Robert had become increasingly disenchanted with the Methodist church. The discord surrounding his radical stand against slavery was part of the problem, but most of the issues were doctrinal. Ten years before, in Ilkley, he had been drawn into Methodism through a mixture of sentiment, emotion, and the stirring hymns of Wesley, - in short, through his heart. Now his head was taking over. The years of reading theology, philosophy and politics had sharpened his critical faculties. He had always baulked at the preaching of eternal damnation and the fires of hell. Now intellectual reasoning pointed to other doctrinal dragons that he needed to slay. By the end of 1857, Robert had developed a liberal theology shaped and refined through discussions with Lucretia Mott, and more recently, and more convincingly, with the Unitarian minister, William Henry Furness.

Furness was a powerful orator, a theologian and author, and a leading light in the Philadelphia abolitionist movement.[1] Robert heard him speak on several occasions at anti-slavery meetings. One stormy Sunday evening he walked to the Unitarian Church in Philadelphia to hear Furness preach. There were so few people present that, contrary to his usual practice, Furness spoke entirely without notes. The spontaneity and sincerity of his extempore preaching spoke powerfully to Robert.[2] A week or two later Robert met Furness at an

[1] Biographical details from http://www.alcott.net/alcott/home/champions/Furness.html

[2] William H. Furness, *Robert Collyer and his Church,* A discourse delivered in the First Unitarian Church in Philadelphia, 12 November 1871, 10.

abolitionist gathering at the home of Edward Davis. Furness later recalled, 'At an anti-slavery meeting, I met a young Englishman, a workman in a neighboring hammer factory and a Methodist class-leader, accustomed to exhort in the religious meetings of his denomination. I was impressed by his thoughtful air and by his acquaintance with the intellectual topics of the day. He was evidently a man who was subsisting on food which his fellow-workmen knew not of, constantly growing, taking into his blood whatever nourishment books afforded him. He was a reader, they said, of the Encyclopaedia Britannica.' [3]

Rev. William Henry Furness. (from William Still, 'The Underground Railroad' ,1872; via Wikimedia Commons)

Furness was twenty years older than Robert, but the older man's vitality and lively mind narrowed the years between them. Over the course of several meetings, Collyer demonstrated his remarkable ability to form genuine friendships across the social divide. Like the warm relationship he had

[3] Furness, *Collyer and his Church,* 9

developed with Lucretia Mott, he now counted Dr. Furness, the most prominent Unitarian minister in Philadelphia, among his friends. Robert became a frequent caller at the Furness house, usually there to dip into the vast collection of books that the owner had put at his disposal, but also, to join Furness and his friends in wide-ranging discussions.

Furness was a powerful advocate for the Unitarian cause, and with Robert as listener, his wise words fell on sympathetic ears. Here was no creed or dogma, no 'fallen creatures', and no eternal damnation. Instead, Robert heard of a faith grounded in the individual's innate capacity for good, personal altruism as perennial as the grass. Here was a faith in which freedom, reason and tolerance held sway. Unitarians believe that divinity is latent in all mankind, and that God is present within, and around, everyone.[4]

In May 1858, this coming together of Furness and Collyer in thinking and friendship was emphasized when Furness asked Robert to take a service at the Unitarian church in Philadelphia. The Rev. Moncure Conway had asked Dr. Furness, an old friend, to conduct his wedding service in Cincinnati.[5] Furness was keen to accept but needed someone to take his services while he was away. He turned to Robert. In part this was a compliment to Collyer's own powers of oratory, but it was also an opportunity to further involve him in Unitarianism. Thus, on Sunday 30 May 1858, Collyer delivered his first sermon in a Unitarian church. The sermon was heard, and remembered, by a nephew of Dr. Furness. The nephew, William Eliot Furness, wrote; 'He (Collyer) was late in reaching the church, and as I remember, he walked from Shoemakertown to Tenth and Locust Streets (the location of the First Unitarian Church). He was rather rough looking, though kindly in his expression, and he came wrapped in a shawl

---

[4] These views on Unitarianism are taken from two pamphlets, *Unitarian views of human nature,* and *A Faith worth thinking about: Introducing the Unitarians,* (London: General Assembly of Unitarian and Free Christian Churches, Essex Hall), and from Dennis Crompton, *Unity in Diversity,* (Manchester: Guardian, 2003), March 28, https://www.theguardian.com/world/2003/mar/29/religion.uk1.

[5] Conway was married on June 1, 1858. He writes in his autobiography; 'We were married by the Rev. Dr. Furness, who travelled from Philadelphia to unite us. A notable event was connected with the visit of Dr. Furness. When I offered him payment he said he would accept nothing for himself, but would give what I offered to a working-man of ability near Philadelphia who for some time had preached for the Methodists. He had become unorthodox, and would preach in the Unitarian pulpit on the Sunday of Furness's absence. The man was Robert Collyer.' *Autobiography: Memories and Experiences of Moncure D. Conway* (New York: Cassell and Company, 1904), 1: 254.

which was crossed behind and the ends over his shoulders. The service was rather longer than usual; I think the habit of Methodism had not worn off so as to induce him to preach sermons which later became less lengthy. To my mind the sermon was too long, but good; it was entirely different from that of my uncle, who never or seldom prolonged the service beyond twenty minutes for the sermon.'[6] Although this account does not sound like a ringing endorsement, the overall reaction to Collyer was favorable. After arriving in Cincinnati, Dr. Furness decided to prolong his visit by another week. He telegraphed home to make arrangements for the next Sunday and received the answer that they were well content with Mr. Collyer and more than satisfied with him as the substitute.

Robert continued with his preaching commitments in the Methodist circuit. Despite all his misgivings, he was finding it difficult to let go of the old faith. It was Lucretia Mott who prompted the final break with Methodism by providing Robert with two crucial insights. The first came during an anti-slavery meeting where Edward Davis was the main speaker. Davis was holding forth and frequently quoting the bible to justify the abolitionist position. Most of the time, however, he misquoted the bible texts and his arguments failed to carry much conviction. Eventually, Lucretia Mott intervened; "You must not try to prove your truth by the Bible, but your Bible by the truth." In that moment, Robert realized that he had to take truth for his sole authority; he should break free from a literal, fundamentalist interpretation of the bible when myth and fable were taken as God's word. The second signpost that pointed him towards Unitarianism came from Mott during a lecture tour.

In August 1858, Lucretia invited Collyer to accompany her on an anti-slavery lecture tour to Yardley and Newtown, near Trenton, Pennsylvania[7]. The time spent together gave Robert plenty of opportunity to discuss his alienation from Methodism, but he appears to have been principally affected by a sermon that Lucretia preached. 'It was at a woods-meeting up among the hills where quite a number of us had our say, and then my friend's turn came. I suppose she spoke for two hours, but after the first moment she never faltered or failed to hold the multitude spell-bound, and waiting on her words...... It

[6] William E. Furness, Address in *Memorial Services for Rev. Robert Collyer, D.D.* held in Unity Church, Chicago, 1912.

[7] Mott was also accompanied by another protégé, Rev James Miller McKim. See Margaret H. Bacon, *Valiant Friend: The life of Lucretia Mott* (New York: Walker and Co. 1980), 57.

was not a speech, but a psalm of life.'[8] The effect of Mott's message, however, was that many people, rather than joining her in trying to awaken the sleeping fires of Quakerism, turned to Unitarianism.[9] It would be a turn that Robert Collyer would soon be taking.

By the autumn of 1858, Robert realized that his differences with the Methodist Church were irreconcilable. He began to think once again of resignation, but not before other events began to overtake him. When, rather belatedly, the Local Preachers' Meeting became aware that Robert had preached at a Unitarian service, they were scandalized. "How can you preach for Dr. Furness, in Philadelphia? How could you find anything to say to these people and yet be true to your Methodism? Collyer replied; "I find it easier to preach to them than to preach at home; for I leap over the fence that bounds the system of Methodism, and as they are already over the fence that has bounded the system of Unitarianism, we all meet in the boundless world of truth and beauty which God has made outside, and it is wonderful how much we find to talk about when we get there."[10]

News of this act of heresy, or treachery, or both, reached higher authorities in Methodism – Robert was reported as a man 'not sound in the faith'[11]. The break could not be postponed any longer. Robert went to the Quarterly Conference in January 1859, determined to resign as a local preacher, but his move had been anticipated and he found himself called up before the Presiding Elder. The Elder was a benign and good-hearted man, but he had some serious charges to lay before Robert. First that he did not believe in eternal hell; secondly, that he rejected the doctrine of total human depravity; thirdly, that he could not agree that a Unitarian was damned because he disbelieved in the Trinity.[12] Robert freely admitted these charges and ended by saying that he had come to the conference prepared to make a statement and present his resignation in any case. The Elder said, not unkindly, "There was no help for it" and accepted the proffered resignation.

---

[8] Homer T. Rosenberger, *Montgomery County's greatest lady: Lucretia Mott* (Norristown, Pennsylvania: The Bulletin of the Historical Society of Montgomery County, 1948) 6: 91.

[9] Bacon, *Valiant Friend,* 226.

[10] Robert Collyer, *The life that now is: Sermons* (Boston: Lee and Shepard, 1874), 121.

[11] Holmes, *Life and Letters,* 1: 178.

[12] Many mainstream church people felt that Unitarians had no right to call themselves Christians by denying the divinity of Jesus in holding onto the one-ness (Unity) of God.

In some respects, Robert felt relieved that a decision had finally been made, but he was also saddened by his severance from the pulpit and the people he had come to love. The worst aspect was that not one person in the Milestown fellowship held out their hand to him, or said a word, despite the intimacy between them built in the church and in their homes through eight years of preaching. For Robert, the immediate prospect of continuing at the forge without the stimulation and challenge of preaching, left him empty and frustrated. He appreciated as never before that much of his self-esteem was founded on his calling as a preacher, but now the pulpits were closed to him. He entered another period of darkness but on this occasion the gloom did not last long. Within two weeks another door opened. The door had 'Dr Livermore' on it, and behind it lay the city of Chicago.

Many weeks before the fateful Quarterly Conference, Robert went down to Philadelphia to attend Furness's church and found a stranger in the pulpit, a Dr Abiel Livermore, who was editor of the Unitarian journal, the *Christian Inquirer*. Livermore had travelled from Yonkers, New York, to help his old friend Dr Furness, and no doubt to win new subscribers to his journal. Furness introduced Robert to the preacher after the service and asked him to come home to dine with them. Robert accepted the invitation gladly. It was an occasion for conversation and conviviality that Robert greatly enjoyed.

Livermore's name was not mentioned again until a meeting with Furness two weeks after the Quarterly Conference. Robert had received a note inviting him to go over to Philadelphia to preach for Dr. Furness who was ill and confined to his house. Robert took up the invitation gladly (the fee would make a useful contribution to his depleted book-fund) and he called on Furness before going into the church to conduct the service. He was greeted with some excitement by Dr Furness who handed him a letter he had received from the Unitarian Church in Chicago addressed to Robert. "The church," he said, "employs a minister-at-large to help the poor of their city. The man they have employed has broken down and can do no more, and now they want a man to take his place. They wrote to Dr Livermore, asking him if he could help them to find a man in the East who could fill the gap. And in his answer, he told them to write to me about a young blacksmith he met here one Sunday, a Methodist local preacher of a liberal mind and make, who might be the man they wanted. So they wrote to me, and I answered their letter; and here is the letter they have sent you in answer to mine."[14] Thanking him, Robert put the unopened letter in his pocket and left for the church.

Robert Collyer in 1859. Author's collection.

After the service Robert read the letter before returning to Dr Furness. It contained a pressing invitation to come out to Chicago to take care of the Unitarian Church's Ministry-at-Large. It gave brief details of the work expected of him, indicated how suitable they felt he was for the job and offered him a stipend of 1,200 dollars per annum. He re-read the figure. Only the evening before, he had received his wages for a month in the hammer factory. The wage packet contained 39 dollars and some cents[13]. When he got back to Furness's study, Robert handed the letter back to him. Furness was surprised. "Hadn't you better take the letter home to discuss with your wife, and then let me know your decision next week." "I don't need a week to make up my mind and consult my wife," Collyer replied, "We will go!"[14]

[13] Furness, *Collyer and his Church,* 12.

[14] Collyer, *Some Memories*, 93.

Robert's confidence in Ann's support was well founded. She said "Amen" to his decision, and Robert began finding out about Chicago. Privately, Ann thought that living in a city would be a marked improvement on the rustic life she had endured hitherto. She looked forward to living in a large community where strange accents and 'different' ways were the norm. She was tired of the prejudices of Pennsylvania and the isolation that they produced.

Robert himself had barely heard of Chicago. One man in the forge had been there; he said the place was all mud and that the drinking water was brought from the lake in barrels and peddled from house to house. He had only spent a few uncomfortable weeks there before deciding that he had had enough and came back East. Robert's boss, Mr. Hammond, had lived in Illinois as a young man and had been to Chicago. He had a similarly low opinion of the place and warned Robert not to go, but that if he went, he will surely return. In anticipation he will keep a fire and anvil ready for him. Robert thanked him but told him that they were going to stay.

The managers of the Ministry-at-Large wanted Robert to start at once. He was able to do this, as he could finish work within the week, but Ann needed time to sell furniture and household goods. These would be provided in the furnished church accommodation in Chicago. She and the children would follow on later. So, at the end of February 1859, Ann and Robert took the train to Philadelphia where Robert would embark alone for Chicago. It was a daunting prospect; setting off for an almost unknown city over 800 miles away to a job for which he had no formal qualifications. Robert was filled with the same mixture of trepidation and excitement as when he had boarded the *S.S. Roscius* nine years before.

13: The Minister-at-Large

Robert waved at the receding figure on the station platform. He felt sadness at leaving his wife and children but there was also excitement and elation at the prospect of his new post in Chicago.[1] Gradually, the figure on the platform became lost in the distance. Robert settled back in his seat and surveyed the Pennsylvania countryside.

At first, the train labored against the gradient as the line climbed westwards through the rugged valleys that course through the Allegheny Mountains. The landscape underlined the struggle between man and nature. Mile after mile of barren countryside was dotted with mines and mills, foundries, and forges. Elsewhere the railway ran by fields and farms, through villages and towns, some with familiar-sounding names like Frazer and Lancaster, but all unknown to Robert. About three hours after leaving Philadelphia, the train reached Harrisburg, and then headed north-westwards along the Susquehanna River. After another hour or so the line forked, and the train turned to the west again, running along the beautiful valley of the Juanita. Late in the afternoon, the train pulled into the railway town of Altoona situated high in the

[1] At the time of its incorporation as a town in 1833, Chicago had a population of only 350. In the decade 1836-1845 there was a large influx of immigrants and by 1847 the population had risen to 16,000. Over the next ten years it grew exponentially and in 1859 (the year Collyer arrived) had reached around 100,000.

mountains. Robert stepped down from the carriage and walked across the tracks to the station building where he used the bathroom and bought some cheese and bread for his supper.

After a short stop, during which a second locomotive was attached to assist in the climb ahead, the journey resumed. The line climbed to the summit of the Alleghenies by toiling up one side of a huge valley and then turning through 180 degrees around the formidable 'Horse-Shoe Curve' to ascend the opposite side. Robert smiled to himself when a fellow-passenger told him the name of the curve. He felt a certain affinity with Horse-Shoe Curve but did not trouble to explain the source of his mild amusement. Climbing the southern slope of the valley the train reached the upper edge of the mountain and rounded it to enter an even higher gorge with dizzying views across the mountain range. Slowly the struggling locomotives hauled the train up to the highest point where the line vanished into a long tunnel piercing the ridge.[2] Once through, the train gathered speed and, travelling at up to 40-50 mph, made its way through wild gorges, around sweeping curves clinging to the mountainsides and into deep cuttings. It passed through the mountain resort of Cresson Springs and entered the Conemaugh valley to reach Johnstown. Beyond the Allegheny Mountains, the line passed through the 'Black Country', a region of coal pits and furnaces. It was late evening, and all was darkness except for the occasional orange glow of the dormant fires at the iron and steel works, or the flicker of gas-lights in half-seen country stations.

About 3am the train reached Pittsburgh. Robert was by now sound asleep, but the shouting of the guard roused him. He dragged on his heavy topcoat, grabbed his two bags and stepped down onto the platform. His breath froze in the cold night air and he stamped his feet in an unsuccessful attempt to keep warm. There was some delay in shunting the cars for Chicago onto the front of the train but an hour later, Robert was huddled in a car of the Pittsburgh, Fort Wayne and Chicago Railroad Company.[3] The journey resumed, and he was soon asleep once more.

---

[2] This section of the line was completed in 1854 and replaced the Portage Railroad that utilized a series of stationary steam engines and inclined planes to haul railway cars up and over the Allegheny mountains.

[3] Prior to 1859, passengers from the Pennsylvania Railroad had to change stations in Pittsburgh. A direct service from Philadelphia to Chicago, albeit with a change of cars, was inaugurated on January 1, 1859 with the opening of a new terminal station in Chicago (on the site of the present Union Station).

Robert awoke around 8.30am as the train pulled into Alliance, a railroad junction where some passengers transferred to the Cleveland train. When the train re-started, he took out a book, *Channing's Discourses* – a parting gift from Dr. Furness.[4] Robert preferred to read rather than watch the dreary panorama of flat prairie that was only occasionally interrupted by a village or small town. The train stopped at Mansfield and he was able to get a welcome hot drink and a sandwich. The next stop was at the Crestline junctions which allowed another exchange of passengers, to be followed by apparently endless prairie.[5] It was dark when the train reached Fort Wayne, and Robert prepared for another night of fitful sleep. When he finally awoke early next morning, they were still passing through the same kind of monotonous prairie country. A couple of hours later, isolated houses marking the outskirts of Chicago came into view, and around 8am the train drew into the terminus station on Canal Street. Forty-four hours and 822 miles after leaving Philadelphia, a tired and rather disheveled Robert Collyer arrived in Chicago.[6]

Robert looked around the station. He needed something to eat and quickly found a stall selling bread rolls and soup. He was due to meet the Unitarian Minister at the church office at 11am, so with some hours to occupy, he bought a newspaper and found the waiting room. He sat on one of the polished wooden benches, gradually advancing nearer and nearer to the stove at the center of the room, as fellow travelers vacated their places. At 10am he picked up his bags, heavy with books, and walked out to the front of the station where he climbed into a vacant horse-cab and asked for 'The Unitarian Church, Washington Street'. The cabman threw him a backward glance, and a fur-rug to cover his legs. After a short time in the open cab, Robert realized that the cold was unlike anything he had experienced in Philadelphia.

The cab ride gave him an early opportunity to take in his new surroundings. The dress of the people reflected the winter season. Fur overcoats were prominent, on both men and women, and fur collars stood high around their faces. Many people, aware that Arctic winds sweep across the prairie and the lake with unbroken violence, were dressed in fur cloaks with the capes drawn over their heads.

---

[4] Channing was a pillar of the Unitarian Church and a prolific author. His *Discourses, Reviews and Miscellanies* was first published in Boston in 1834.

[5] The junction was with the Cleveland, Columbus and Cincinnati railroad.

[6] This account of the journey is adapted from William Smith, *A Yorkshireman's trip to the United States and Canada* (London: Longmans, Green & Co. 1892), 193.

The cab crossed a low swing bridge that seemed to hover just a few feet above a sluggish river, and the cab proceeded into the main commercial district of Chicago. Robert's first impressions were far from favorable. He thought back to New York and Philadelphia where the streets and buildings showed grandeur and order, qualities that seemed largely lacking in these first glimpses of the city. In some streets both carriageway and sidewalks were planked, and even the main streets had wooden sidewalks. These appeared to change level with almost every block, sometimes one foot, sometimes three feet and sometimes five. The ascents or descents were made by steps, or by short, steeply inclined boards with or without cross-pieces of wood to prevent slipping. He learnt that the city had been built on a bog, an area of swamp at the mouth of the Chicago River, and only three or four feet above it. To achieve a higher level, some buildings were lifted bodily using screw-jacks and Robert was amazed to see buildings in the process of levitation.[7] Everywhere he looked, a constant stream of horse-drawn omnibuses, public carriages and hacks passed back and forth. It was an impressively busy city.

After its slow progress through crowded streets, the cab finally reached the Unitarian Church of Chicago. On seeing it, Robert's heart sank. The church was a small frame-built structure, albeit with four Doric columns or pilasters and a steeple, but it paled in comparison with the Philadelphia church, a handsome stone structure with a Classical facade and columns, and a Greek temple compared to this humble building.[8] He walked around to the side entrance and pulled on the doorbell. Shortly afterwards the door opened to reveal a small, bespectacled man with a slightly comic, over-large moustache and a severe parting down the center of his brilliantined hair. With a limp handshake, he introduced himself as Charles Gregory, Secretary to the Trustees of the Ministry-at-Large.[9] He took one of Robert's bags, and led him down a dim corridor to the church office.

---

[7] This massive engineering program was supervised by George M. Pullman, who was later to gain immortality through the construction of the railroad sleeping-car. When Collyer arrived in Chicago he witnessed the lifting of the entire Marine Block and the Tremont Hotel.

[8] There is a full description of the First Unitarian Church building and its early history in Alfred T. Andreas, *History of Chicago from the Earliest Period to the Present Time* (Chicago: The A.T. Andreas Company, 1885) 1: 343 and 2: 439.

[9] Between 1859-60, Charles Gregory was Secretary to the Trustees of the Ministry-at-Large. Other Officers were Henry Tucker (Treasurer), E.W. Willard, Amory Bigelow, Jonathan Burr and J.L. James.

Once in the small untidy office, George Noyes, the Minister, welcomed Robert disconcertingly as "Brother Collyer". Noyes was a tall, slightly bent man with a lined and sallow face. He explained that he had started the Ministry-at-Large in October 1857 with the appointment of Reverend William Hadley, supported by two volunteer ladies.[10] Hadley had done sterling work and brought several aims of the Ministry to fruition, but he had been forced to resign after a little more than a year through the stress of the job. Robert put this ill omen on one side telling himself he was made of stronger stuff. Noyes told him that as Minister-at-Large, "You must look after the poor, - the Lord's poor, our own poor, and the devil's poor; for you will find them all in Chicago."[11] He added proudly that the Ministry was "the only private agency for general relief in the city at that time."[12] Noyes went on to explain how he had come West two years before to take charge of the church, and found a congregation aggrieved by the sudden and unexplained resignation of his predecessor, the Reverend Rush Shippen.[13] He felt the church was too inward-looking and needed to develop its social work through a Ministry-at-Large. Although Noyes made much of his two-year's work at the church, Robert formed the impression that he was a man with regrets about moving from New York, and keen to return. Robert's hunch was soon to become a reality.

Noyes brought the conversation to a close and suggested that he and Robert go to the house that the church had rented for Robert and his family. Noyes took one of Robert's bags and with a farewell to Mr. Gregory they set off along Clark Street to the hackney stand where Noyes hired a cab. Crossing the van Buren Street Bridge into the West Side, the cab took them further west to

---

[10] The Ministry-at-Large had its origins in Boston in 1822 when some young men formed 'The Association of Young Men for their own Mutual Improvement and for the Religious Instruction of the Poor.' Two years later this ponderous title was shortened to 'The Association for Religious Improvement.' Largely through the efforts of the Unitarian minister, Rev Joseph Tuckerman, who was appointed in 1826, the Ministry-at-Large became a model for enlightened help for the poor and was adopted in many other cities.

[11] Collyer, *Some Memories*, 95.

[12] Wallace P. Rusterholtz, *The First Unitarian Society of Chicago: A brief history* (Chicago: Privately published by the First Unitarian Church, 5650 South Woodlawn Avenue, 1979) 2.

[13] The Rev Rush R. Shippen was minister between 1849 and 1857. In 1844 Shippen was the first student to enroll in the new Unitarian Meadville Theological School in Pennsylvania and was appointed at the age of 21 to the Chicago church.

Clinton Street where it turned south. The horse trotted along at a steady pace for several blocks before the cabman hauled on the reins and steered it into a narrow side street where they came to a stop in front of a substantial three-story terraced house. They unloaded the bags and, after asking the cabman to wait, Noyes handed Robert the keys to the house. Robert pushed open the heavy front door. In the hallway, standing on a small table was a large patterned bowl containing a mass of holly twigs heavy with bright red berries. Each of the downstairs rooms was aglow with polish and suffused with the scent of lavender. Noyes explained with pride that in anticipation of Robert's arrival, some of the church ladies had spent several days working in the house. Robert was impressed; this was truly a warm and practical welcome from the church. After a quick tour of the house, Noyes took his leave, but not before inviting Robert to take the Sunday service in two weeks' time.[14] An invitation to preach was totally unexpected and sent a nervous flutter through him. Nevertheless, with a parting handshake, he accepted the challenge.

Next morning Robert had an amiable meeting with his assistant, Miss Newcomb, together with some volunteers from the church and decided on a plan of action. He began by getting to know the scope of the job and the people he had to work alongside and started work straight away. His own humble origins and his ability to communicate in straightforward, homely terms made him a natural pastor to the poor. In the weeks that followed he became recognized and accepted in the shanty town around the mouth of the river, a place that for many immigrants provided the first foothold in the new country. Down by the docks he could walk into a smoke-filled bar or tavern without embarrassment, he could talk to drunks and down-and-outs without patronizing them. He could offer help and motivation. For some people, a talk with Robert Collyer was a life-changing event.

Collyer soon discovered the power of 'public relations'. Less than two weeks after starting in the post, he wrote to the newspaper, the *Chicago Press and Tribune*, to alert readers to the existence of a Ministry-at-Large and indicating how they could help. The letter is a foretaste of Collyer's early mastery of communication in which he combines anecdote with an unequivocal appeal to the reader's better self. 'A poor woman came yesterday to see if I could help her. Her husband is a painter; they came to this city from Holland, just as the hard times were setting in. Since then they have struggled to get a living, which she tried hard to tell me in touching broken English; "Will you come to see us,

[14] Sunday March 13, 1859

and see how he can paint? He can do anything." It was evident to me that no amount of ill-fortune could destroy her faith in him. I went, of course, and found by the specimens shown me, that he was a man of ability.....He had some small pictures of considerable merit, which he has painted just for bread; two were waiting to be finished. No more paint, no more money. I was glad to make that possible. He has a family of three children here; they will be glad to go into the country or stay in the city. I trust this will meet the eye of some helper of the faint-hearted, who will give him a trial. Other cases are waiting to be noticed. I am their Pastor, they are members of my church: I want help for them to help themselves.'[15] Collyer published further letters in March and April, letters that combined moving 'case histories' with a challenge to the reader; 'Cannot something be done? It seems to me that with all our provision for the souls of the good, we might also do a larger percentage for the suffering, even if also a sinner.'[16]

While Collyer put all his energies into getting to grips with the new job, he did think from time to time about that first sermon he had to deliver. He decided that he did not need to spend precious time in the preparation of a new sermon, so he sought out the notes of one that he had used before in the Milestown church.[17] Nevertheless, when the day came he entered the pulpit in fear and trepidation. He thought himself little more than an artisan who was now faced by a sophisticated and potentially critical congregation. Although he got through the sermon without faltering, he had no sense of the 'gift of words' he had received in the humble farmhouse in Wharfedale. Yet, the address was well received. People recalled many years later how that first sermon had made such an impression on them.

Within a month of Robert's arrival, the Rev. Noyes called a meeting of members of the church and told them that he intended to resign and return East. Despite the members' best efforts to persuade him otherwise, Noyes had made up his mind to go.[18] Reluctantly, the Society accepted his resignation, and Noyes left shortly thereafter. With hindsight, it could be that Noyes had

[15] 'The Ministry at Large', *Chicago Press and Tribune,* 3 March 1859

[16] 'The Ministry at Large' and 'An urgent want' in *Chicago Press and Tribune,* Mar 9 and Apr 28, 1859

[17] The sermon was based on the text, Isaiah 9:3; "They joy before thee according to the joy in harvest."

[18] Rusterholtz, *First Unitarian Society Chicago,* 3

learned of the imminent departure of many of his most influential parishioners to form a separate North-side church and was fearful of the consequences.

The establishment of other Unitarian churches in Chicago had been a theoretical possibility since April 1857. At that time, the church meeting had passed a resolution that they would mortgage the land on which the original Unitarian church stood and, if required, contribute two quarter shares of the proceeds towards the building of new churches in the North and West Sides. The 'mother-church' would retain its half share. The following month, William Larrabee, Treasurer of the Galena and Chicago Railroad called a meeting of North Side residents interested in the formation of a new Unitarian church.

By this time, Chicago's North Side had become a desirable place to live, attracting into its leafy avenues many wealthy citizens, some of whom were Unitarians. Thus, the residents who attended Larabee's meeting — all men, for only men had been invited — were notable for their wealth and standing in the community.[19] Other meetings followed, and by December 1857 the trustees had decided on a constitution and agreed a name, 'Unity Church'. As this was to be the second Unitarian church in Chicago, the original became increasingly recognized as the 'First Church'.

In June 1858, a quarter of the value of the First Church lot was conveyed to the trustees of the proposed Unity Church, but apart from an occasional business meeting, no action was taken. However, Collyer's arrival prompted renewed interest. Among the listeners at his first service in Chicago, were several members of the embryonic North Side church. Their positive reaction to Collyer's preaching was the signal for the trustees to swing into action.

By April 1859, Robert was busily building up the work of the Ministry-at-Large, while the First Unitarian Church were coming to terms with the Rev. Noyes's resignation, and the North Side 'Unity Church' was about to become a reality. However, Robert's current preoccupation was the imminent arrival of Ann and the children from Pennsylvania.

Ann had stayed on in Shoemakertown until the end of school term before selling most of the furniture and arranging the packaging and shipment of their remaining belongings. Now the family were to be re-united. Robert met them

---

[19] Those attending the meeting were Benjamin F. Adams, William M. Larrabee, Eli Bates, Nathan Mears, Gilbert Hubbard, Samuel S. Greeley, William H. Clarke, Captain Samuel Johnson, Benjamin F. James, Samuel C. Clarke, Henry Tucker, George Watson, Augustus H. Burley and Edward K. Rogers.

From Samuel S. Greeley , B.F. Adams and W.G. Lewis, *Historical sketch of Unity Church, Chicago* (Chicago: Privately published, 1880), 2.

at the Canal Street station after their own prolonged ordeal by train. He saw Ann, holding baby Harriet in her arms, step down from the train and he ran towards her. He hugged her and smothered her in kisses while Samuel and Emma stood by. Then it was their turn. Robert stood with his arms encircling the two of them and hugged them close while they buried their faces in the warmth of his coat. The babble of questions that began at the station seemed to go on for several days in their new home.

A well-thumbed 'carte de visite' of Robert Collyer c.1859. Author's collection.

Following the departure of George Noyes, the First Church sought help from Unitarian headquarters in Boston in maintaining their services. Preachers would come over from New England, usually for a month at a time, to take the weekly services. Sunday by Sunday, Robert attended morning service and heard a succession of sermons delivered by the lions of the Unitarian faith. These sermons were Collyer's theological school. "Each one," he wrote, "had his message and his lessons for me, and how greedily I drank them in!"[20] However, the pulpit could not be filled by visiting preachers every Sunday, and on these occasions, Robert would be expected to stand-in.

In early May, the activists in the North Side project had arranged to rent a small Baptist Church on the corner of North Dearborn and Ohio Streets for use on Sunday afternoons. A deputation approached Robert and invited him to occupy their pulpit "for a few months, till a permanent minister could be settled." They indicated that they intended to build a new church and that it would be well endowed; they could then attract a good man to take charge of the parish, leaving Robert once again to give his whole time and energy to the Ministry-at-Large. Robert accepted, and arranged to preach at the inaugural service on May 29.

The response by the North Side congregation to Collyer's preaching was warm and immediate.[21] Although the Baptist building was relatively small, it did have 250 'sittings'. Such was the appeal of Collyer's preaching, however, that before the summer was out, the place was full to overflowing. Furthermore, the North Side neighborhood was growing rapidly, and the sponsors could see that a larger building was required. The group began a subscription list, a vacant lot on the north-eastern corner of Chicago Avenue and North Dearborn Street was bought, and construction began.[22]

The new Unity Church was ready for use before the end of the year. The building was of wooden construction and cost the relatively modest sum of $4,000, yet it could hold a congregation of 450. The first service was held amid the ice and snow of Christmas Eve, 1859. The Rev. Dr. George W. Hosmer of Buffalo preached the sermon and dedicated the new church.

Robert felt that the official opening of the new church was the right time to withdraw his temporary assistance. In a letter to the Unity trustees, he

[20] Collyer names among these visiting preachers; Dr Briggs, Dr Thompson, Dr (Edmund H) Sears, Charles Brigham, Mr Woodbury and Dr Horatio Stebbins of Portland, and "more I do not remember." Collyer, *Some Memories,* 102.

[21] Address by Samuel S. Greeley in *Memorial Services for Rev Robert Collyer D.D. held in the Unity Church, Chicago,* (Chicago: Privately published by the Unity Church, 1912) 17.

[22] Lot 15 of Block 1, Bushnell's addition to Chicago, was purchased on August 20th.

indicated that he was anxious to be free from the work of preacher and that they should appoint some well-accredited man to be the permanent pastor. He offered to do occasional preaching at Unity, as he was continuing to do at the First Church but insisted that he needed to concentrate on his duties as the Minister-at-Large. Within days, the trustees called Robert to an evening meeting to discuss the matter. They acknowledged that he had been engaged to occupy the Unity pulpit on a temporary basis, but were equally emphatic that for him to withdraw, at the very moment when his work was finding permanent foundations, would be preposterous. The building was theirs, but the new Unity Church as a body of worshippers was Robert's creation and he must be its minister.[23]

While he was initially completely against the idea, Collyer's resolve was weakened by the trustees' confidence in him and their insistent pleadings. In considering the way forward, he saw three potential obstacles in the path to the pastorate at Unity Church. Firstly, there was his obligation to the Ministry-at-Large at the First Church who, after all, paid his salary. Second was his lack of formal theological education. He regarded himself as an 'uneducated' man, an artisan who could not fulfil the expectations of a cultured and demanding congregation. Finally, he questioned his own *bona fides* as a minister of religion. In June 1859 Collyer had been recognized as a Unitarian minister by the Western Conference in Milwaukee but, and this was a big 'but' in Robert's mind, he had not been formally ordained.[24]

The first potential obstacle was easily removed. The First Church magnanimously agreed that he should continue as Minister-at-Large, retaining overall supervision of the work but passing routine tasks over to assistants. While the Unity Church could contribute some money towards Robert's stipend, the First Church agreed to continue to pay the major part of his salary until Unity was on a surer financial footing. As for the other impediments, the Unity congregation knew the quality of his preaching and had no misgivings about his lack of formal education or ordination. However, this vote of approval from the trustees did not entirely satisfy Robert. In response to his continued misgivings, the trustees made a proposal to Robert, "Will you agree to this — that we shall write to any ministers in our body you may name, and

[23] Holmes, *Life and Letters*, 1: 216.

[24] Collyer attended the Western Unitarian Conference held in Milwaukee from 5 - 18 June 1859. On the last day of the Conference, Collyer was formally welcomed by the President, Rev. Dr. Hosmer of Buffalo, "on his first fellowship with this conference and his union with the Unitarian Churches". *Chicago Press and Tribune*, 21 June 1859

seek their counsel as to what you ought to do?" Collyer agreed to this and said he would stand by their answer. He named four men to be consulted - Dr. Eliot of St. Louis, Dr. Hosmer of Buffalo, Dr. Bellows of New York, and Dr. Clarke of Boston, who answered with one voice that he must take the church.[25] Thus, in January 1860, the unqualified, un-ordained and initially unwilling Robert Collyer was formally called to be the Minister of Unity Church.

By March 1860, Robert was firmly established in his new post at Unity and had completed his first year in the Ministry-at-Large for the First Church. His combined income now exceeded $2000 a year, a king's ransom compared to the hard-earned wages in the hammer factory. Collyer gave a formal report on his year as Minister-at-Large to the trustees; 'The Free Night School had a regular attendance ranging from 80 to 130 per night over the winter. They came from all parts of the city, some up to two miles away, and about one third are girls and young women while the rest are boys and men, from 10 to 45 years of age. The Ministry provides all school material where it is needed.'

`The Ministry is keeping a Sunday School for all poor children that will come — from 170 to 200 are in regular attendance. These children are gathered from the poorest homes from all quarters of the city. The majority are German — a few Irish. When this school was first gathered, most of them were very ragged — some worse than that. But the influence of the school has been good. We have insisted upon the virtues of a clean skin, a good temper, and a mind to work. There is a great improvement, at least skin deep. To assist them, we have given out a large number of new garments. Four sewing societies belonging to the two Unitarian and the Second Universalist Churches have worked for us, as well as private workers.[26] Besides this, each child, so far as possible, has had one pair of new shoes. About 160 pairs have been given out to our scholars.'[27]

---

[25] Collyer, *Some Memories*, 110.

[26] The Universalist and Unitarian Churches have always been strongly associated. After their official foundation in 1793, the Universalists spread their faith across the eastern United States and Canada. The Universalist preacher, Thomas Starr King, is credited with defining the difference between Unitarians and Universalists thus: 'Universalists believe that God is too good to damn people, and the Unitarians believe that people are too good to be damned by God.' The two Churches merged in 1961. From M.W. Harris at http://www.uua.org/info/origins.html

[27] The shoes were donated by Doggett & Bassett, Henderson & Co., Wadsworth & Wells, and Selah Reeve Esq.

`The Ministry is engaged in finding homes for all the poor or vagrant and neglected children that can be found ready to go. Some of these are picked up by our helpers; some are brought by the police, or by kind-hearted neighbors; some mothers bring them, saying they cannot provide for them or keep them out of the streets. They range from a few weeks to 16 years of age. We covenant that each child sent to a home shall be well cared for, well clothed, sent to school three months in each year, and trained to work. That when a girl is free at eighteen she shall receive fifty dollars. When a boy is free at twenty-one he shall receive 100 dollars. Over the past year, we have found homes for 128 children, mostly from six to fourteen years of age. Some of these have run away again. But a great number have done well, and we are constantly receiving pleasant letters about our children from parties who have taken them.'

'In the past year we have had over 500 applications for help, and have placed in situations 146 boys and men, and nearly 300 girls. Some of them were sad cases of poverty and suffering, brought on by their own careless habits, or the bad training of foolish parents. We have tried to enter into their sorrows — have talked to them of cleanliness, temperance and carefulness. We have married, baptized, buried the dead, sent some to the poor house, some to the noble home for the friendless, or the orphan asylum. We have found courtesy and a ready hand to help us on all sides, and this work is still growing broader and deeper, almost without further thought than our daily duty.'

`Besides this, we do work that cannot be printed. We have tried to gain the confidence of that large class of sinful women, and yet more sinful men that abound here, and we have not quite failed. When we try to sum up this work, it seems very small for the harassing care and time it has cost us, but we believe the right method of treating these poor women is not yet discovered. We have tried to help six in the past year, we think in two cases only have we done much good.'[28]

In one case, Ann Collyer became personally involved. Robert writes, 'A man came one day to see if I could do anything to help a poor girl who had been left in a wretched den to die. I went at once to see her, and found she was, as we say, a 'lost woman'. I could find no refuge for her anywhere in the city. So when I came home, I told mother (Ann) my trouble. She was silent some time after I had said; "Can you do anything?" And then she answered: "There

---

[28] Robert Collyer, *Some account of the Chicago Ministry-at-Large from its foundation to the present time* (Chicago: Privately published by the Trustees, 169 Randolph Street, 1860)

is only one thing we can do: we have a spare room, we must take her in. It is hard. Here are the children; but we can keep the poor creature apart in that room, and I will look after her." So this was done. In about a month she was well. We wanted to find her a place to work. Mother often told me in the after time how she had spoken to her about the life she had lived and the life she might live, but (she) could make no impression on her heart or mind. She left us, with no thanks even when she was well, and went to her own place. She was still a 'lost woman'.'[29]

[29] Collyer, *Some Memories*, 97

14: The Iowa Tornado

During May 1860, Chicago began to reveal its hot and sultry side. At times, the city was stifling. Ann, now in an advanced state of pregnancy, found the heat particularly distressing. Out on the prairies the early arrival of summer heat had an ominous aspect. Hundreds of miles to the west of Chicago, in Cherokee County, Iowa, the heat had built up through the last three weeks of May. Around mid-day on Sunday June 3, there was a sudden stirring in the air. The zephyr became a breeze, and the breeze became a wind. As the disturbance moved eastwards, the wind gathered pace. Massive volumes of heated air shifted and turned and began to take on a rotary motion. Moving forward with increasing speed and ferocity, a vortex developed in which the centrifugal forces began to exert a huge sucking effect on any objects it encountered. A tornado had been born. At the same time, a second tornado was in the process of creation about 12 miles away, and the two converged as they moved eastwards through Hamilton County. Somewhere near the Wapsipinicon River, the tornadoes merged to form a single column of immense force and destructive capacity. 'Twisting and writhing, with an undulating motion and accompanied by a dismal roaring, like that of a mighty cataract but infinitely more menacing, it traversed Cedar County, utterly wiping out every natural and artificial object in its path.'[1]

Although only half a mile to one mile in breadth, this super-tornado wreaked terrible destruction across Iowa, as over the next few hours it swept

[1] From Nettie Mae, *Memorable Tornado of 1860* at http://www.rootsweb.com /~iaclinto/tornado.htm, and Linda Suarez, *Hardin County – Cyclone of 1860* at http://www.rootsweb.com/~iahardin/misc/cyclone.htm

hundreds of miles eastwards. In New Providence township, Hardin County, only two houses were left standing, about 30 having been scattered like kindling wood over miles of prairie. Fortunately, only a few people were hurt as most were attending a Quaker meeting in New Bangor, 12 miles distant. In Union Township, the storm hit Michael Devine's house, a two-story structure built of brick, and levelled it to the ground instantly killing four of the nine persons inside. Searchers discovered the body of Mrs. Devine some distance from the house, with the head severed from it. The head was found several hundred yards away the following day. Nearby, Mrs. Christ's house was torn to bits and scattered over the prairie, but the family took refuge in the cellar and escaped death, although all sustained injuries.

Tornado of 1860. Illustration in Benjamin F. Gue, 'History of Iowa From the Earliest Times to the Beginning of the Twentieth Century' (1903). via Wikimedia Commons.

Clinton County suffered the tornado's most devastating effects. Many small townships were destroyed, and sheep and cattle killed in large numbers. Dwellings and barns were ground to pieces as completely as if they had passed through a rock-crushing machine. Among the wreckage, the tornado left the severed head of an infant and an adult's arms and legs brought from many miles westward. The whirlwind took up three people bodily and they vanished without trace. In the sparsely populated country between DeWitt and Camanche, a distance of only 15 miles, 28 persons were killed and 51 wounded. Camanche, a small town with a population of 1200, suffered the full fury of the tornado and was almost totally destroyed.[2] Eye-witnesses described whole buildings taking off into the air. One citizen saw a horse flying through the air about twenty feet off the ground, followed by a cow at the same height. A Mr. Butler saw his stable building carried away while the horses remained tied to a rail. Even the dead could not rest in peace; in the cemetery the wind wrenched tombstones out of the ground and hurled them hundreds of feet into the air.

Throughout Iowa, some 175 people lost their lives and 329 were injured, and the total damage was estimated at $945,000. In Illinois, a further thirty-five people were killed and many more injured. By the time the tornado reached the north-eastern corner of Iowa, it had lost much of its power, and its remnants became diffused and harmless somewhere over southern Wisconsin and Lake Michigan.

News of the tornado and the devastation it had caused over a 180-mile tract of Iowa, soon reached Chicago. The Board of Trade quickly established a relief fund and the citizens responded with great generosity. After just two weeks of collecting, a substantial sum had been raised and it was felt timely to send someone to Iowa to disburse funds to the neediest. The person chosen for this humanitarian task was Robert Collyer.

The fact that the Board asked Collyer to take the money out to Iowa, speaks volumes for the respect in which he was held. Although he had only been Minister-at-Large in Chicago for a little over a year, the members of the Board must have already recognized him as a man of integrity who would not only

[2] Camanche was the first governmental seat when the County was formally organized in 1840. However, following the building of the Chicago, Iowa and Nebraska Railroad in 1855, a tract of land purchased by the company adjacent to the Mississippi crossing at Little Rock, became the site of a settlement, named Clinton in honor of DeWitt Clinton, governor of New York State. Clinton grew rapidly thereafter and soon became the new County seat. See http://www.villageprofile.com/iowa/clinton/05his/topic.html

spend the money wisely, but would also serve as an ambassador for the people of Chicago. He accepted the task but with some trepidation for Ann, who was now coping with the new baby, Anna, as well as the other children. Ann, however, could see that Robert had his mind set on going and so, as usual, she gave Robert her blessing. At least she now had a live-in helper, an Irish girl called Bridget (Biddy) Ryan, and Robert estimated that he would be only be away for seven or eight days.[3]

Robert travelled via the Chicago, Iowa and Nebraska Railroad to the town of Camanche, or what was left of it. A scene of complete devastation greeted him. Although few buildings had escaped the effects of the tornado, the intervening two weeks had seen a flurry of activity and some buildings and houses had been made habitable again. Some families were in rudimentary shelters constructed from the remains of their houses while others managed in makeshift tents. Many people had left the town to stay with friends or relatives. Robert made his way to the partly destroyed, but still functioning, Waldorf Hotel where he was met by Mr. N. B. Baker, the man coordinating the relief work. He told Robert about some of the human tragedies that had resulted from the devastation of the town. He described the funeral of the twenty-two victims, their coffins lined up for a service attended by two thousand mourners. The crowd then joined the procession of grief-stricken relatives who trudged to the burial ground where the bodies were committed to the long row of freshly-dug graves. Others had died of their injuries since the mass funeral, taking the death toll to over thirty. Baker conducted Robert on a tour of the devastation. He pointed out the hardware store in First Street where the ground floor with all its contents was carried into the river and lost, while the upper floor had dropped down whole onto the foundations as though placed there by builders. One house on the river-bank had been lifted bodily off its foundations and whirled around into the river, disintegrating as it fell and drowning the three occupants. He showed Robert one area where formerly a group of frame-houses stood; now not a single house remained, the ground was strewn with splintered wood, shingles and fragments of plaster.[4]

Taking advice from Mr. Baker, Robert hired a wagon and an experienced driver, and filled the cart with foodstuffs, medical supplies, tools and clothing. He purchased some of the food at the only two stores still carrying on business, but also took some from a stock-pile of sacks of flour, sugar, and corn, and jars

---

[3] Census return June 16, 1860. Chicago 8th Ward, page no. 66.

[4] Details from *Harper's Weekly* (New York: June 23, 1860), 392-4.

of preserves donated by the citizens of neighboring towns.[5] The clothing had either been made by groups of women volunteers or been given in house-to-house collections. Amazingly, the tornado had torn the outer garments from many of its victims even though they themselves had survived relatively unscathed. Robert stayed at the Waldorf and had an evening meeting with other local worthies and together they planned his route through the stricken area.[6]

The journey was generally westward, but they had to pursue a zigzag route to take in the worst of the devastated towns and villages, with occasional diversions to find accommodation for the night. Robert was armed with a list of contact persons and addresses where he and his driver could stay overnight. Thus, there followed a week of trekking through scenes of hardship, sorrow, pain and courage, and thankfulness for help given and blessings received. A newspaper reporter noted that as Collyer moved among the sufferers "his cheerful presence brought scarcely less encouragement and comfort than his gifts."[7]

One such visit was to a farmer, a man who had prospered sufficiently to have built a new house out of brick just a few months before the tornado. Collyer writes; 'The tornado had literally crushed the brick into small fragments and wrecked everything about the place, which was strewn with the fragments and splinters, and the tires of the wagon wheels were twisted as if some strong machine had twisted them round and round.' When Collyer visited the man he was there alone, the wife and children were sheltering at another house outside the line of the storm that at this point was only half a mile wide. Collyer goes on, "You were not hurt then," I said, "or the wife and children?" "No," he answered as one still in the shadow of a great awe, "and I will tell you why. When we came here, the Indians used to tell about these tornadoes; and we have had some bad storms, but nothing like this before. And I would think the thing over and wonder what we should do if one came along. Well, it came to me sudden, one day, what to do. You see that sort o'cave in the rise near by? That was the idee that came to me. We would dig in there and make a root house with a good strong door. Then if the varmint did not jump

---

5 The settlements of Dubuque, Davenport, LeClaire, Keokuk, Rock Island, Moline, Savannah, Mt. Carmel and Wheatland sent generous contributions.

6 The local relief aid distribution committee comprised N.B. Baker, C.H. Toll, O.A. Anthony, Horace Anthony and T.W.J. Long.

7 Account from the *Clinton Herald* reproduced at http://www.rootsweb.com/~iaclinto /tornado.htm

on us too sudden, we would rush in there and shet the door. Well, things began to look skeery up above, sir, in the week before that Sunday afternoon, and it was stifling on the prairie, so I began to look out for squalls. I had told my woman how I felt, and warned her to be ready with the children if the thing should come along. Well, about three o'clock I was sitting on that hump a-watching, and all at once I see her away out yonder, comin' whirlin' head on, black and angry, and I ran and shouted, "Ma, here she comes!" She was ready with the children. There was no time to spare. We rushed for the root-house and shet the door. First there was a roar; and then it was still, and then another roar; but we were safe in the root house, and, when we came out, things were what you see."[8]

After a journey of about 100 miles, Collyer reached the town of Cedar Rapids where he paid off his driver and caught a train back to Chicago. Robert returned to his church work, but he was soon aware of a gathering storm whose effects would turn out to be far more devastating than the Iowa tornado.

[8] Collyer, *Some Memories,* 113.

15: "The Sanitary"

In May 1860, the Republican National Convention met in Chicago to select their Presidential candidate[1]. New York senator William H. Seward was the favorite going into the convention. On the eve of the ballot, however, the campaign staff of Abraham Lincoln, as well as some members of the Illinois delegation, bartered with key delegation leaders to secure Lincoln's nomination. The Mayor of Chicago, John Wentworth, packed the galleries of the convention with Lincoln supporters while Seward's backers were absent for a parade. The cheers from the gallery helped convince the delegates of Lincoln's strong support. On May 18, the third day of the Convention, nominations were presented. The third ballot gave Lincoln of Illinois 231 and a half votes with 233 votes necessary for nomination. At this point, the Ohio delegation switched its four votes in favor of Lincoln. Thus, by the narrowest of margins, Abraham Lincoln became the Republicans' Presidential candidate. The party's anti-slavery stance, although moderated by Lincoln's pragmatic attitude, was anathema to the Southern States. A fuse had been lit that within a year would explode at Fort Sumter.

Southern rights men were willing to adhere to the Union as long as their pro-slavery views received national sanction through the medium of the Democratic Party. When it became clear that the traditional partisan allegiance

---

[1] This was the first national political convention to meet in Chicago. The meeting was held in the 'Wigwam', a temporary wooden structure, built on the south-east corner of Lake and Market Streets at a cost of $5000. See http://www.chipublib.org/004chicago/timeline/firstconv.html

would not protect them from northern power, they chose (sometimes reluctantly) to sever their ties to a Union, which in their eyes, had been taken over by the enemies of the Constitution.[2] Notwithstanding widespread fears that a Republican victory would prompt secession, Lincoln won a comfortable victory in the Presidential Election of November 1860 owing to his strong performance across the North. Before the close of the year secessionist fears were realized; South Carolina was the first state to go, Mississippi, Alabama, and Florida soon followed and by the time a Confederate government had been organized in Montgomery in February, the three remaining states of the deep South – Louisiana, Texas and Georgia – had left the Union. With the formation of a separate government under the Presidency of Jefferson Davis, the secession movement gathered momentum, and confidence. The Confederate authorities sought the removal of U.S. troops from all federal forts but the outgoing President, Buchanan, declined to accede to the Southerners' demands. The Confederates threw up a blockade around Fort Sumter in Charleston harbor. On March 5, Lincoln, on his first day in office, learnt that if action was not taken, Fort Sumter would be starved into surrender.

The new President advocated some form of relief expedition but did not wish to precipitate war with the Southern States and equivocated over the issue. With the Confederates running out of patience, Lincoln wrote to Governor Pickens of South Carolina stating that an attempt was to be made to re-supply Fort Sumter. On receipt of the news from Pickens, President Jefferson Davis demanded the immediate surrender of the Fort. In the early hours of April 12, the Confederate commander in Charleston, General Beauregard, began the bombardment of the fort. The Union expeditionary force arrived on the scene later in the day, but it was too late. The battered fort surrendered on April 14, and the next day, amid a general clamor for action, Lincoln called on the Northern states to provide 75,000 'ninety-day' militiamen to suppress the rebellion against federal authority. Southern impatience and a tenacious determination to save the Union had finally inaugurated Civil War.

In Chicago, news of the attack on Fort Sumter came through by telegraph on Sunday, April 14. Consequent upon the fort's surrender, Lincoln issued his call to arms the next day. He called on all loyal citizens to defend the National Union and popular government, and "to redress wrongs already long

---

[2] Robert Cook, *Civil War America: Making a nation, 1848-1877* (London: Longman, 2003) 100-111.

endured."[3] Mass action followed. Throughout the North people swarmed on to the streets, into public squares and into meeting halls. On the following Sunday, they crowded into the churches.

When Collyer entered his church, he could not see the pulpit. A great Union flag completely enveloped it, and there was another draped behind where he would stand. More flags hung about the organ, while others hung from the iron bars that traversed the church just below ceiling level. Normally, the iron bars were a source of irritation to Collyer. The builders claimed that they were necessary to strengthen the structure, but after completion of the building, Robert had taken an immediate dislike to them, claiming them to be an example of the Dutch *Deformed* style of architecture. However, on this day, draped with the Stars and Stripes, he found them beautiful to behold.

Collyer had racked his brain for a suitable Bible text from which to preach his sermon, and eventually settled on "He that has no sword, let him sell his garment and buy one." For the first hymn he chose, 'Before Jehovah's awe-ful throne,' and for the second, 'America', while after the benediction they closed with 'The Star-spangled Banner.' Normally the singing at Unity was poor stuff compared to the rousing noise heard in Methodist chapels. Most of the congregation paid lip service to singing and let the choir do all the work. He had set out to correct this and had made a little headway, but some in the congregation had told him that lusty singing was 'not good taste' and he had let the matter rest. Nevertheless, that morning, the large congregation sang as if they would lift the roof, despite the iron rods. Collyer's hunger for a joyful sound was amply satisfied. The bombardment at Sumter had broken the ice, and the waters gushed free. Emotions normally held in check were loosened in a tide of patriotic fervor. That very evening many young men from the church went to enlist.

The Illinois troops were typical of the enthusiastic but ill-organized volunteer brigades mustered throughout the Union. They had four cannon and twenty-four horses, but there were no arsenals in the State of Illinois to equip the men with guns and ammunition. The 400 volunteers assembled with squirrel-rifles, shotguns, single-barreled pistols, antique revolvers, - anything that looked as if it would shoot. In addition, the Chicago war committee borrowed fifty ancient muskets from a Milwaukee militia company. The troops were placed under the control of a 'General' Richard Kellog Swift, a prominent

[3] Carl Sandburg, *Storm over the Land,* extracts from *Abraham Lincoln: The War Years 1861-1865* (London: Jonathan Cape, 1944), 27.

citizen but a man without military training or knowledge. However, he did have with him as aide, a Captain Joseph Webster to whom the Governor gave the authority to supersede General Swift at any time "should it become necessary."[4]

Eight days after the fall of Sumter, volunteer troops were dispatched from Chicago to the town of Cairo. Situated in the extreme south of Illinois at the confluence of the Ohio and Mississippi rivers, Cairo was considered a place of great strategic importance. The motley collection of volunteers, dressed in their everyday clothes and overcoats, set off to their 'secret' destination at 11 o'clock at night from the Great Central Passenger Depot amid the cheers of the people and the screaming of steam-whistles.[5] Thanks to travelling overnight, they arrived at Cairo ahead of the rebels. They were none too soon in their occupation of the town. Many of the inhabitants were sympathetic to secession and would have been glad to welcome Southern instead of Northern troops. The South was in earnest, and the North now began to believe it.

Robert Collyer believed fervently in the defense of the Union, and during the next two months used every opportunity, from the pulpit and the meeting platform, to encourage recruitment and support for the war effort. He preached sermons on 'Our Relation to the War,' 'Woman and the War,' Christ and the War,' and 'God and the War.' He spoke at a great rally at the Bryan Hall; he presided over a meeting at the Briggs House for the organization of a women's nursing corps and met a committee of citizens to discuss problems of relief. These were everyday events as Collyer toiled unceasingly as citizen, preacher and Minister-at-Large for the Union cause. In addressing a huge open-air gathering outside the Court House, Collyer said that being a minister he could not go to the front as a soldier, nor could he let his son (Samuel) go as he was only fourteen, but he had a hundred dollars in gold to give to a good man who would go in his place. The next morning a young man came to Collyer's house and said that he would like to accept the offer and would send the money to his sick mother in Canada. He enlisted in a Chicago regiment, and was killed

---

[4] Augustus H. Burley, *The Cairo Expedition,* a paper read before the Chicago Historical Society on 11 November 1890, reproduced in Mabel McIlvaine ed., *Reminiscences of Chicago during the Civil War* (New York: The Citadel Press, 1967), 51.

[5] The Depot had been built on land formerly occupied by Fort Dearborn near the mouth of the Chicago River. It served the Illinois Central, the Michigan Central and the Chicago, Burlington & Quincy Railroads.

two years later (in November 1863) at the battle of Lookout Mountain, North Georgia.[6]

Meanwhile church and family life continued to provide Collyer with satisfaction and structure. His reputation as a pulpit figure continued to grow. A fellow minister, Moncure Conway, wrote to him from Cincinnati in October 1860 declaring that, 'I can never be persuaded that (Chicago) is the right place for you,' believing that he should set his sights on a more prestigious appointment back east.[7] Collyer, however, was happy and settled. A letter of February 1861 to Flesher Bland, his old Addingham friend and now a Methodist Minister in La Chute, Quebec, gives some insight into Collyer's frame of mind.[8] He wrote, 'We are all well, thank God for that; the baby (Annie) grows hugely, is now near 9 months old, and has got four teeth. The other three are all well, so am I, so is Mother; our life jogs on quietly. I have plenty to do and plenty of robust health to do it. The winter is my busy time and keeps me full handed. This winter we have three schools open and I have done a good deal for the poor.... And my people tell me I have preached the best sermons they ever heard, so you may well believe I will hardly fail to be spoiled. Sure enough my church is filling.'

Collyer was hungry for news of the War and every morning he pored over the newspapers. Nevertheless, he also found time to satisfy his passion for book reading. In June 1861, he writes: 'I have just completed the Encyclopaedia Britannica, a grand work in twenty-one volumes, begun in 1853. Also, I have got a fine copy of Milman's *Latin History*, of Bacon's works, of Burke, Addison, Junius, Virgil, Homer, Demosthenes, and some others.'[7]

Despite Collyer's belief that a minister's place was at home with his people, he was soon to revise this stance. In August 1861 he found himself on the fringes of battle, but not as a combatant. He had responded to a call to serve in the United States Sanitary Commission.

---

[6] John Haynes Holmes, *The Life and Letters of Robert Collyer,* (New York: Dodd Mead and Company, 1917), 1: 246.

[7] Correspondence of Moncure D. Conway, 1 October 1860, Special Collections, Dickinson College, Pennsylvania MC 1999.6 / 04.

[8] Henry Flesher Bland was born on 23 August 1818 in Addingham, Yorkshire, son of Anthony Bland and Martha Flesher; m. 1846 Emma Levell in Addingham, and they had five sons, of whom Salem G. Bland and Charles E. Bland became Methodist ministers; Flesher Bland died 29 December 1898 in Smiths Falls, Ontario. From http://www.biographica.ca

On the morning of April 25, 1861, Dr Elizabeth Blackwell, the first woman Doctor of Medicine in the United States, called together a group of New York women to organize an 'Aid Society'. Their immediate concern was for the conditions endured by volunteer soldiers in the numerous camps pitched around Washington. In an emphatic response to Lincoln's call to arms, thousands of troops began to make their way to the capital, where they were housed in commandeered buildings or makeshift, tented camps. The crowded camps were filthy, with garbage scattered everywhere and fly-infested latrines laid out too close to the cooking tents. Consequently, epidemics of disease broke out and entire units came down with dysentery and other diarrheal diseases.[9] Through her friendship with Florence Nightingale, Blackwell was aware of the lessons of the Crimean War. The intervention of a British Sanitary Commission, sent out by Prime Minister Palmerston to investigate the high mortality in the Crimean military hospitals, had a profound effect on the incidence of diseases like cholera, dysentery and typhoid that were killing ten times more soldiers than died of battle wounds.[10]

The New York meeting attracted ninety-two women, including the leading ladies of New York society, and two men were invited, Dr Elisha Harris, the Superintendent of Hospitals on Staten Island, and Dr Henry Bellows, Minister of All Souls Unitarian Church. The result of this meeting was a call to interested women to attend a public meeting the following Monday morning. A notice appeared in the Sunday newspapers announcing the meeting and 4000 women gathered at 11 am to hear Dr Bellows invite no less a figure than the Vice-President of the United States, Hannibal Hamlin, to take the chair. The women then formed themselves into the 'Women's Central Association for Relief' with Dr. Valentine Mott, one of the world's great surgeons and President of the New York Academy of Medicine, as its president. This placed the highest authority in American medicine behind the women's efforts, but the military establishment was reluctant to take advice from a group of amateurs, especially women amateurs. They had hoped to send nurses, but the War Department wrote to them that no arrangements had been made to receive such nurses and it was an impossible proposal. General John Dix, in command of the New York volunteers, threw cold water on the project even though his wife was a member

[9] Stephen B. Oates, *A Woman of Valor: Clara Barton and the Civil War* (New York: The Free Press, 1995), 17.

[10] Mark Bostridge, *Florence Nightingale: the Lady with the Lamp* at http://www.bbc.co.uk/history/british/victorians/nightingale_01.shtml.

of it. However, the women were undismayed, and initiated a letter-writing campaign. Gradually the sheer number of letters of protest encouraged Bellows and the medical advisers to the women's group to take the matter to Washington. There they would petition Lincoln to appoint the Board of Managers of the Women's Central as the nucleus of a United States Sanitary Commission.[11]

Bellows and his colleagues spent several days lobbying in Washington. They met first the Surgeon General, then the Secretary of the Treasury and finally had two meetings with President Lincoln himself.[12] Although they felt that they were moving ahead, the War Department still regarded them as "weak enthusiasts, representing well-meaning but silly women" but with thousands of soldiers in the field, the Department was struggling to maintain control.[13] It was grossly understaffed and ill-prepared for war and the top military cadre were much more concerned with the forthcoming struggle than with sanitation.

While Bellows kicked his heels waiting for some sensible response, events conspired to aid the proposed Sanitary Commission's cause. Every day brought weeping women to Washington to recover the bodies of their dead. Every day, trains left the capital with a load of corpses packed in ice – and the battles had not even started. Bellows faced the War Department again, "We understand," he said, that on 4 July, President Lincoln will go before Congress and ask for 400,000 volunteers. Our own investigations show that, of the men already recruited, one half will be dead of camp diseases before the first of November. Do you think you can go before the country and ask the wives, mothers, sweethearts, sisters, fathers and neighbors of these men to send more of them into this shambles?" The harassed officials finally gave up and told the President to let the women clear up the mess. On 9 June, the Secretary of War, Simon Cameron, approved a document providing for the appointment by President Lincoln of a 'United States Sanitary Commission' with power to oversee the welfare of the volunteer army, and to serve as a channel of communication between the people and the government. Branches of the Sanitary Commission and Ladies Union Aid Societies were soon established in all the major cities of the Union. Hundreds of thousands of boxes and barrels

---

[11] Walter D. Kring, *Henry Whitney Bellows* (Boston: Skinner House, 1979), 227-239.

[12] The Surgeon General was William A. Hammond, and Mr Salmon P. Chase was Secretary to the Treasury

[13] Kring, *Henry Bellows,* 233.

of hospital dressings, warm clothing, drug supplies, food delicacies, books and tracts were forwarded to the camps, Army hospitals and Commission convalescent homes. The threat of a winter epidemic of scurvy in the camps was countered by the dispatch of tens of thousands of bushels of potatoes, turnips, onions, cabbages – and lemons.[14]

The Sanitary Commission was established with two main functions, preventative and relief work. In the former role, inspectors immediately set about advising on the proper placement of camps and the provision of adequate drainage; they gave instruction on personal hygiene and inspected the food supply, tested the drinking water and provided for the proper disposal of refuse. These measures were to have a striking effect on the death rate from disease. Along with these measures went the work of relief. Wherever the wounded were gathered, there went the representatives of the Commission to assist the hard-pressed surgeons and nurses in the dressing of wounds, giving medicines, making beds, writing letters, comforting the dying and supervising the disposal of the dead. It was to this relief work that Robert Collyer was called in a personal invitation from Rev. Henry Bellows.

Collyer read the letter from Bellows with mounting excitement. Here was a way in which a minister of religion could *directly* serve the Union cause. Naturally, he discussed his 'call-up' with Ann, and she reluctantly acquiesced. On the following Sunday he presented the facts surrounding his invitation to the Unity congregation who with one voice declared that he must go. It was Sunday July 21, 1861, the day when the Civil War erupted into a bloody conflagration along the banks of an insignificant creek just 20 miles from Washington. The name of the creek was the Bull Run.

---

[14] Charles H. Lyttle, *Freedom moves West: A history of the Western Unitarian Conference* (Boston: The Beacon Press, 1952) 110.

16: Into battle

The Confederate Government, further strengthened by the secession of Virginia, Arkansas and North Carolina, had moved its seat in the last week of May 1861, from Montgomery, Alabama, to Richmond, Virginia, to be nearer the Border States where the heaviest fighting was likely to be concentrated. Into Richmond streamed regiments from all parts of the South. The cry in the South, "On to Washington!" snarled straight into the cry from the North, "On to Richmond!" From the windows of the White House, Lincoln's telescope caught the Confederate flag flying over the town of Alexandria, just eight miles down the Potomac River, where several heavy guns and 500 troops had been advanced from Richmond. The Confederates built riverside batteries to blockade vessels moving up and down the Potomac. The provisional army called together by the Virginia convention was assembled and preparing for battle.

In bright moonlight on May 24, at two o'clock in the morning, squads of Union cavalry crossed the bridges leading from Washington across the Potomac into Virginia. Infantry and engineers followed, and they began the work of fortifying every hill for miles around with defensive trenches for the protection of the ten-mile-square District of Columbia that now lay isolated within the surrounding Slave States. The South reacted with anger to the Union advance into Virginia. The Confederates considered this move to be an 'invasion', and immediately began their preparations for retaliation. Meanwhile, more Union troops gathered around Washington.

On July 6, 1861, the Secretary of War notified Lincoln that sixty-four volunteer regiments of 900 men each, besides 1200 regulars, were in readiness. However, not everyone agreed on the degree of readiness. For instance, the head of the Union army, the veteran General Winfield Scott, favored waiting until a larger army, better trained and better prepared, could win victories that would be decisive. Nonetheless, the clamor by public and press for a decisive battle with the Southern army forced Lincoln and his Cabinet to overrule Scott. The commander of the Union army, General Irvin McDowell, asked for more time to drill and discipline his troops, but Lincoln told him: "You are green, it is true, but they are green also."[1] Lincoln ordered an advance into Virginia, and Alexandria was recaptured.

The Battle of the Bull Run, Sunday July 21, was anticipated almost as a gladiatorial event by a large and eager public. The day and place of combat had been announced beforehand, and crowds of spectators rode out of Washington in their buggies laden with picnic baskets and equipped with spyglasses to survey the 'inevitable' Union victory. At three o'clock that afternoon McDowell thought he had the battle won. An hour later, his army was going to pieces. That night in Washington, Lincoln heard eyewitnesses tell what they had seen from saddle, buggy, or gig on the twenty-mile ride back from the battlefield. Strewn along the roads for miles, were hats, coats, blankets, haversacks, canteens, rifles, broken harnesses, and upturned wagons – the evidence of thousands of soldiers in panic and retreat. McDowell's staff-man recorded 16 officers and 444 men killed; seventy-eight officers and 1046 men wounded; and fifty officers and 1262 men missing in just one day of fighting.

After the hot sweltering Sunday of the battle, came a Monday of drizzling rain. Across the Long Bridge over the Potomac, from daylight on, came lines of bedraggled men. Hour after hour, these silhouettes of defeat shuffled into the capital. A Captain Noyes described, "Stragglers sneaking along through the mud inquiring for their regiments, wanderers driven in by the pickets, some with guns and some without, while everyone you met had a sleepy, downcast appearance, and looked as if he would like to hide his head from all the world."[2] The Union hospitals in Washington, Alexandria and Georgetown were crowded with wounded, sick and discouraged soldiers.

A few days after the battle, a train of two-wheeled ambulances clattered into Washington from the battlefield. The Medical Department had dispatched them to collect the hundreds of wounded soldiers who had been abandoned

---

[1] Carl Sandburg, *Storm over the Land,* extracts from *Abraham Lincoln: The War Years 1861-1865* (London: Jonathan Cape, 1944), 37.

[2] Robert E. Denney, *Civil War Medicine: Care and comfort of the wounded* (New York: Sterling Publishing Co., 1995), 36.

where they lay. The civilian drivers told stories of grotesque sights; swollen corpses rotting in the July sun, and parts of human bodies scattered about the fields. In some ways, the dead were the lucky ones. For the wounded, the journey back to Washington dumped in the two-wheeled carts and carried along rutted lanes and roads would have been agony. The 'ambulances' deposited their cargo of wounded in old warehouses, redundant churches and schools taken over as 'hospitals' where they would receive the most rudimentary care.[3] Amputations were often carried out without the benefit of anesthesia. Chloroform was in short supply, and in any case, some of the Generals felt that its use was 'un-manly'.

Congress, other politicians, and the press began to apportion blame for the catastrophic events at the Bull Run. Harper's Weekly declared that 'the great blunder taught us the folly of going into battle under civilian leadership. In selecting company and even field officers, our militiamen often attach more weight to wealth and political or social influence than to bravery or soldierly aptitude. We have the best evidence to prove that the march to Bull Run, and the fight there, were both undertaken in deference to the popular craving for action. The wretched result must serve as a warning for the future.'[4] In the camps around Washington, despondency and ill-discipline prevailed. Many of the officers had decamped to hotels in the city where they thronged the bars and left their troops to their own devices. In the camps, infectious diseases were rife, and the death rate soared. More soldiers lost their lives to bacteria than bullets. It was to these 'death camps' that Collyer had been summoned to represent the Sanitary Commission. He arrived in Washington in early August and was to remain there for six weeks.

Coinciding with Robert's arrival came news that Lincoln had sacked the octogenarian General Scott and installed General George McClellan as the new commander. McClellan had fought in the Mexican War. He was youthful and vigorous; a man of authority and self-confidence. He modelled his proclamations on Napoleon's style and believed in the value of discipline, maneuvers and strategy. He was the man of the hour. The arrogant young general proved to be a brilliant organizer. In the weeks that Collyer spent with the troops, he saw them transformed in discipline and spirit. They became a true fighting force that McClellan proudly dubbed 'The Army of the Potomac'.

---

[3] Stephen B. Oates, *A Woman of Valor: Clara Barton and the Civil War* (New York: The Free Press, 1995), 22.

[4] *Harper's Weekly*, 1861, August 10, 499.

Robert was asked to visit the camps and look closely into their sanitary condition and report back to the Commission. They gave him a small team of fellow inspectors, and a soldier to take them from camp to camp. Collyer reckoned to have visited them all. The sights that he witnessed repeatedly through his tour of inspection must have appalled him. On every side, dirt and disease; foul tents in which the healthy and the sick shared water and food and, in their ignorance, spread contagion from one to the other. Nothing was known of bacteria, viruses and the spread of infection, and the link between typhoid and polluted water was not known. In 1861, typhoid fever caused seventeen percent of all military deaths.[5]

Union Army in winter camp. 'The troops have built log huts in preparation for severe conditions - wind, rain and snow.' Valley News Echo, Hagerstown, Md. January 1862.

One sunny Saturday morning Robert set off with his soldier-guide to visit a camp somewhere towards the Maryland line. As they went past the White House toward the bridge, his soldier said, "See them feet, sir?"

There were perhaps half a dozen pairs set with their soles towards them at two open windows, and his man said, "That's the Cabinet a-settin'. See the big feet in the middle o'that window? Them's Old Abe's."

They crossed the bridge and headed, as his man thought, straight for the camp. After some time, he realized that he had taken a wrong turn in the woods

[5] Denney, *Civil War Medicine*, 9.

and did not know the way. "Better go right on," Robert said, "We shall get out of the woods, and then we can take our bearings."

The soldier took the buggy forward for a while, until they came to an opening in the woods and saw a ridge ahead of them planted with cannon. "That's a rebel battery," he whispered. "What'll we do?"

"Turn around," Robert whispered, "and make a bee-line, if you can, for the river."

This the good fellow did, and they were fortunate. They got safely back to the city, and Collyer told the story of their hairs-breadth escape from the rebel battery. "Where was it?" his listeners enquired. After some discussion it became clear that this was the Munson's Hill Battery, a battery armed with 'Quaker' guns – logs on wheels painted to look like cannon, and Collyer's 'narrow escape' became a source of general amusement.

Collyer returned to Chicago in early October, but only for a few days. The Commission had appointed him 'agent for the Missouri front' and had asked him to go to St. Louis and thence through Missouri to inspect the camps and hospitals there and bring back a report. The Union campaign in Missouri had been almost as catastrophic as the Bull Run in the east. The commander of the Union army was John Charles Fremont, the adventurer, failed millionaire, and former Presidential candidate whose political campaign Robert had been so keen to support back in Pennsylvania. At the outbreak of war, Fremont had been in France, but he came straight back to Washington where Lincoln made him a Major General and sent him westwards. Setting up headquarters in St. Louis, Fremont went on to secure the state capital Jefferson City and began to formulate plans to capture the entire Mississippi basin. The plans proved over-ambitious, and Union soldiers found themselves in another disastrous battle. Acting independently, detachments under the command of Brigadier General Nathaniel Lyon embarked on an ill-advised attack on a superior force of rebel troops at Wilson's Creek near Springfield in the south of Missouri. The Confederate army prevailed and within four hours, the Union side suffered 1,235 casualties and retreated in disarray.[6]

[6] Shelby Foote, *The Civil War: 1 Fort Sumter to Perryville* (London, Pimlico, 1992), 95.

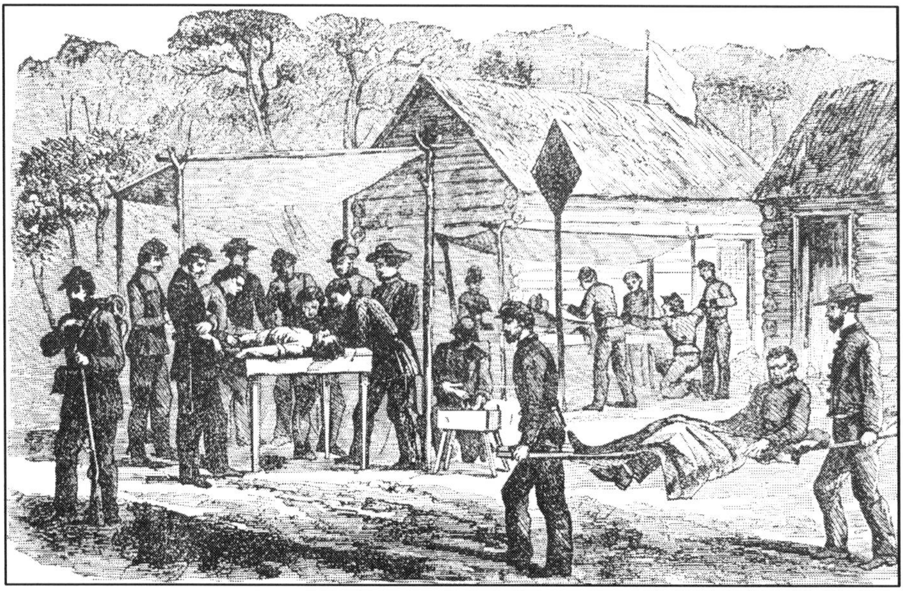

'Bringing in the Wounded' A field hospital treats casualties from the Union Army. Valley News Echo, Hagerstown, Md. January 1862.

Collyer's first port of call was Jefferson City, to inspect the military hospitals there. He found them 'in the most fearful condition you can imagine. I cannot stop to tell you of the scenes I saw,' he wrote, 'it is enough to say that one poor fellow had lain there sick on the hard boards and seen five men carried away dead, one after another from his side. He was worn to a skeleton; worn through so that great sores were all over his back, and filthy beyond telling.'[7] Collyer then went to the country around Wilson's Creek to hunt out and care for the sick and the wounded and take them back to St. Louis. However, the land was devastated, as though by a plague of locusts. Collyer writes, 'This was a hard task; the troops seem to have eaten the land clean to the bone. I was never so hungry, so far as I can remember, before or since. All we had to eat going down was hard tack. When the train halted for a few minutes, the men who were helping me with the sick – good fellows, but so hungry – said, "Yonder is a tavern; we will go and forage for victuals." They went, and presently came on the dead run, holding something by a string, with a man running after them,

[7] John Haynes Holmes, *The Life and Letters of Robert Collyer* (New York: Dodd Mead and Company, 1917), 1:
257.

shouting bad words. He was the tavern-keeper, a German; and it was a piece of pork they had on the string. The train had begun to move slowly. They had just time to board the train, so had the tavern-keeper; and this is how I came to know he was saying bad words when I could not hear them. The soldiers told me they wanted to buy the pork, which was roasting before the fire, and he would not sell it at any price. So, one of them cut the string, and they ran off with it. He calmed down after another polyglot of blasphemy, and sat up to help them eat his pork; and, when they had dined on that and the hard tack, I said to one of them, "Now let's pay him for the pork." So we paid him, and he got off at the first station to take the train home. *No,* I did not eat any of that pork.'[8] However, Collyer's hunger was satisfied later the same day.

'Toward sundown a bad headache came on; and, when we came to a long wait at the station, I must needs find some good soul who would make me a cup of tea. A man on the platform pointed to a house where he thought I could have one, and, asking there, the woman said, "I will give you your supper for a quarter." I told her this was what I wanted, so she got me my supper. It was not good but the best she had. I found chatting with her, that she was a member of a small white church near by. So, for the humor of it I said, "I suppose you entertain the ministers now and then when they come round?" "Yes," she said, "I entertain 'em all and never take a cent. I would scorn to charge a minister." Whereat I said with a most winsome smile, "I am a minister, ma'am."

She looked me over sharply. The grime of a week was on me; I was unshaven also, and looked much more like a tramp. So she said promptly, "You are no minister."

I drew a lot of letters from my pocket, laid them in her hand, and said, "Read the address, please, on those letters."

She read them. "Yes, I suppose you be a minister; but be you for the North or the South?"

"For the North," I answered, "every time."

"Then," she answered, "you got to pay for your supper. I am for the South every time. I don't feed Yankees for noth'n'; and if my husband out there wa'n't a coward, he would be fightin' for the South this day." So I paid for my supper, and my head was better.'

Fortunately for Collyer, this tour of duty was short. Returning to St. Louis, he made his report to William Greenleaf Eliot, a fellow Unitarian Minister and

---

8 Robert Collyer, *Some Memories* (Boston: American Unitarian Association, 1908), 123.

friend, who superintended the Western Sanitary Commission, and then made straight for Chicago. It was the last week in October 1861.[9] During that first week back home, he wrote a long letter to Flesher Bland in Canada.[10] He wrote, 'Of course soldiering even as a civilian is not an easy life,..... but it was such an opportunity as can only come once in a lifetime for seeing men under strange, new circumstances. I came into contact with about 50,000 all told and found camps like homes, a few nearly perfect, a good many that needed to be amended, and the rest dirty, disorderly and disorganized. I found men whose pure steadfast goodness went with them and shone from them under all circumstances, officers who had taken to arms because they had failed shamefully in everything else, and officers who were as true as steel, unbending as granite, tender as a woman. I saw hundreds of men sitting in the golden Sunday sunset listening to the prayer or sermon as it poured from the heart of the preacher, or helping to raise the hymn with a heartiness that destroyed all discord as the sound swept up through the great arches of heaven. And many of the same men in the weekday uttering blasphemies that smote you with a sudden pain as when you tread on a thorn. I saw chaplains in immaculate white cravats, men who would hardly soil their fingers to save a soul, preaching to perhaps forty men instead of a whole regiment and even they suspecting that the sermon was meant for somebody else; and chaplains whose every sermon was a week long and was made up of genuine, hearty loving helpfulness, writing letters for the men to wives and maidens far away, watching by and comforting the sick, receiving the photograph and Bible and last message home from the dying. I have seen the sick left by their own officers to rot in squalor and destitution, and an old black man or woman come in and bear them off to their poor homes and nurse them back to life.'

'Our cause so far does not prosper. We have met with little besides reverses and mostly very sore reverses. It is dark days for America and all the darker for our fears. Our rulers are more tender for slavery than they are for freedom. I think they are shamefully backward in dealing with the matter, but I think the word emancipation will have to be said and stood to before we get through and we shall have a real republic in the end. I see by the paper this morning that Cameron has authorized the employment of slaves as soldiers by our army

[9] Dr. Eliot came to St. Louis in 1834 to establish a Unitarian Church in the city. His major claim to fame is his founding of the Washington University (originally the Eliot Seminary) in 1853. Like Collyer he was a fervent abolitionist and champion of Women's Rights.

[10] Holmes, *Life and Letters,* 1: 258.

in the South. If that is true it is full of significance and will do more for abolition than any other thing that has been done except the rebellion itself.'

By the end of October, Fremont was to be relieved of his command. The defeat at Wilson's Creek was the major factor in his dismissal, but Lincoln had also been embarrassed and annoyed by a proclamation that he had issued. Fremont already had a reputation as an adventurer and romantic, now amid war, he became a loose-cannon. Without any consultation, he drafted a radical new edict to the effect that all insurrectionists found above a line drawn through the middle of Missouri would face court martial and death by firing squad. Furthermore, all Missourians who were 'proved to have taken an active part with their enemies in the field' would have their property confiscated and their slaves, if they had any, declared freemen. Fremont's pledge of freedom for slaves met with an enthusiastic response in many quarters in the North, but caused a furor in the Border States, and apoplexy in the administration in Washington. The President decided enough was enough. On October 28 he sent orders for his dismissal. Fremont's one hundred days of command in Missouri were at an end.[11] The next day he issued a farewell address and set off for St. Louis to join his wife. When she was told of his downfall, she remarked, "Oh if my husband had only been more positive! But he never did assert himself enough. That was his greatest fault."

Although Fremont's maverick behavior was his eventual undoing, some of his military stratagems were sound. Lincoln was particularly impressed with a plan to take control of the Western rivers. During the winter of 1861-2, with the Army of the Potomac apparently frozen into immobility, he ordered preparations for attacks on Confederate positions along the Tennessee and Cumberland Rivers. Earlier, Lincoln had called to Washington a St Louis man, James B. Eads, who knew the Mississippi intimately – he had salvaged numerous ships embedded in the mud and sands using a diving-bell of his own invention and asked him how best to carry on a war against the riverside forts. Eads, working under a government contract, employed 4000 men on his project. In one hundred days he had ready eight iron-plated, steam propelled gunboats.

---

[11] Foote, *The Civil War,* 1: 99. After the war, Fremont lost his fortune following a series of bad investments mainly involving railroads. Thereafter his wife supported him until his partial rehabilitation in later life. In 1878 he was made Governor of the territory of Arizona, a post that he filled for 5 years. He then settled in California but died in relative obscurity in New York in 1890.

A post of the U.S. Sanitary Commission. The photograph conveys an appearance of order and gentility far removed from the horrors of the field hospital. The 'staged' photograph may have been arranged to encourage volunteers to come forward. Valley News Echo, Hagerstown, Md. July 1862.

On February 6, 1862, a flotilla made up of these and other gunboats escorted a line of steamships up the Tennessee River carrying eighteen regiments under the command of Brigadier General Ulysses S. Grant. Young men crowded the decks watching the passing scene. The 18,000 troops, a motley collection of recruits made uniform by the dark blue of the Union, were drawn from Iowa, Indiana and Illinois, from Nebraska, Ohio and Missouri; students and shopkeepers, bankers and butchers, farmers and factory hands; American, Scandinavian, German and Irish. Disparate, but united in their vision of a single flag, the Union flag, flying over the land from the northern origins of the Mississippi down to the Gulf of Mexico. The gunboats stopped opposite Fort Henry, bombarded it with exploding shells, and the troops marched in and tore down the Confederate flag. The garrison had already left for Fort Donelson, twelve miles away on the Cumberland River. Grant marched his army the short distance towards Fort Donelson. *En route*, the weather was so warm and balmy that thousands of soldiers threw away their blankets, overcoats, or both. Meanwhile the gunboats had a long passage to undertake to approach

Donelson and share in the attack; first down the Tennessee to its junction with the Ohio River, then along the Ohio and up the Cumberland River. Other gun-boats that had been undergoing repairs in Cairo were dispatched to augment the attack.

While Grant waited for the gun-boats, and for another 10,000 reinforcements in transport ships to arrive, the weather turned bitterly cold. The now ill-equipped troops huddled in small groups close to hedgerows, under trees, and in abandoned houses and barns to shelter against the icy blast. They could not light fires for fear of revealing their positions, and the conditions became extreme. Some soldiers froze to death before a shot was fired in the attack on the fort.

After a week of waiting and watching, the gun-boats arrived. However, as they steamed up-river they came under heavy fire from Confederate cannons placed on a bluff overlooking the bend of the Cumberland on which the fort stood. Furthermore, the river was mined, and the submerged mines presented a further threat. The fort itself was no fortress; constructed as it was with timber stockades around a low wooden building, it offered no defense against an army. However, the fort occupied a strategic position commanding the river and the Confederates were determined to fight for this position. By February 11, the first skirmishes were followed by a series of surging Union attacks hurled at the Confederate positions and by their counter-attacks. With nightfall, the heavy fighting ebbed away.

Two days later, the transport ships arrived with their precious reinforcements. Grant now had 27,500 troops facing 17,500 Confederates, the latter arranged in an arc around Fort Donelson and the small town of Dover nearby, with their backs to the river.[12] It was toward this vulnerable rearguard that the Union gunboats aimed their shells, but the flotilla had been increasingly disabled by Confederate cannon fire and had to withdraw down-river to re-group. On the land, through ice and fierce winds, the fighting continued, but Grant's superior numbers allied to a new resolve in his troops gradually gained the upper hand.

On Sunday, February 16, 1862, telegrams detailing the progress of the battle trickled into the War Department in Washington. General Simon B. Buckner, commanding Fort Donelson, had sent a message to Grant asking for 'terms of capitulation'. Grant replied; 'No terms except an unconditional and immediate surrender can be accepted. I propose to move immediately upon your works.'

[12] Foote, *The Civil War*, 1: 201.

Buckner surrendered the fort and 13,828 prisoners. The battle losses were: Union, 500 killed, 2108 wounded, 224 missing; Confederate, 231 killed, 1534 wounded. The victory secured Kentucky for the Union, gave a foothold in Tennessee, and propelled Union troops 200 miles forward into Confederate territory. More than anything else, it lifted the gloom of the North.

Throughout the Northern states, outpourings of people celebrated with bonfires, fireworks, bells ringing, meetings, speeches, and subscriptions for the wounded.[13] This was certainly how the people of Chicago greeted the news. Collyer saw; 'men shaking hands everywhere, and breaking into laughter that ended in tears, and in tears that ended in laughter.' Nonetheless, he realized that this victory had been won at a terrible price. Robert knew what would happen next. He could picture the battlefield littered with bodies, and the gore-drenched field-stations crowded with wounded soldiers. He knew that the Sanitary would call him into service and, if he went, he would have to face the full horrors of battle and confront his personal nightmares. He did not have to wait long. Straightaway, the Chicago Sanitary Commission convened an emergency meeting with the Board of Trade to coordinate relief efforts. An immediate appeal to the citizens led to $3000 being donated for the wounded, and the Commissions' officers set about buying food and medical equipment. Within thirty-six hours of news of the surrender, Robert and a group of volunteer surgeons and nurses, set out for the battlefield.[14]

---

[13] Sandburg, *Storm over the Land*, 60.

[14] Seventeen physicians left on the first train out of Chicago. Sarah E. Henshaw, *Our branch and its tributaries; being a history of the work of the Northwestern Sanitary Commission and its auxiliaries, during the war of the rebellion* (Chicago: Alfred L. Sewell, 1868), 52.

17: Battle-scarred

The town of Cairo, Illinois, provided the focal point for the Sanitary Commissions' relief work. In parallel with the preparation of the gunboats, Dr. Aigner of the Commission proposed that floating hospitals should be prepared to accompany the waterborne attack on Fort Donelson. These 'hospital steamers' were now ferrying back the wounded down the Cumberland from Donelson to Cairo[1]. Furthermore, the Commission in Chicago having news of an impending battle, had been sending stores to their depot in Cairo for several weeks. Thus, it was to Cairo that Collyer and the Chicago volunteers headed.

For Collyer and his colleagues, the rail journey was to be long and tedious, but it began amid much excitement at the Passenger Depot at the end of Lake Street. Crowds of well-wishers waving flags and banners cheered as the train left the station. With a crescendo of steam, the straining locomotive hauled the train along the low breakwater that carried the track along the edge of Lake Michigan to the southern limit of the city. Robert scanned the frozen lake and the ice-bound ships before settling back to his reading as the train made its sluggish progress across the great, dreary stretches of snow-clad prairie. Over

---

[1] The Commission's agent in Cairo, Rev E. Folsom of Chicago's Second Presbyterian Church, fitted out several steamers as hospital ships including the *City of Memphis, Hazel Dell, Franklin, War Eagle* and *City of Louisiana.* Sarah E. Henshaw, *Our branch and its tributaries; being a history of the work of the Northwestern Sanitary Commission and its auxiliaries, during the war of the rebellion* (Chicago, Alfred L. Sewell, 1868), 53.

seven hundred miles of railroad later, Robert stepped down into the mud of Cairo.

There was not a vestige of ice or snow to be seen and, for the first time in his life, Robert got a clear realization of the effects of latitude. He considered Cairo to be a 'mud-hole' and his opinion of the place was remarkably like that of Charles Dickens written after a visit some twenty years before: "At the junction of the two rivers, on ground so flat and low and marshy that at certain seasons of the year it is inundated to the house-tops, lies a breeding-place of fever, ague and death... a hotbed of disease, an ugly sepulchre, a grave uncheered by any gleam of promise: a place without one single quality, in earth or air or water, to commend it: such is this dismal Cairo."[2]

Mud seemed to characterize Cairo, the unpaved streets churned to liquid by innumerable carts, horses and mules. Supplies and munitions moved one way and the sad detritus of battle, including 'those long boxes that hold only and always the same treasure,' moved the other[3]. It was a place filled with noise, clamor and confusion; a city hideous to enter and a relief to leave behind. However, the Chicago party had to wait several hours before they could board the steamer that would take them to Donelson. At the dockside, Robert came face to face with the aftermath of battle. Four crude coffins, nailed together in haste, held the bodies of four officers sent home for burial. As he stood nearby, Collyer saw a young man approach, evidently the brother of one of the officers. There was some doubt over the identity of the body, so the coffin was opened. Robert glanced at the handsome, but distressed face of the soldier and then turned to the pallid face in the coffin. There could be no doubt that they were sons of the same mother. The man in the coffin must have died instantly. There was no contortion of agony, indeed he had the look of one who had just fallen asleep.

Sitting on the bank by the quay, with his feet in the mud, a young soldier stared at the coffins before him. His head was swathed in a turban-like bandage soaked in blood. Robert asked him, "Are you from Donelson?"

He answered in a matter-of-fact way; "I was in the battle, where I got a bad clout on my head. So they sent me down the river, and I'm going home to Indiana."

---

[2] Charles Dickens, *American Notes for general circulation,* (1842), Reprinted in Penguin Classics (London: Penguin Books, 1985), 215.

[3] John Haynes Holmes, *The Life and Letters of Robert Collyer* (New York: Dodd Mead and Company, 1917), 1: 263.

"Can I do anything for you?" asked Robert.

He looked up shyly. "Can you give me a bit of tobacco?"

Robert didn't have any, but gave him money to buy it. He took it quietly.

"You're real good, sir. Would you like to see ma head?"

Robert shrank back, but the soldier was already unwinding the turban. There was a purple bruise, turning yellow at the edges, high up on his forehead.

"The bullet didn't go in then?" asked Robert.

"No, sir: ma head was too thick for the bullets of them rebs. It flatted and fell off. I got it here in my pocket."

He pulled out the deformed bullet and laid it in Robert's hand, saying with a touch of pride, "That ain't no use agin a head like mine."[4]

At last, Collyer and the others boarded the steamer and snatched some precious sleep. A journey of 160 miles up the Ohio and Cumberland Rivers brought them to Donelson and the work they had come to do. It was sunset. They immediately went in search of the men and boys from Chicago. Robert found a group from his own church crouched around a low fire. They welcomed the visitors with hugs and laughter, and some self-conscious tears. They gave them coffee, which the soldiers drank as though it were nectar and the visitors as if it were senna. They exchanged tales of the fighting and news from the City until the late hour demanded that they find rest in one of the Commissions' tents.

Early next morning, General Joseph Webster escorted the Sanitary Commission party over the battlefield. [5] Almost a week had elapsed since the battle and most of the human wreckage had been cleared away. However, through the open fields and in among the splintered trees, discarded equipment, dead horses, harnesses, shot and shell, littered the ground. Collyer saw three men lying in a gully waiting for burial, while at the edge of a copse, eleven dead Union soldiers lay in a line where they fell. The Commission group reached a long mound with pieces of board here and there. Sixty-one soldiers from the Illinois companies lay side by side under that mound. Robert

---

[4] Robert Collyer, *Some Memories* (Boston: American Unitarian Association, 1908), 142.

[5] Joseph Dana Webster served in the U.S. Army during the Mexican War but resigned in 1854 and entered business in Chicago. He was President of the Commission that planned the new sewerage system for the city and the elevation of buildings that George Pullman carried through so successfully. He entered the Union Army at the outbreak of war and soon rose to become General Grant's Chief of Staff, a position he occupied with distinction until the Autumn of 1862.

dismounted to read some of the inscriptions, not chiseled into gravestones but scrawled in lead-pencil onto the crude wooden crosses. 'John Olver, 31st Illinois', he read, and wondered if a brave son of the Oliver family had been misrepresented in death. He came to the crest of a hill where the citizens of Dover had buried their dead ever since they settled on the banks of the Cumberland. Here were headstones of white marble and grey limestone, whose permanence made the crude crosses marking the battlefield graves seem even more pathetic. Saddened and sickened, the small group on horseback followed their guide down into Dover.

Collyer writes, 'The little town of Dover was full of sick and wounded. There was no adequate comfort of any kind: many were laid on the floor, most were entirely unprovided with a change of linen, and not one had any proper nourishment. What we carried with us was welcome beyond all price. The policy of our commanders was to remove all the wounded on steamboats to Paducah, Mound City, and other places on the rivers: and it was part of my duty, with several other gentlemen acting as surgeons and nurses, to attend 158 wounded men from Fort Donelson to Mound City[6]. I may not judge harshly of what should be done in time of war like this in the West: it is very easy to be unfair. I will simply tell you, that, had it not been for the things sent up by the Sanitary Commission in the way of linen, and things sent by our citizens in the way of nourishment, I see no possibility by which those wounded men could have been lifted out of their blood-stained woolen garments saturated with wet and mud; or could have had any food and drink, except corn-mush, hard bread, and the turbid water of the river.'[7]

The wounded men were packed into the main saloon of the steamboat. They lay in long rows with hardly space between them to place a foot. Robert and the other attendants picked their way among them, knowing that they all required their help but could only respond to the most urgent cries. Some were unable to cry out. A young soldier had the lower part of his face badly injured; he could not open his mouth and he was dying for lack of fluid and food. His blue eyes fixed on Robert and he gesticulated at him, first pointing to his injured mouth and then to his stomach. For a few moments, Robert stood by, seemingly unable to help. Then he remembered that as he rested in one of the

[6] Mound City, Illinois, lay about seven miles north of Cairo on the Ohio River. The Military Hospital was established in 1861 in a converted warehouse. Over 2000 soldiers were treated there after Pittsburg Landing. Henshaw, *Our branch and its tributaries,* 46.

[7] Robert Collyer, *Battlefield of Fort Donelson: A narrative sermon,* In *Nature and Life* (Boston, Horace B. Fuller, 1867), 274.

state-rooms he had seen a small silver funnel on a shelf above his head. He thought that in better times it was used to decant wine. He retrieved the funnel and made up a jug of milk in which he dissolved several spoonful's of sugar and laced it with some whiskey. Robert bent over the soldier and explained what he was about to do. The man could not answer, but his eyes showed understanding. Robert introduced the spout of the funnel into a slit at the corner of the man's mouth and began to pour the milk slowly into it. With a gurgle, the milk passed down the man's throat, and his eyes shone in appreciation. Robert returned twice a day to repeat the process and he saw the young soldier's body slowly recover. Before he left the steamer, the surgeon told Robert that he was confident the boy would do well. On another occasion, one of the Illinois boys pleaded with Robert. He had been told by the surgeon that his arm must be amputated. Tearfully, he explained to Robert that there was only him and his old mother at home on the farm and he could not see how they would manage if he only had one arm. Robert called the surgeon back to the soldier who begged to keep his arm no matter what the pain. Again, before Robert left the steamer the surgeon assured him that the arm would be saved.

Not all soldiers fared as well as these. Robert attended one man who had lost an arm and, as he laid cool wet linen on the stump, the man told Robert in a weak, halting voice that he had left a wife and two small children at home and he would never see them again, unless in heaven. He looked pleadingly at Robert. "I've always tried to be a good man," he said, "but I've never been one for church."

"Never you fear, you will go right home to God, your Father and mine," Robert told him.

After some more words of comfort, Robert backed away leaving him in the care of Mr. Williams, a Presbyterian deacon and a neighbor of the Collyers' in Chicago. At the end, the man raised his hand and closed his eyes. The good deacon gently took hold of the proffered hand and laid it softly across the man's chest. A moment later, all was still.[8]

Another boy lay in the bulkhead shot through the lungs. He had been moved out of the saloon because his cries were so distressing. All day long and into the night he kept up an incessant wailing, but at last the pain ebbed away and he called Robert to his side. "I shall die now; and will you do me a great kindness? Write to my father when I am gone." He named a small rural nook

[8] Collyer, *Some Memories*, 148-9.

in Indiana as the address. "Tell him I owe such a man four dollars and 50 cents, and such a man owes me four dollars; and he will make things straight as I came away in such a hurry. And father must draw my pay and keep it all." Then he lay silent for a while, but stirred again and said, "I have been dreaming about home, and had a drink out of the old well in our yard: it did taste so good." And then while Robert looked on, the lad's eyes grew dim, and he passed from them.[8]

Such was the work of the Commissions' volunteers on board the steamer. When required, Robert acted as a surgeon's assistant and grew adept at the job. At other times, he walked the decks with cool water and soft lint and linen, or with morsels of bread and cups of wine. It was an act of Communion; a Last Supper devoid of liturgy but powerful to a dying man. Robert's words often meant more than food to these wounded men. They spoke of home and family, and he of blessing and eternity.

After a passage of four days, the steamship docked in Mound City and discharged its frail cargo into the care of the huge base hospital there. Robert's thoughts turned to home and family and he decided to return to Chicago. He arrived there on Friday, March 1. On the following Sunday, he stood in the Unity pulpit and told his people about the triumphs and tragedies of this terrible campaign. Just over five weeks later he was back at the battlefield.

With the loss of Forts Henry and Donelson in February, the Confederate commander General Johnston withdrew his disheartened forces into west Tennessee, northern Mississippi and Alabama to reorganize.[9] In early March, the Union side responded by ordering General Grant to advance his 'Army of West Tennessee' on an invasion up the Tennessee River. Occupying Pittsburg Landing, Grant entertained no thought of a Confederate attack. However, on April 3, realizing that Grant would soon be reinforced, Johnston launched an offensive. Advancing upon Pittsburg Landing with 44,000 men, Johnston planned to surprise Grant, and cut his army off from retreat to the Tennessee River. On the morning of April 6, the Confederates stormed forward and found the Union position unfortified. Johnston had achieved almost total surprise. By mid-morning, the Confederates seemed within easy reach of victory, overrunning one frontline Union division and capturing its camp. However, stiff resistance on the Federal right entangled Johnston's brigades in a savage fight around Shiloh Church.

---

[9] Based on James M. McPherson (ed), *The Atlas of the Civil War* (New York, Macmillan, 1994), and from http://www.civilwarhome.com/shilohdescription.htm

Shiloh's first day of slaughter also witnessed the death of the Confederate leader, General Johnston, who fell at mid-afternoon, struck down by a stray bullet while directing the action on the Confederate right. At dusk, the Federal reinforcements reached Pittsburg Landing, and crossed the river to file into line on the Union left during the night. On April 7, Grant's army, now fed with over 22,500 new troops, renewed the fighting with an aggressive counterattack.

Taken by surprise, the Confederate General Beauregard managed to rally 30,000 of his badly disorganized troops and mounted a tenacious defense. Inflicting heavy casualties on the Federals, Beauregard's troops temporarily halted the determined Union advance. However, strength in numbers provided Grant with a decisive advantage. During the night, the Confederates withdrew, greatly disorganized, to their fortified stronghold at Corinth. Possession of the grisly battlefield passed to the troops of the victorious Union Army. They were satisfied to simply reclaim Grant's camps and make an exhausted bivouac among the dead.

Casualties upon this brutal killing ground were immense. Union losses were 1754 killed, 8408 wounded, 2885 captured - total 13,047; Confederate losses were 1723 killed, 8012 wounded, 959 missing – total 10,694. Of the 100,000 soldiers engaged in this conflict, approximately one in four had been killed, wounded or captured. Casualties were 24%, the same as at the battle of Waterloo. Yet Waterloo had settled something, while this one seemed to have settled nothing[10].

When the news came through to Chicago of the battles at Shiloh and Pittsburg Landing, the volunteers of the Sanitary Commission were once again called to assemble for embarkation to Cairo. Collyer was in a dilemma. Racked with anxiety, he wrestled with the decision. Could he possibly refuse to go? He had, of course, discussed his misgivings with Ann, but he could not find the words to express the true depth of his fears. For her part, she had not seen the mangled bodies, she had not heard the pitiful cries that punctuated Robert's fitful sleep. Reluctant as she was to push Robert into acceptance, Ann's talk of patriotic duty persuaded him that he must report for service.

When Collyer arrived at the station, a large group of volunteers was already gathered. The group eventually numbered fifty-two citizens and clergymen who had volunteered as 'nurses' (fifty male and two female), and sixteen

---

[10] Shelby Foote, *The Civil War: 1 Fort Sumter to Perryville* (London, Pimlico, 1992), 350.

surgeons.[11] Collyer was chosen to be director of the nurses because, as they said, he knew the ropes. With Mrs. Eliza Porter, a formidable woman who directed the operations of the Chicago Sanitary Commission, Collyer had been instrumental in establishing the Chicago Protestant Female Nurse Association with the aim of recruiting and screening nurses for the increasingly needy military hospitals.[12] Their initiative, however, had not yet borne fruit and there was a dire shortage of trained nurses willing to serve.

The Sanitary Commission provided the Cairo party with 104 boxes of hospital supplies. They left Chicago by special train at 5pm on April 9, the day the news of the battle came through, and reached Cairo at 8am the next morning. The Commission had a breakfast waiting for them but had not been able to organize a boat to convey the company to the battlefield. Two representatives of the Commission started for Pittsburg Landing, but the main party were unable to leave until the morning of April 11 aboard the 'Lousiana'.

Among the company of 'nurses' on-board ship was Mr. Dwight L. Moody and some fellow members of the 'Christian Commission'.[13] Unfortunately, Moody was one of the few men that Collyer disliked. He felt guilty about his ill feelings towards a fellow Christian, but through a mixture of intuition and experience, Robert felt deeply suspicious of Moody's motives and sincerity. Having shared the platform with Moody on several occasions, Robert saw in him too much Christian fundamentalism and too little humanity.

Moody had arrived in Chicago as a shoe salesman in 1856.[14] A short dapper man with receding dark hair and large, bushy sideburns, Moody turned up at the Plymouth Congregational Church and immediately revealed his ambitions by renting four pews. Over the succeeding weeks, he filled these pews with young men and boys that he met at the YMCA. Soon afterwards, he asked the church Elders if he might become a Sunday school teacher. He was told that he could — if he brought his own scholars. The next Sunday he marched into the church at the head of eighteen ragged boys whom he had collected during the week.

---

[11] The numbers are in dispute. Collyer mentions 48 'nurses' and 18 surgeons but the *Chicago Daily Tribune* April 10, 1862, names 16 surgeons and 52 nurses. http://www.uttyler.edu/vbetts/chicago_tribune.htm

[12] Theodore J. Karamanski, *Rally 'round the Flag: Chicago and the Civil War* (Lanham, MD: Rowman and Littlefield, 2006), 101

[13] See http://www.edinborough.com/Life/Commission/Moody.htm

[14] Frederick B. Meyer, *Dwight L. Moody* in *The Sunday at Home* (London: The Religious Tract Society, 1900), 301.

In 1860, Moody gave up selling shoes in favor of saving souls and became a full-time evangelist, sleeping at night on a bench in the YMCA to keep down his personal expenses. At the outbreak of the Civil War, Moody approached the YMCA board of directors about creating an organization to minister to the troops and formed the United States Christian Commission in November 1861. Just as the Sanitary Commission had responded promptly to the call to Pittsburg Landing, so members of the Christian Commission had reacted with equal urgency. On this journey, Rev Robert Patterson and a Mr. Jacobs accompanied Moody.[15]

As they went upriver, Moody approached Robert, "Brother Collyer, we're going to hold a prayer meeting. Will you come and join us?" Robert could hardly refuse, so he put a positive slant on his reply. "Gladly," he said and went with Moody to the saloon. Early in the meeting, Moody gave an address. The thrust of his message was that they were going to the battlefield to save souls or those men would die in their sins. The clear inference was that these men would go to hell if they were not 'saved' for Christ. When Moody sat down, Collyer rose to his feet and said, "Brother Moody is mistaken: we are not going there to save the souls of our soldiers, but to save their lives and leave their souls in the hands of God." There was complete silence when he sat down.

After a pause, a Congregational minister from Chicago, the Rev. Dr. Patton, rose and said, "This is the way the Unitarians always go to work, from the surface inward; but we go directly to the heart first, and then work out to the surface, pray with him, and point him to *the thief on the cross*."[16] Collyer rose the instant Patton sat down and said, "My friends, we know what those men have done, no matter who or what they are. They left their homes for the camp and the battle, while we stayed behind in our cities. They endured hardness like good soldiers, while we were lodged softly. They have fought and fallen for the flag of the Union and all the flag stands for, while here we are safe and sound. I will not doubt for a moment the sincerity of my friend and yours who has just spoken; but I will say for myself that I should be ashamed all my life long if I should point to the thief on the cross in speaking to these men, or to

---

[15] By 1865, Moody had risen to Presidency of the Chicago YMCA and in that office directed the building of its new headquarters, Farwell Hall. Despite Collyer's misgivings, Moody continued to prosper as an evangelist and, in due course, he was to command an international reputation as a preacher.

[16] This was a reference to the biblical account of the thief being crucified next to Christ who was granted eternal life by his dying acknowledgement of the kingship of Christ – 'Jesus remember me when you come into your kingdom'. Luke 24: 42.

any other thief the world has ever heard of." This time when he sat down, there was a roar of applause.[17]

The 'Louisiana' arrived at Pittsburg Landing at 4pm on the afternoon of Friday, April 11, four days after the battle. The Landing was simply a road leading from the river up a steep bank into open countryside. A fleet of 30 or 40 transport steamers lay along the shore, two or three deep. It had been raining for days; it was raining still; and everything looked indescribably melancholy. Weary, bedraggled men huddled together in sodden tents. On the battlefield, which ran down to the river-bank, lay groups of wounded men, uncared for in the mud. Those who had been carried to shelter lay in crowded tents with their wounds unattended.

The ground was churned into an almost impassable mire. For a mile or more up the river edge, a procession of steamers discharged their cargoes up the steep and slippery bank. Troops, provisions, forage, litters, ambulances and artillery, the reinforcements and supplies of a vast army struggled on to the land through the mud and rain. Soldiers on horseback stumbled through the mud while some of the wagons interlocked their wheels and overturned each other. Wounded men on litters were borne painfully down the slopes toward the ships. Dead men lay in pitiful neglect, unburied, even un-noticed.[18]

Collyer set about exploring the battlefield. 'Right up the bank, I found five or six dead men, some wrapped in their blankets, (the soldier's coffin,) and some bare of all but the garments they wore when they died. The rain beat pitilessly down upon them all day long. I stopped to look at them for a moment - common men, not beautiful when they were alive, ghastly now that they are dead, in the mud and rain; but I think of a time I can easily remember, when they must have been very beautiful to some poor mother, waiting, perhaps even now, to hear from her boy who has gone beyond her life and ours, into the great Hereafter. I pick up a scrap of paper that lies near one, and make out that it is a letter, written from a place called Prairieville, by a father or brother. There are words of hearty, homely cheer in it, but the letter and the man were alike silent beyond a certain line. At the crest of the bank, I came to the tents of the men and more signs of the awful day - dead bodies here and there still unburied, and limbs, shattered and cut away, useless debris even to the living, who, a week ago, held them at priceless worth. But we cannot dwell with the dead; and our great purpose is to see whether we cannot save some brave

---

17 Collyer, *Some Memories*, 127.

18 Henshaw, *Our branch and its tributaries*, 66.

fellows who are near to death. The steamboats are gradually filling with wounded men, and to care for them is our sole business. On the boat, as we came up the river, we got into working order. Doctors and nurses were classified and organized, each doctor had his own nurses to go with him, wherever he went "God bless the Sanitary Commission," many a brave man said in my hearing, and I feel like echoing that cry.'

'We found the steamboats loaded with wounded men, and almost destitute of stores. The army officers here, as everywhere, are like the foolish virgins — lamps out and no oil. The wise virgins, this time, did give of their oil — they were there for that purpose. Drs. Rea, Lynn, Ingalls, Gillette and Miller, with thirteen nurses, were detailed to the 'Hiawatha' to take charge of, I think, 285 wounded. I went with them, and what was done there is a fair sample of how things are done all round. We found the steamboat bare - no beds, no medicines, no stores. ... From the army supply, we were able to get flour, and swap it with another boat for bread, sugar, beef tea, lint, sponges, soap, towels, quinine, nitrate of silver, 100 bed sacks, sixty to eighty cots and a few minor articles. From the Sanitary Commission we get isinglass, plaster, morphine, spirits, sponges, chloroform, wine, brandy, apples, butter, ale, eggs, lemons, oranges, solidified milk, jellies, apple-butter, soft rags, (one of the most precious treasures after a battle) sheets, drawers, shirts, pillows, pads, buckets, brooms, pearl-barley, sago, adhesive plaster, tea, (first rate), quilts, blankets, comforters, bed sacks, undershirts, and a vast number of minor articles. These things did not come in sparse measure, but in plenty - not with vast labor and running miles to get them; but Mr. Patton and Dr. Douglas were there and put them on board for us, and then said heartily, "Now can we do anything else?" This, however, is not true of all the boats. Cincinnati sent three or four fitted up most generously with everything. St. Louis has two equally good. But the Government boat, put in at the last moment, is a deplorable thing. The 'City of Memphis', sent down ahead of us, and bare of supplies and nurses, lost forty men, if I am rightly informed. Our boat, cared for by the Sanitary Commission, and the Chicago surgeons and nurses, lost only one, Captain Stephens, of Dixon (Illinois), who said to me a little while before he died, "I was not fit to go on the field; I had the flux very bad and was weak; but I felt that I was needed, and that my country might not count me unfit, so I went through it. My leg was taken off, and I shall die, but I am peaceful. I have done my duty."' [19]

[19] Robert Collyer, 'To Pittsburg Landing and back: The Sick and Wounded.' Letter to the Editors, *Chicago Daily Tribune*, 1862, April 18.

The Hiawatha took the wounded soldiers to the hospital at Mound City, the first leg of their journey back to Chicago. Unfortunately, for many wounded soldiers returning from the battlefield this proved to be the last leg. Many died during surgery or in the immediate aftermath from blood loss and shock, while others succumbed to infection. Hundreds of dead Union soldiers were buried outside the hospital.[20] With the transfer of wounded into the care of the hospital, Collyer and the others had finished their work. The weary group transferred from Mound City to Cairo, and immediately boarded an Illinois Central Railroad train back to Chicago.

Collyer arrived home, exhausted and perplexed. "War is hell, the great commander said. Yes, I would answer, war is hell. And I turn to the seer's vision in the Holy Book and read there was war in heaven.... And then I ask, What do these things mean?"[21] Although the war was to continue for another three years, Collyer never returned to the battlefield.

---

[20] The U.S. Government bought 10 acres of land outside Mound City in 1862 and created a National Cemetery. The dead from the Military Hospital were reburied here along with 4800 other Civil War dead.
www.state.il.us/hpa/Illinois%20History/Lamszus.pdf

[21] Collyer, *Some Memories*, 151.

18: Distant Thunder

The summer and autumn of 1862 witnessed a succession of battles in a war that had become one of dogged attrition. The Union side based its strategy on its greater financial and industrial resources and larger population. Lincoln and his generals knew that in a sustained war of large set-piece battles along shifting fronts, the Union army would probably prevail, whatever the cost. However, August 1862 saw a second bloody reverse for the Union troops at the now-infamous Bull Run. Once again, Northern soldiers, cowed and broken, straggled into Washington. Three thousand convalescent soldiers were moved out of Washington to make way for the casualties. Floors in the Capitol building and in the Patent Office were cleared to accommodate the torn and mutilated men. The War Department called on Northern cities for surgeons, volunteer nurses and more hospital supplies. Naturally, the Sanitary Commission answered this call, but Robert resisted it. Instead, he channeled his energies into fund-raising for the war-effort and speaking at public meetings, rallies and recruitment meetings.

Through his speeches and sermons, often reported in full in the newspapers, Collyer became well known throughout Chicago. He was widely regarded as the focal point for the citizens' response to the Civil War, an icon of their concern, patriotism and generosity.[1] While Collyer's belief in the Northern cause never wavered, his confidence in Lincoln and the Union

[1] In one newspaper report, the sermon is headed by an editorial note: 'We give place to the following sermon at the request of a large number of citizens, not the parishioners of Mr. Collyer. His views are historic, striking and sound, and should command the attention of the reader.' Holmes, *Life and Letters,* 1: 283.

generals was frequently equivocal and on occasions, non-existent. These misgivings sometimes surfaced in his sermons when a thread of frustration and despair ran through them. Privately, he wrestled with his self-imposed detachment from the conflict. As a non-combatant, Collyer had volunteered for the one form of war service open to him but having witnessed the agonies of wounded and dying men, he knew that he could not face the human detritus of battle again. Yet almost daily, he spoke in public of the noble cause, the nation's expectation, the heroism of battle and the sainthood of sacrifice. His words were powerful and persuasive. The meetings brought forward waves of recruits, but he knew that all too few of these eager young men would return home. Perhaps Robert's tireless work towards the war effort and the endless round of meetings and rallies was his way of reconciling words with actions. In himself, the duplicity gnawed at his soul.

The war was devouring men at an alarming rate. The Second Bull Run was followed by an even bloodier battle. On September 17, 1862, McClellan's 90,000 strong Union army met a Confederate force only half this number under General Robert E. Lee at Antietam Creek, Maryland; the only time that a Confederate Army invaded the North. Both sides lost around 12,000 soldiers in a single day of fighting, but if McClellan had pursued Lee's flagging troops as they retreated south across the Potomac, an outright Union victory could have been secured. As it was McClellan chose to rest and re-group, and an opportunity to end the war was lost.

Later in September, Lincoln issued an Emancipation Proclamation. While the President had earlier shelved Fremont's bold declaration of freedom for the slaves, Lincoln now published a full and unequivocal proclamation to the effect that on January 1, 1863, all slaves in States, or parts of States, in rebellion against the United States 'shall be then, thenceforward, and forever free.'[2] Although the Southern States were clearly outside Northern jurisdiction, they reacted with extreme anger. The Confederates argued that Lincoln was violating private-property rights and, by inference, the proclamation was inviting Negroes to kill, rape and burn their southern masters.

The blood-letting continued. The armies came together on December 13 at Fredericksburg where the Confederates easily repulsed a Union attack. The fields around Fredericksburg, now churned into mud, were flushed crimson with the blood of 12,000 dead Union troops. The distant thunder of battle rolled

---

[2] Shelby Foote 1992 *The Civil War: 1 Fort Sumter to Perryville.* (London: Pimlico, 1992), 707.

across the North, the clouds of defeat dark and threatening. In Chicago, Collyer attempted to deflect its echoes by his leadership and inspiration.

Collyer began to travel across the Eastern states delivering his brand of patriotic fervor at public meetings and in special sermons. According to the barometer of Northern successes and reverses, and his own temperament, the content of his sermons would be at times optimistic and inspirational or at others, despondent and critical. On one of these latter occasions, he gave voice to a savage indictment of Lincoln and his conduct of the war. In a lecture entitled 'Night and Morning' delivered to the Parker Fraternity at the Tremont Temple Baptist Church in Boston, Collyer launched an excoriating attack on the Administration.[3] "Such a sight as this democracy has presented," he cried, "of mistaken confidence and broken hope, this world never saw. (Our people) have said to their executive, tell us what you want done and we will do it. Striplings and strong men and grey-headed men have marched out joyfully to death for their great inheritance. Money has been poured out in such floods as were never seen in the world before. The woman has stood up grandly by the man as her great mother in the forests of Gaul or Britain did in the old time. And yet our record, from first to last, has been one long black night, with but here and there a star. Vultures have been all about us ready to gorge themselves on the distracted nation when it should die... Our great commanders have been made out of epaulettes and apathy. They have been recklessly winning battles on paper, and losing them in the field... I know very little about state affairs. The President, cabinet and commanders may have done the best they knew. I believe the President has done his best. I trust in Abraham Lincoln as I trusted in my own father who rests in heaven. But I cannot shut my eyes to three cardinal principles of action, which our President has followed, so far as I can understand him, which to me seem to be radically wrong."

Collyer went on to elaborate on these three articles of his indictment. Firstly, Lincoln had selected his cabinet largely from the rejected candidates for the presidency at the Chicago convention, "I cannot believe that these men are the best that could be found in all the nation to stand at the head of money and ships, and munitions of war, simply as men. Their training has been entirely of another sort; they are only political preachers, and for such men to unite in a firm, strong way to carry on the war is difficult, or perhaps impossible.[4]

---

[3] October 23, 1862. Holmes, *Life and Letters*, 1: 289.

[4] Others have placed a contrary interpretation on this move, for example, Doris Goodwin posits in her book *Team of Rivals* that by using his rivals for the Presidency as

Secondly, Mr. Lincoln had gone not only to the rejected candidates for his cabinet, but to the milk-poultice party (the Bell-Everett Constitutional Union) for his policy ... a party that wanted to pat and tickle, while events that followed ... summoned the nation to strike quick and hard. There was but one way out of this trouble; the country was prepared for that way from the start. The Milky-Way was not it, and Mr. Lincoln went that way for his policy." The third indictment and "the mistake most fatal of all, was that Mr. Lincoln went to the pro-slavery democrats for his generals — or, in other words, the men who are placed in every one of the most important commands are men who have wanted ... to see the South victorious in the particular thing for which she has plunged us into this dreadful agony of a civil war." Amid the darkness, however, Collyer saw streaks of light of which the President's Emancipation Proclamation was the most conspicuous. He recognized these signs of hope and acclaimed them with a resounding "God bless Abraham Lincoln!" "The Night, now and forever," he said, "is not the Master but the subject of the Day ... and the Day has begun to break upon us."

Collyer's listeners might not have agreed with his analysis, but they applauded his powers of oratory. As a consequence, a few weeks later he received an invitation to preach in the great Music Hall pulpit in Boston, a pulpit that until recently had been filled by the Unitarian hero, Theodore Parker. Parker was a controversial but charismatic preacher who regularly attracted audiences of over 2,000 to the Music Hall. Since his untimely death from tuberculosis in 1860 (at the age of fifty), Parker's church, the 28th Congregational Society in Boston, had been seeking someone of equivalent stature as his replacement. Invitations to preach were sent out far and wide so that the pulpit would be filled every Sunday, and at the same time the congregation could audition a prospective successor to Parker.

Collyer accepted their invitation willingly and in due course undertook the long train journey to Boston. He spent a couple of days looking around the city and had meetings with some of his 'brother' ministers. When Sunday morning arrived, he made his way along Tremont Street towards the Music Hall, filled with trepidation.[5] Once on the platform he was faced by a huge crowd that filled the vast hall, and after speaking for two or three minutes he was overtaken by the fear that he could not be heard. He paused and held out his

---

cabinet members, Lincoln kept the North united throughout the war. Doris K. Goodwin, *Team of Rivals* (New York: Simon & Schuster, 2005), 319.

[5] The Music Hall was built in 1852 and situated in Hamilton Place off Tremont Street. It is now the Orpheum Theatre.

hand, pointing to a man in the far-away top gallery who was leaning forward listening. "Can you hear me, sir, up there?", Collyer enquired without forcing his voice. The man nodded his head with emphasis. The audience, as one, broke into a broad smile, and Collyer went on confident that they could at least hear what he had to say. It was soon evident that they had enjoyed the sermon; many of those who filed past him at the exit gave him a warm handshake accompanied by effusive thanks. He went home elated. He had been heard in Music Hall.

Collyer photographed in Boston 1862. (Holmes, 1917)

Collyer had created a big impression on his listeners in Boston and within a matter of days a letter arrived on his desk imploring him to be the minister at Music Hall. He was surprised and flattered by the invitation, with its un-stated promise of fame and great financial rewards. He asked the Trustees in Boston for two weeks grace so that he could consider his position and discuss a possible move with Ann and the family. His reply to the Boston folk, dated December 22, 1862, says a great deal about his feelings for the Unity Church and his own state of mind. Collyer wrote; 'I can remember but one other decision in my life that has cost me so much painful searching thought, and that was when I went out from my home and kindred, to seek a home in this new world. My answer after this most painful, and I believe sacred searching is — I cannot come. Perhaps it is not *needful* that I should say more than this: and that the matter should rest just where it is. If your letter had felt like the cold formal thing that is usually sent on such errands, I *should* say no more; but there is so much in it to touch my best nature, as well as in others that have come to me touching the same thing, that I cannot but ask you to listen while I tell you what is in my head and heart to compel this answer. My church in this place has grown up with me. Your letter has revealed to me, as I never knew before, how it has grown down in my heart. A very small company of men and women gathered round me at the start three and a half years ago. I was just out of the blacksmith shop. They held on to me: built me a church; defended me; loved me; bore with me. They have taken the most untiring interest in all I have done, given me more than I ever asked for, done more work and given more money for benevolent purposes than I ever dared hope for. My sermons (poor as I believe them to be) they have listened to with a fresh unflagging interest, never under any circumstances dropping asleep. I have rejoiced with those that did rejoice, and wept with them that wept; every house in my Parish is a sort of home to me. I know its history for three years as much as a man ought to know. The manifestations of their love to me since I mentioned your letter has been so deep, so unbearable if I had resolved to leave them (and it would tear the most delicate fibers of my own heart so much to leave them under these circumstances) that I have no choice of answers, I must say *No.*'

This would not be the last invitation to tempt Collyer away from Chicago, but at least in the short term he had resolved the dilemma.[6] He would stay. In

[6] Over the next two years he received invitations to fill several major pulpits in the Unitarian church including a second invitation from Boston and one from the Second Church of Brooklyn, N.Y. following the death of Collyer's friend Nathan A. Staples. When the great preacher T. Starr King died of diphtheria, Collyer was considered for

the meantime, his work in support of the war effort continued - even if this support took some unexpected turns. One such resulted from the military suppression of a newspaper, the *Chicago Times*. The *Times* was a scurrilous anti-war paper whose editor, Wilbur Stacey, promoted extreme racism and civil disobedience. Nevertheless, the paper enjoyed a wide constituency — Chicago was a Democrat city with a Democrat Mayor and most Northern Democrats were pro-slavery and therefore anti-war. Furthermore, the *Times* was the municipality's official organ. On June 2, 1863, General Ambrose E. Burnside (of whiskery 'side-burns' fame) issued an order to General Sweet, Union commander at Camp Douglas — the military headquarters in Chicago — to take charge of the *Times* office and prevent any more issues of the paper. As soon as the news got out, vast crowds of people gathered on the streets to demonstrate their support for the *Times*; by evening the thoroughfare from State Street to Dearborn Street was blocked by a solid mass of people shouting, "Stacey! Stacey!". The demonstrations continued throughout the following day and the public mood was angry and threatening. Crowds surrounded the office of the rival *Chicago Tribune* with a view to preventing its publication. Meetings were hurriedly convened, and representations made to the President. Two days later, June 4, General Burnside announced that the President had rescinded the *Times* military order. The result of all this was that the circulation of the *Times* was greatly increased! [7]

Much as Collyer hated the *Times,* he hated suppression of free speech even more. The following Sunday he preached a sermon upholding the freedom of the press and censuring Burnside for his attempt to silence the Times, a sermon that demanded a great deal of courage. Most, if not all, his parishioners saw the *Times* as the mouthpiece of the enemy and a cruel 'thorn in the flesh' of right-minded people. Collyer warned them that he was "about to preach a sermon which his conscience had made him preach, but which he felt sure would cost him some dear friends, the loss of whose love would be a sore trial." Then with tears streaming down his cheeks, he launched into an attack on military

---

the First Unitarian Church of San Francisco but Henry Bellows thought that he "would be a good man , if he had more education and eloquence of manner." Walter D. Kring, *Henry Whitney Bellows* (Boston: Skinner House, 1975), 285.

[7] Frederick F. Cook, *Suppression of the Times,* reprinted from 'Bygone days in Chicago', in Mabel McIlvaine, *Reminiscences of Chicago during the Civil War.* (New York: The Citadel Press, 1967), 151

autocracy, and extolled the great freedoms that had drawn him from the old oppressions of England to the land of the free.[8]

His prediction about losing friends proved correct. One old church member wrote accusing him of 'prostituting himself to the *Chicago Times*, of being a convicted liar (in going in the teeth of all I had said before), and of selling myself for gold.' Others, fortunately in the great majority, saw his strength of feeling and the underlying reasons for his stand, as he continued to fight the good fight for the Northern cause in the weeks and months that followed.

Despite Collyer's withdrawal from the Sanitary Commission he could not always keep the thunder of war at a distance. Its echoes were plain to hear when Collyer visited the forlorn Camp Douglas. The camp was built in the summer of 1861 as a gathering place for volunteer troops and for their early military instruction, but this use was short-lived. Immediately after the capture of Fort Donelson in February 1862, the commandant, Colonel Tucker, was ordered to prepare the camp for prisoners of war. Over the next few days, almost 9,000 rebel troops arrived at the Camp, with a further influx in April from Pittsburg Landing. A committee was formed to oversee the prisoners' welfare and, inevitably, Collyer was asked to serve on it. Although the welfare committee, and a 'self-appointed detachment of benevolent ladies', strove to maintain reasonable standards of care among the prisoners, mortality was high.[9] Periodic attacks of 'camp fever' swept through the primitive wooden barracks and conditions during the long winter of 1862-3 were harsh. Many of the Southern troops had no experience of the cold weather that faced them in Chicago, and they were ill-equipped to withstand it. As a result of the harsh conditions, some four thousand men died at the camp; they were buried in unmarked paupers' graves in Chicago's City Cemetery.[10]

Through his weekly visits to the Camp, Collyer spent many hours talking to the prisoners. He found them dejected and forlorn but still true to their own side. "We were raised in the South," they would say," and so were our folks. We belong there just now as you belong in the North, and we fought for our rights. There was no other way, and we'll fight again if we get the chance. Can you blame us?" Collyer did not blame them, and he chose not to pass these

---

[8] Holmes, *Life and Letters,* 1: 295.

[9] William Bross, *History of Camp Douglas,* a paper read before the Chicago Historical Society, June 18, 1878, in Mabel McIlvaine, *Reminiscences of Chicago during the Civil War,* 161.

[10] In 1867 the remains were transferred to Oak Woods Cemetery about 5 miles south of the camp.

comments on to the Federal guards. The U.S. Government gave the prisoners the option to join the Northern navy and be set free, but very few of them took the option. When Collyer asked one of them; "Why do you not join our navy and be free?", he answered incredulously, "How can I do that? I could never go home again and look my folks in the face."[11]

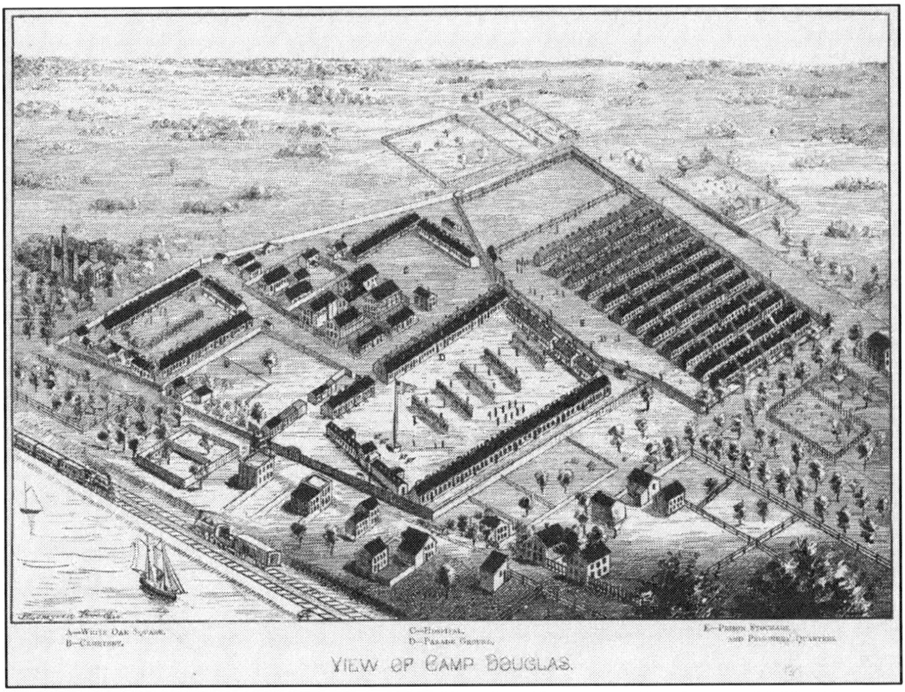

'Bird's eye' view of Camp Douglas created by the Blonogren Brothers c.1862. Chicago History Museum collection via Wikimedia Commons.

Many of the rebel troops were country born and raised, and those who could not write would ask the volunteer helpers if they would write a letter home and tell the folks they were prisoners in Chicago but alive and well. Sometimes a soldier would blush and stammer as he told them what to write. The object of his letter would be a young woman; perhaps he could not express the words he held in his heart and the volunteers would help him out. Collyer became quite expert at these letters. He lost himself in the task and forgot for a

[11] Collyer, *Some Memories,* 131.

short while that he was a middle-aged clergyman as he returned to the days of his youth and wrote the words of a love-sick swain.

Once, on a morning visit to the Camp hospital, Robert saw a boy soldier – not even a young man, beckoning him over to his bedside. He was very weak. Collyer recalled the conversation; "Be you a minister, sir?"

"Yes," he answered.

"A Methodist?"

"No."

"A Baptist?"

"No."

This seemed to be the extent of his knowledge, for the boy asked, "What be you, then, sir?" When Collyer replied; "I am a Unitarian," the boy looked at him with a touch of wonder and said; "I never heard of them. What do you believe, sir? I am dying, and would like you to help me if you can." Then in the simplest language, Collyer told him of, "his faith in God our Father and of his Christ who came to tell us of his Father's love for all his children, not here and now alone, but forever here and hereafter." When Collyer had finished, the boy drew a long breath and between sobs, for he was crying now, said; "That is good, and I thank you, sir. Will you come to see me again, when you are in the camp?" Collyer said, "Yes," but the next time he came, the boy was gone.[12]

---

[12] Collyer, *Some Memories*, 132.

19: Massacre in Kansas

Early in September 1863, Collyer had to confront the aftermath of war yet again. As with the Iowa Tornado Relief, he had been called upon to represent the citizens of Chicago in an expression of concern and charity towards a devastated community, but this time it was man-made devastation. A marauding band of pro-slavery guerrillas from Missouri under the leadership of William Quantrill had killed about 140 men and boys in the small town of Lawrence, Kansas.

The state of Kansas owes its origin to an Act of Congress in 1854 that organized the land west of Missouri into two Territories, Kansas and Nebraska. From 1854 onwards, Chicago, like many cities in the North and East, contributed numerous settler families to the Kansas Territory in general, and to Lawrence in particular. The influx of largely anti-slavery migrants brought the Territory into smoldering hostility with neighboring Missouri, a slave state. Incursions by Missourians were commonplace; sometimes they were simply groups of pro-slavery rabble-rousers intent on manipulating elections, but other raids had a more malign purpose and ended in bloodshed. In January 1861, Kansas entered into full statehood under the Union flag and soon afterwards joined the war against its Southern neighbors. Nevertheless, the Civil War was no justification for Quantrill's unprovoked and unauthorized raid on Lawrence and the massacre that ensued.

A wave of sympathy swept through Chicago, and the citizens swiftly responded with generous donations. Collyer was entrusted with a large sum of money for 'the relief of those who had survived the massacre and were in need of help'.[1] He travelled to Kansas with Jeremiah Brown, a man who knew the area well and had many relatives there, including the Unitarian minister in Lawrence, John Stillman Brown. Jeremiah was half-brother to the legendary John Brown, the militant abolitionist whose soul has been marching on since his death by hanging in December 1859.

After a long and complicated journey by rail and stagecoach, the two men arrived in Lawrence and made their way to the Unitarian minister's house. There, Collyer was introduced to the Rev. Stillman Brown and to another minister, Rev. Richard Cordley, Pastor of the Congregational Church. Unlike the Rev. Brown, who had been away from Lawrence on church business, Cordley had been an eye-witness to the massacre, and the visitors spent that first evening listening to Cordley's account of the mayhem and murder that took place on August 21, 1863.

Cordley later wrote a full account of the massacre.[2] 'Quantrill assembled his men at Columbus, Johnson County, Missouri on August 19. The roll was called, and 294 men responded. They were organized in four companies under four 'captains'. Two of these captains were the notorious Bill Todd and Bill Anderson, the most desperate and bloodthirsty of the border chieftains. The raiders moved towards the Kansas border crossing over at about 5 pm. On the night of August 20, they struck directly across the prairie to Lawrence. About 11 o'clock they passed Gardner on the old Santa Fe trail. Here they burned a house or two and killed a man. Quantrill took a boy from a house near Captain's Creek and compelled him to lead them to Lawrence. They kept this boy during their work in Lawrence, then Quantrill dressed him in a new suit of clothes, gave him a horse and sent him home.'

'Quantrill and his men entered Franklin, four miles east of Lawrence, at the first glimmer of day. They passed quietly through the village, leaning over upon their horses so as to attract as little attention as possible. A few persons saw them, but in the dimness could not make out who they were. Distinctly heard, however, was the command: "Rush on, boys, rush on! It will be daylight before we are there. We ought to have been there an hour ago."

'About two miles east of Lawrence they passed the farm of Rev. Snyder, a minister of the United Brethren church. Here a couple of them left the main

---

[1] Collyer, *Some Memories*, 130.

[2] Richard Cordley, *A History of Lawrence, Kansas, from the first settlement to the close of the Rebellion* (Lawrence, KA: E.F. Caldwell, Laurence Journal Press, 1895), 198-232. See also www.etsu.edu/cas/history/docs/lawrenceka.htm

body and rode through his gate, found him in his barnyard and shot him. About a mile from town they met young Hoffman Collamore, the son of the town's Mayor. He was riding out early to his father's farm to spend the day shooting game. He was a young lad of about sixteen. They halted him and asked him where he was going. Suspecting nothing, he made an indifferent reply and kept on. At that they began firing at him. He put spurs to his pony and dashed out into a field. Soon one bullet hit the boy and another the pony, and they both fell headlong. The boy lay as if dead until they passed and then he crept away. He was severely wounded in the thigh, but recovered.'

'As they drew near to the town they seemed to hesitate and waver. Two horsemen were sent in advance of the troop to see that all was quiet. They rode through the main street without attracting attention. They were seen by several persons but excited no suspicion. They returned to the main body and reported the way clear. When they came to the high ground facing Massachusetts Street the command was given in clear tones, "Rush on to the town." Instantly the whole body bounded forward with the yell of demons. They came first upon a camp of unarmed recruits for the Kansas Fourteenth regiment. They had just taken in their guards and were rising from their beds. On these the raiders fired as they passed, killing seventeen of the twenty-two. This diversion did not check the general advance. In all the bloody scenes which followed nothing surpassed for wildness and terror that which now presented itself. The horsemanship of the guerrillas was perfect. They rode with the ease and abandon of men who had spent their lives in the saddle amid rough and desperate scenes. The riders sat with their bodies erect and arms free, some with a revolver in each hand, shooting at each house or person they passed. On each side of this stream of fire were men falling dead or wounded, and women and children, half dressed, running and screaming, some trying to escape from danger, and others rushing to the side of their murdered friends.'

'The attack could scarcely have been made at a more unfortunate hour. People were just awakening from their sleep, and could hardly comprehend what had come upon them. The men of Lawrence were organized into a militia company, but the Mayor had insisted that the arms should be kept in the armory instead of being carried home by the members – and the guns remained inaccessible.'

'The raiders dashed along Massachusetts Street, shooting at every person on the sidewalk, and into almost every window, until they came in front of the Eldridge Hotel. The firing now ceased and there was silence for a few moments. Captain A.R. Banks, provost marshal of the state, opened a window and displayed a white sheet and called for Quantrill. Quantrill rode forward and Captain Banks surrendered the house, stipulating for the safety of the inmates, mostly strangers. The raiders ransacked the hotel, taking what they found in the rooms and robbing the guests of their valuables as they came out. Once assembled, the guests were marched to the corner and ordered to go to the City Hotel where they would be safe.'

Ruins of the Free State Hotel after the sacking of Lawrence. State Historical Society of Missouri via Wikimedia Commons.

'Quantrill evidently regarded the Eldridge house as the citadel of the place, and considered its surrender equivalent to the surrender of the town. The raiders then scattered all over the town. They went in bands of six or eight, taking street by street and house by house. The events of the next three hours find no parallel outside the annals of savage warfare. History furnishes no other instance where a large number of such desperate men, so heavily armed, were let loose upon an unsuspecting and helpless community. They were not restrained even by the common rules of war, and went about their work of death with the abandon of men with whom murder was a pastime and pity a stranger. Instead of wearying of their bloody work, they grew more brutal as the work proceeded, for they secured liquor at some of the stores, and added the recklessness of drunkenness to the barbarous purpose for which they came. They killed whom they met without knowing who they were or caring what they were. They said their orders were "to kill every man and burn every house." They did not quite do this, but they went to work as if this was their intent.' At the end of the slaughter, 140 men lay dead; 80 women made widows and 250 children lost a father.

Two weeks after the carnage, Collyer arrived in Lawrence with the Chicago Relief Fund in his luggage. Over the next three days he went about the task of distributing the money to the eighty widows. He devised a scale of payments that reflected the number and age of any children, and whether the house had been destroyed. By these means he hoped that all would receive in proportion to their loss and need. He heard the women's own accounts of their ordeal. Their horror and grief were palpable. Some were too shocked and numb to talk about their involvement. Their thanks for the money from Chicago were heartfelt, and in many homes Collyer's words of sympathy and support were valued no less highly.

Collyer also arranged for the bodies of sixteen men who had gone out from Chicago to Lawrence, to be transported back to their 'home' city for burial. Having completed their work in Lawrence, Collyer and Jeremiah Brown headed back to Chicago, but that was not the end of the matter. On the following Sunday, Collyer stood on the platform of the Bryan Hall for the memorial service that preceded the burials. Sixteen caskets draped in flags lay in a line alongside him as he faced the vast audience that packed the Hall. He had been asked to take the sermon, 'but there was no text that day and no sermon of the old pattern, only the story in simple sentences of what we had seen and what they had done. You felt the great heart beating the grand Amen, and in the psalms and songs. I can never forget that Sunday.'[3]

On October 23, 1863, Collyer wrote 'that he was just back from Lawrence, Kansas, and tired to death.'[4] In truth, his health was broken yet again and it was several weeks before he could consider himself back to 'normal'. At least the expedition to Lawrence was Collyer's last direct contact with the Civil War. For the first time since accepting the pastorate at Unity he was now able to give his full attention to the church, even if he had to first regain his energy and enthusiasm.

In a perverse way, Collyer's guilt-ridden decision not to undertake further service with the Sanitary Commission acted in his favor. His presence week by week in the Unity pulpit served to strengthen his reputation as a preacher and

---

[3] Collyer, *Some Memories,* 131.

[4] In a letter to Rev. Jasper Douthit from Holmes, *Life and Letters,* 2: 11.

inspirational leader. His activities on the public platform gained him further accolades. He was widely perceived as the 'voice of Chicago'. Naturally, many citizens were drawn to Unity Church to hear the great man Sunday by Sunday. This led to a problem. 'The church is full – very', he wrote in November 1864.[5] In February 1865, there is the first suggestion of a possible solution, 'We are full – have no pews left, and propose to build afresh – want a church twice as large, and hope we may get it – have a committee out to see after subscriptions which bids fair to do something handsome.'[6]

[5] In a letter to Miss Alice Baker from Holmes, 2: 18.

[6] Holmes, 2: 18.

20: Murder and mourning

By November 1864, the war was reaching its final stages. General William T. Sherman led the Union army through Georgia, and after taking Atlanta and leaving it in flames, a two-pronged attack advanced through the State. The Union troops destroyed everything in their wake so that the country could offer no succor to the diminishing Confederate army. Savannah fell shortly before Christmas, and Sherman's army continued northwards into the Carolinas, meeting little opposition. In April 1865, Mobile, Selma, and Montgomery in Alabama fell to Union forces. At the same time, General Sheridan prepared to join General Grant for a conclusive assault on Lee's army. In Virginia, Grant finally succeeded in seizing the railway line supplying Richmond. Forced therefore to abandon both Petersburg and Richmond, Lee retreated westward, hoping to join with the Confederate army of Joseph Johnston in North Carolina. On April 9, Grant's Union army of 50,000 men blocked his way, and Lee with only 10,000 troops saw the futility of battle. Lee wrote a note asking Grant for an interview 'with reference to the surrender of this army'. Thus it was, that at the McLean house on the edge of Appomattox village, 95 miles west of Richmond, Lee gave over his army to Grant. With Lee's surrender, the remaining Confederate armies quickly collapsed, and the war was ended.

In all, 620,000 Americans had been killed in action or died of their wounds or disease — 360,000 from the North; 260,000 from the South — a lost generation of American manhood now committed to the earth. Their graves marked and unmarked, a testimony to their loyalty to a cause that few could articulate but that led them to cut each other down in the bloom of youth. It was to this vanished generation that Lincoln directed his thoughts and made 'reconciliation' between the survivors his constant watchword - 'Malice toward none and charity to all.' There were those who considered Lincoln's magnanimity in victory, and his search for accommodation and compromise in restoring the Southern states to the Union, as signs of equivocation and weakness. Whether Lincoln would have his way, or his radical opponents would control the reconstruction of the South, were still matters for conjecture by the evening of April 14, 1865.

Thursday, April 13, had been a day of victory celebrations in Washington with a holiday for workers, and parades and marching bands. April 14 was Good Friday. In the evening, the President and Mrs. Lincoln took a carriage ride to see the lights of the city. Calcium lights burned from the buildings and bonfires lit the streets. Rockets flew into the sky and sent their showers of light onto the crowds below. On the Friday morning, a Cabinet meeting discussed the reunion of North and South, Lincoln set the tone, 'we must extinguish our resentment if we expect harmony and union.'[1] That evening the Lincolns, in the company of two friends, went to see a comedy play – *Our American Cousin,* then running at Ford's Theatre in Washington. During the play, an out-of-work actor named John Wilkes Booth, quietly opened the door of the President's box and, standing close behind him, fired a single-shot derringer pistol at Lincoln's head. The lead ball crashed through the left side of the President's skull and lodged behind his left eye. Lincoln's crumpled body was carried into a house across the street from the theatre where he lingered, unseeing and unconscious, until the next morning. The President died at 7.21am on April 15.

Throughout that day, the telegraphs carried the news of the President's assassination to every newspaper office in the land. The shockwave ran through the newsrooms and offices, out onto the streets, and passed from person to person so that by the time the special editions appeared most readers were already aware of the tragedy. The reaction was unprecedented. People wept openly. Anger mingled with tears was the reaction of many, while others expressed despair at the prospects for the country.

The mourning over Lincoln was vast and intense. The body was embalmed and taken on board a funeral train that was to retrace the 1,654-mile route that Lincoln had travelled from his hometown as president-elect in 1861. The train left Washington amid much pomp and ceremony on April 21, six days after his death. Over its twelve-day passage, (the train proceeded at only 5-10 mph) to Springfield, Illinois, many millions of people saw the funeral procession and

---

[1] quoted in Chicago Historical Society's account of the last days of Lincoln. See http://www.chicagohs.org/wetwithblood/return/ford1.htm

thousands took part in it. The funeral train made stops at all the major towns, and several minor ones. At almost all these stopping places, the coffin was carried a variable distance from the train and placed on a catafalque. These repositories were invariably ornate, their grandiosity reflecting the municipal pride and wealth of the host city. Elevated in rococo splendour, the coffin would be opened and the body 'lie in state' for a varying length of time. Each city had its own funeral service. Local dignitaries and military men back from the war, presided over a succession of ceremonies that too often indulged their self-importance to the point of excess. The ceremonials competed in their grandeur and showiness. The words and songs frequently evoked sentimentality bordering on mawkishness. Nevertheless, they provided an opportunity for a huge outpouring of genuine love and respect from a nation in deep shock and dismay.

Collyer took the news of Lincoln's death as an intense, personal bereavement. For him Lincoln embodied the Union cause and the country's future. The impending Northern victory would signal an end to fighting, but who was to shape the peace? Suddenly, all Collyer's optimism evaporated, and he sank into a trough of despondency. His gloom was all-pervasive. He lost sleep, awakening in the early hours with his mind in turmoil. Over the following days, Collyer was overtaken by constant tiredness as all his energy and powers of concentration drained from him.

On May 1 it was Chicago's turn to host the funeral procession. Although Robert was at a particularly low ebb, he felt compelled to take his appointed place in the ceremonials. The Lincoln train, comprising nine carriages with about 300 mourners on board, arrived in Chicago at 11am. A military band played a funeral march as the coffin was moved from the train onto a platform under an elaborate three-arched canopy that itself had cost $15,000 dollars to construct. Then the silver-handled casket was transferred to a funeral carriage bearing a stuffed American eagle and pulled by ten horses bedecked in black mourning blankets. The carriage, flanked by a military escort, was positioned behind the band. As the band struck up yet another funeral march, the first groups in the huge procession of thirty-six thousand people began their slow progress down Michigan Avenue.[2] Collyer and the other members of the clergy walked in one of the leading groups, their marching uncoordinated and halting as, with bowed heads, they tried to keep step with the muffled drumbeats of the band.

---

[2] 'Lincoln Funeral', https://chicagology.com/prefire/prefire005/

President Lincoln's hearse accompanied by young women dressed in white pass beneath an ornamental arch at 12th Street in Chicago. United States Congress image via Wikimedia Commons.

It took four hours for the groups at the rear of the procession even to begin their march. By this time, the head of the slowly elongating snake of people had passed along Lake Street and Clark Street to the Court House, where the President's body was to be placed for public view. Apart from a large military contingent, the marchers were a mix of ordinary people and Chicago officials, from 10,000 schoolchildren wearing black sashes, to the Mayor, John Wentworth, who was one of the pallbearers. An estimated 120,000 people witnessed the procession.

Black and white flags hung from the windows and the chandeliers of the Chicago Court House; and the walls were covered in black crepe. Decorative banners bore the inscription: 'He left us sustained by our prayers; he returns embalmed in our tears; Liberty's great martyr'.[3] The pallbearers placed the

[3] 'Lincoln's coffin in the City Hall, Chicago', see https://rememberinglincoln.fords.org/node/1139.

coffin in the center of the building directly under the dome of the rotunda. Collyer, with a group of fellow clergymen, entered shortly afterwards. They joined the line of people that snaked across the floor of the Court House towards the catafalque. As he neared the coffin, Collyer was overcome with grief. He had a deep sense of sadness, only partly explained by his proximity to Lincoln's inert body. He shuffled close to the catafalque and leant over the open coffin. Lincoln's mouth was locked in a grim half-smile, the chiseled jaw and the small beard jutting upwards in a last gesture of resolve. As he studied the familiar features of the President's face, a wave of nausea swept over him as he discerned a part-foul, part-perfumed smell. He grabbed his handkerchief and pressed it to his nose and mouth, moved out of line and hurried towards the exit. The President was putrefying.

Shortly after Lincoln's death, two medical men who claimed to be expert embalmers, Drs Charles Brown and Harry Cattell, set about the grim work of preserving the President's body. They incised his jugular veins and opened the blood vessels in his groins.[4] Using a metal cannula tied in the femoral artery, they flushed the entire vascular system with a strong chemical preservative. Then, they cut open the body, removed the organs, and filled the cavities with more preservative fluid. Finally, they reflected the scalp, opened the skull and removed the brain. Thus, the President had been converted into a largely hollow shell. Now, sixteen days after death, the embalmers' work was found wanting. The skin of the ears and scalp had a slight green tinge. While the be-suited body was surrounded by white satin and strewn with roses, magnolias and lilies, their sweet scent could not neutralize the smell of incipient putrefaction, as Collyer could readily testify.

At 6pm, members of the military guard opened the doors to the public. Throughout that evening and night, thousands of people filed past the coffin pausing to discern the President's features, to shed a tear or even to say some words, a spoken prayer or a simple goodbye. The next morning saw a huge increase in the number of people wanting to view the body and by noon the line of mourners extended for over a mile from the Court House. At 8pm the Court House was closed, with thousands of people still waiting to get into the building, and the coffin was escorted back to the depot of the St Louis and Alton Railroad. The 'Lincoln Special' was destined for its final stop, Springfield, Illinois.

---

4 https://www.mentalfloss.com/article/31845/preserving-president-abraham-lincoln-grave-robbers-and-excellent-embalmer

Next morning the train reached Lincoln's hometown and the body was moved in solemn procession to the State House. It was a sweltering hot day and the discoloration of the President's face had become even more apparent. The funeral organizers enlisted the help of Mr. Thomas Lynch, an undertaker from St. Louis who had been brought to Springfield to construct the funeral carriage, to disguise the obvious deterioration. Lynch got to work with rouge chalk and amber and restored the face to a near normal color.[5] Shortly after 10am, the front doors of the State House were opened to the long line of mourners. After twenty-four hours of public viewing, and further treatment of the body by the undertaker and embalmer, the coffin was sealed and taken to the Oak Ridge Cemetery. There, twenty days after his death, Lincoln's body was finally laid to rest. The iron gates and the heavy wooden doors of the tomb were closed and locked.

In the aftermath of Lincoln's funeral, Collyer felt adrift and lost. Although the prospect of a new church building should have enthused him, it seemed to have the opposite effect. Collyer writes; 'I was tired with the long strain of such service as I could render in the War, and the church and parish, but did not tell the people, or indeed quite know myself; but the truth is I was preaching *tired* sermons, some of them so poor and fatuous that they made me sick, and I burnt them off-hand. The wise heads in the church knew what was the matter; and on a Saturday evening (in June) one of them came to see me and said, "We want you to take a good rest this summer, to go over to your old home and see the folk; and here is a check for your expenses." The money the church gave me … would have been equal to three years' steady work at the anvil, so generous they were and eager to send me home rejoicing.'[6]

---

[5] From *The route of Abraham Lincoln's Funeral Train* at https://rogerjnorton.com/Lincoln51.html.

[6] Robert Collyer, *Some Memories* (Boston, American Unitarian Association, 1908), 169.

21: The Home-coming

Robert leant against the forward rail of the *S.S. New York* and peered through the morning mist towards the Liverpool waterfront. All his long-suppressed yearnings for the sights and sounds of England welled-up, and he realized to his embarrassment that tears were trickling down his face. The years of frustration, the recurring bouts of depression and the haunting nostalgia, were laid aside as with mounting anticipation and excitement he urged the ship towards the dock.

Every waking minute of the three weeks prior to his departure had been filled with preparations. The first decision Robert had to make was the most difficult; should he go for so long without his family. He put the proposal to Ann, but she knew that he had to go by himself, not because of expense — thanks to his beneficiary he had ample funds — but because the children were too young to travel, and her place was with them. Ann knew how important this trip was to Robert. She gave him her blessing; Robert would travel alone.

The prospect of the vacation in Europe had an immediate and beneficial effect on his state of mind and morale. The travel arrangements, the planning of his itinerary and the numerous purchases he had to make, were a source of excitement, and distraction. He also had to write numerous letters to old friends, and to Unitarian contacts in America and England. The tonic effect of his adventure began with the knowledge that he was going home. His depressed mood and anxiety lifted over a matter of days. A letter to a friend summed up his feelings; 'I am going to lie among the heather and hear the lark, and drink in at old wells, and eat oat-bread and milk, and hunt up old cronies, and tumble round in a river I know of, and go to the church where I was baptized, on one or more Sundays, and hear the parson preach — he does not mind that I am a heretic, and if he did I should not care — and there is a little tavern where the landlord knew my folks forty years ago, and I shall put up with that landlord for a spell, as it is a pleasant place, and haunted by pleasant ghosts as anybody didn't see, and I shall toddle through some woods I know of, between an old abbey and an old tower, where I used to go a-courting.' On July 1, 1865, Robert Collyer sailed from New York to bring these dreams to reality.

On board he contented himself with reading a succession of books, some academic, some frivolous, from the English section of the ship's well-stocked library. Now, with the dockside in Liverpool approaching, he could hardly wait to get on the train to Leeds.

Collyer's mother. A photograph taken shortly before her death in 1874. (Holmes, 1917)

Collyer's mother was now living with her daughter Maria and her family in Leeds. The cab dropped Robert outside the house in Emerald Street,

Holbeck.[1] He recalls that he walked straight in; 'no knocking at that door of all the doors on the earth. She was sitting in the same old chair where I had left her; but I think it was not the same house, and her hair was white as snow. I said, "Mother." She looked up with a touch of wonder, and said, "my lad, I do not know thy face, but that is thy voice." And then she rose up and kissed me, while the tears ran down her fine old face.'[2] Whether or not the home-coming was as Collyer described it is a matter for conjecture. The house was not the mother's original home in Leeds that he knew, and his reference to 'that door of all doors' does not ring true, after all it was a strange door, in an unfamiliar part of Leeds. Whatever the circumstances, he was soon 'at home' and, sitting by the fireside. He quickly lapsed into the old familiar Yorkshire dialect, a way of talking that he had taken so much trouble to put aside when he first went into American pulpits.[3]

Collyer arrived at the Shires' house on a Thursday.[4] The following Saturday he made for Ilkley picking up Dobson's coach from Briggate, in the old center of Leeds. 'William Dobson was the whip,' he wrote in a letter to Flesher Bland.[5] 'He did not know me and I did not tell him who I was, but just rode along and drank in the pleasure of the old familiar things. I remembered standing back in 1850 on that fine point where turning from Leeds you see such a noble reach of Wharfedale all at once, and wondering if I should ever see it again, and if so under what circumstances. When we came down from Bramhope and the view burst on my sight, the old memory came back as though it were yesterday. Otley was not altered in the least .... they have pulled down the White Horse and are building a good hotel on the site, but all else was unchanged. In Burley too, the things looked just as usual. The Red Lion and the Malt Shovel, the shops and houses, and the very trees stayed still in their old place with the old look on them. But, of course, Ilkley was the great point. As I rode up I would see places where I used to wander reading and dreaming. Then I saw a field I helped to drain, the tower of the old church, and the town. As we rode into the village .... outside a new house, I saw a man and said at once, that is John

[1] Maria's husband was John Shires an overlooker in a local flax-mill, and the family lived at 14 Emerald Street. They had four children, Maranda, Robert, Mary and Martha. Maria was pregnant at the time of Robert's visit and she gave birth to a son, William, later in 1865. (personal communication, John Shires, Beverley, East Yorkshire 2005).

[2] Collyer, *Some Memories*, 169.

[3] Collyer, 171.

[4] Probably 6th July

[5] Holmes, *Life and Letters*, 2: 55.

Dobson. When we had got away from the coach, I went back to that house, and asked the man if I could have lodgings.[6] He said, "Nay, we are full". Then he looked at me and I at him. Then he caught at his heart and sat down and said, "I feel faint, but I know you". You may be sure he was glad to see me.'

Accommodation was soon found in a boarding house owned by a cousin – Michael Dobson, but run by a manageress. Michael's attention was elsewhere. He had put a lot of money and all his energies into building a 'hydropathic' hotel on the edge of Ilkley Moor which he called 'Craiglands'. The enterprise left Michael in poor health and he died shortly after Collyer's visit. The building of Craiglands was a response to the hydrotherapy boom that now gripped Ilkley. Robert remembered its beginnings with the building of Ben Rhydding Hydro in nearby Wheatley. Under the charismatic Dr. William McLeod, the Hydro had virtually doubled in size, and four new Hydros had appeared – Wells House, Craiglands, Troutbeck, and The Grove (later called The Spa).

Brook Street, Ilkley, in 1862 – with part of Brook Terrace on the right. Author's collection.

[6] The house was Hollybank House, Leeds Road. John Dobson was by now a lodging-house keeper and, with William Dobson, proprietor of the Ilkley-Leeds coach.

Unlike Otley, Ilkley had changed dramatically. The stream running down Brook Street had been culverted so that the village now boasted a broad main street lined by new shops and houses. John Shuttleworth, who had founded a local newspaper, the *Ilkley Gazette,* occupied one of the four shops in the handsome Brook Terrace at the foot of the street. On the opposite side, William Bell's old grocery shop had been demolished to be replaced by a splendid hotel, the Crescent. The most impressive development, however, was the building of a railway from Leeds to Ilkley and the appearance of an imposing station right in the center of the town. The rail service was to be inaugurated the following month. It would halve the time taken to travel to Leeds and mark the demise of Dobson's coach business.

The photograph purports to show the first train to leave Ilkley for Leeds. The inauguration of the service, on August 1, 1865, was accompanied by great celebrations any signs of which are totally lacking here. It is nevertheless one of the earliest trains to leave for Leeds. Author's collection.

Robert stayed a few days in Ilkley looking up old friends. On the Sunday, he visited the Methodist Chapel (on the corner of Bridge Lane and Addingham

Road); 'It is very little changed; on the outside not at all; on the inside slightly. A man named Way was in the pulpit. I thought he was a narrow way.' [7]

Collyer then returned to Leeds to await the arrival of his brother, John. The reunion had a great influence on John's life, for he resolved to follow Robert's lead and emigrate to America. Robert next went up to Washburndale, the focus of much of his nostalgia. 'I knew what I wanted to see and to do when I came there. There was one well at which I would drink my fill. Then there was the great holly-bush on the hill, where as a boy I had gone year after year to look at the blackbird's nest, where one year, that brigand, the cuckoo, had laid an egg, and when I went one evening to see how the fledglings fared, there was the young cuckoo sprawling all over the place, while the young blackbirds lay on the grass below. There was also that shadowy reach in the stream where the water came down from the moor to turn the great overshot wheel for the factory, and at the mouth of the tunnel the biggest trout I ever failed to catch. He would look at me and shake his tail, as if he would say, "It is no use: I am here to stay," and then float quietly into the tunnel. Then there were those swallows that came every year to build their nests under the eaves of one house right in the sun's eye, and went away when the summer waned, after sitting in council on the roof-tree, - went I knew not where, and even my father could not tell me. And there was the one oak-tree in the pasture where I would sit and dream, when the fit was on me, of the great and wonderful world beyond the valley and the moors. I seemed to own that oak.'

'So I would dream of these in my new life, and wonder if they were all there as when I left them. Well, I lost scant time when I came to my old home-nest; and, will you believe me, the blackbird's nest was there in the holly-bush, and the old birds were busy feeding their young. I stood quietly at some small distance. They did not seem afraid of me, and I wondered if they had chirruped the tradition down of the boy who came to look at the nest and never harmed or robbed them. Yes, and the same old trout was there or another perhaps not quite so big. But he knew the old trick with the tail after taking my photograph on those eyes and floated away in the dark. The beryl brown water in the well was sweet, and I drank my fill. But the swallows came no more to build their nests under the eaves. The once quiet home had been turned into a noisy beer saloon, and they would not stay, the good swallows.'

'There was the oak on the slope of the pasture too, my oak: but it seemed to have grown smaller in many years. I was staying with the owner, who

---

[7] Holmes, 2: 57.

remembered our family and kept the inn (the Hopper Lane Hotel). He went with me over the place, and, when we came to the tree, I said, "It is not nearly so large, sir, as it was when I was a boy." But he answered: "It is larger. Your eyes are not the same: they are the eyes of a grown man." But before we left the pasture he said: "It may be the tree needs some more nourishing after all. But, whether or no, for the sake of old lang syne I will spread a load of manure about the roots, happen that will help it to grow a bit faster." And after I came home I heard this had been done.'[8]

The landlord of the inn also brought Robert up to date on the fortunes, or more properly, misfortunes of West House mill. In 1858, the Crowthers of Halifax bought the empty flax-mill, together with the old corn mill and fourteen cottages. Many of the cottages that were vacated in the 1840s and -50s had been demolished. A pair of large, semi-detached houses, Westhouse Villas (later Skaife Hall), stood on the site of the row of cottages that included Collyer's old home. The Crowthers' converted West House into a silk mill but it was never more than a modest success. There were only thirty-two employees, very different from the West House mill of Robert's boyhood.[9] Robert visited the mill but the people at work were strangers. 'There was not a face I knew, not one, and yet this was where I was once as well known to everybody as I knew my own kinsfolk, for it was here that I began my life. Again in fancy I saw in one of the great dusty rooms of the factory a little fellow about eight years old working away from six o'clock in the morning till eight at night, tired sometimes almost to death, and then not tired at all, rushing out when work was over, home to some treasure of a book.'[10]

While he was in Washburndale, Robert also took the opportunity to visit his old schoolmaster Willie Hardy at his home in Fewston. Willie remembered well the reluctant mathematician who now stood before him as a minister of the church. The boy's preference for reading over arithmetic had brought a rich reward.

There were two trips to Addingham, Flesher Bland's former home village, and just two miles from Ilkley. Robert told him about the visits; 'the first with my mother in a carriage, by way of Fewston and Bolton Bridge, and then again

---

[8] Collyer, 174.

[9] The later stages of West House mill are documented in Bernard Jennings, *A history of Nidderdale,* (Huddersfield, Yorkshire: The Advertiser Press, 1967), 253.

[10] Quoted in Tom Bradley, *Yorkshire Rivers. No.10 The Washburn* (Leeds: Tom Bradley, 1895), 27.

from Ilkley by foot through the fields and along that bit of old Roman road.[11] That time I went to see Brother William (Bland). Addingham looks just as it did. ...In your shop window was a bill about services in the Ranter chapel, when a woman would preach and silver be thankfully received on entering the gallery.[12] The very old gaol with the old date remains, and Sailor Bill's hotel, and all the rest of 'em.'[13]

'William was very glad to see me. We had a very pleasant chat all about you....... He would honour a dog that had seen Flesher. He lives on seeing you again. He grows like what I remember his father was in 1838; he will be very like him in ten years. ... I was very busy going about ... But I saw Bolton Abbey and all the beauty of that region. Walked from the (Bolton) Bridge over through Blubberhouses, by Darley to the railroad, and rode with mother over the same road to Hopper Lane and Fewston. Drank in at all the pores of my spirit the good renewal of my childhood.'[14]

Collyer spent over a week in Wharfedale, exploring old haunts and enjoying chance reunions. One Sunday morning in Ilkley, he met an old member of the Methodist Chapel as he walked up Church Street. Collyer greeted him gladly, but the man replied, "I don't know ye, sir."

After Collyer had introduced himself, the man said, "I am ever so pleased to see ye, sir. I am going t'chapel, and the preacher has sent word he cannot come, he is badly. Ye were a 'Local' (Preacher) when ye left us: do ye preach a bit still?"

"Yes," Collyer answered, "I am still a preacher."

---

[11] The remnant of Roman road commences just beyond Lumb Beck Cottage and extends for 1.5 miles westwards. Alison Armstrong, *Country walks around Addingham* (Addingham, Yorkshire: Addingham Civic Society, 1992), 11.

[12] In the 1851 census, Henry Flesher Bland and his wife, Emma, occupied a shop in Front (Main) Street described as a Grocer, Draper and Calico manufacturer. They emigrated to Canada in 1858. The term 'Ranters' was a term applied to the Primitive Methodists. They met in a chapel room that was part of the Oddfellows Lodge up Lodge Hill. Kate Mason, *Addingham: from Brigantes to bypass* (Addingham, Yorkshire: Addingham Civic Society, 1996).

[13] The public house was officially called 'The Sailor'. The old village 'lock-up' or gaol was in a building erected in 1666.

[14] The 'railroad' ran from Pateley Bridge, along the Nidd Valley to Harrogate and thence to Leeds. Kenneth Hoole, *Railways in the Yorkshire Dales* (Clapham, North Yorkshire: The Dalesman Publishing Co. Ltd., 1978), 67.

"Then ye will come and take our man's place. We shall be ever so glad to hear you again after all these years."

Then Collyer told him that, "he was no longer a Local, but was settled over a church in Chicago of quite another brand."

The old man's face fell as he said, "What made ye leave us?"

Collyer asked him, "Do you remember telling me that I should reason myself out of the Methodist body if I did not change my methods, and I think your words had come true." They clasped hands and said their goodbyes. Collyer was never to see him again.

As it happened, on this Sunday, Robert had chosen to attend worship in the old Parish Church, All Saints. He was drawn to this sacred place by his boyhood memories and the sense of history and continuity that it engendered; 'joining in the ancient psalms and liturgies that in their essence and spirit had been said and sung there for more than a thousand years. Where through the latticed windows I could glance toward the small God's acre where the dust of Roman, Saxon, Dane and Englishman rested after life's fitful fever. There were pillars carven by the Northmen standing in the sun and Roman inscriptions to the emperors built into the walls – inscriptions from the Roman temple that stood on the selfsame spot – while among the dust of the rude forefathers was that of our Longfellows who had been baptized in the ancient font, and when their time came, had been buried there for more than two hundred years.'[15]

Before leaving America, Collyer had obtained letters of introduction from the Rev Everett Hale in Boston to two Unitarian ministers in England, Robert Spears and William Gaskell.[16] He posted the letter to Gaskell from Leeds but decided to deliver the letter to Spears personally when he visited his church in London. Robert also wrote to Unitarian ministers in Leeds and Pudsey, and preaching engagements were arranged at their churches. Thus, in between visits to his old haunts in Wharfedale, Washburndale and Nidderdale, Robert had a series of preaching engagements both in the north of England and in

---

[15] from Robert Collyer, *Where the light dwelleth* (London: The Lindsey Press, 1908), 157.

[16] Edward Everett Hale (1822-1909) was minister at the South Congregational (Unitarian) Church in Boston for 43 years. He began his Unitarian ministry in Worcester, Massachusetts, but at the time of Collyer's correspondence with him, he had moved to Boston. He was well connected in Unitarian and literary circles and had visited England on several occasions. Collyer's acquaintance with Hale dated from the first Unitarian Conference that Collyer attended in June 1859.

London. The first of these, at the Mill Hill Unitarian Chapel in Leeds, was undoubtedly the most meaningful.

A group of Presbyterians founded Mill Hill Chapel in 1674, two years after Charles II's Act of Indulgency gave dissenters the right to worship. One of the most eminent of the Mill Hill ministers was the Rev Joseph Priestley who was born into a weaving family in Birstall, Leeds, in 1733. He moved to Mill Hill in 1767 receiving a stipend of 100 guineas a year and a house situated just north of the chapel.[17] The house was next door to a brewery and this gave Priestley, who was interested in science, the opportunity to study 'fixed air' (carbon dioxide) that accumulated above the vats. In the 1770's he discovered several new 'airs' including nitrous oxide or laughing gas. At the same time, he was publishing radical books on political philosophy that preached the virtues of individualism and civil liberty, and inspired Jeremy Bentham's principle of 'the greatest happiness of the greatest number'.[18] Priestley left Leeds in 1772.

By the 1840's, the 1,000-strong congregation of Mill Hill Chapel had outgrown its dilapidated accommodation. Hamer Stansfeld, former Lord Mayor of Leeds and the entrepreneur behind the building of Ben Rhydding Hydro in Ilkley, laid the foundation stone for a new chapel on the same site in 1847. When Collyer preached for the first time at Mill Hill, John Dobson came over from Ilkley to hear him. 'He had kept track of my life through the fifteen years and was well aware of the change in my Christian fellowship; but he did not turn a hair. My mother also went with me that morning; and I still remember so well, as we walked home arm in arm after the service, she said, "I am not sure that I understood all thy sermon, my lad, or can believe as thou does; but I do believe in thee." Then she squeezed my arm, and I was quite content'.[19]

Collyer preached on three other occasions in Leeds and twice at the nearby Pudsey Unitarian Church. Towards the end of August, he was already regretting that he had arranged so many preaching engagements. He was eagerly anticipating his forthcoming holiday on the Continent - three weeks exploring France, Germany and Switzerland, but before that he had to fulfil two more commitments, for William Gaskell in Manchester and Robert Spears in London.

---

[17] http://www.millhillchapel.org/about-us/chapel-history/

[18] Richard Cavendish, 'The death of Joseph Priestley', *History Today*, 54: February 2004, 48.

[19] Collyer, *Some Memories*, p. 170.

22: London, Manchester, and Switzerland

Collyer's first ever journey from Leeds to London was an interesting, if not always scenic, affair. The early stages of the six-hour train journey from Central Station passed through a succession of grim industrial towns with only distant views of open countryside. After Doncaster, a railway town dominated by the locomotive works of the Great Northern Railway, the towns became more widely separated and the landscape opened out. Nevertheless, the rolling countryside was pock-marked by coal mines and spoil-heaps and canal-side mills and factories. Through the Midlands, pastoral countryside became more evident, but there were frequent stops to take on water in market towns that, viewed from the railway, showed more evidence of poverty than any prosperity created through their market-squares. Through Bedfordshire, Hertfordshire and Middlesex, farms and fields dotted with neat villages became the prevailing theme until the northern outskirts of the sprawling capital were reached.

At King's Cross station, Collyer took a cab to his destination, the *Crown Inn,* in Essex Street. The cab journey was a slow and staccato affair; they crawled down Grays Inn Road, halting every few minutes in some bottle-neck that gradually resolved, only to be repeated at the next junction. Collyer later learnt that the building of the extension to the Underground line from Farringdon

Street to Moorgate was the cause of the problem.[1] Collyer had never seen such a crowded city; he was struck by the haphazard arrangement of streets lined by a jumble of houses, tenements, inns, and shops, and the thousands of people who jostled along the pavements, spilling out of alleyways, and criss-crossing the roads by weaving through the sluggish procession of horse-drawn vehicles. Crossing Holborn, the cab went down Fleet Lane to Fleet Street, thence into The Strand where it took a left turn into Essex Street. *The Crown* was just beyond Essex Street Chapel, England's first Unitarian church, and a room had been booked for Collyer by a secretary at the headquarters of the British and Foreign Unitarian Society, just around the corner at 178, The Strand.[2]

Next morning, was a Sunday, and Collyer headed for Robert Spears's church in Southwark. With time in hand before the service, he walked down through the narrow archway, the 'Watergate', at the foot of Essex Street and, skirting round the construction work on the embankment, gained his first sight of the Thames. He paused several times to take in the scene while crossing Blackfriars Bridge, but the stench from the river dissuaded him from unnecessary lingering.[3] A short walk down Blackfriars Road brought Collyer to Stamford Street, and shortly thereafter he reached the Unitarian Church. The church exterior immediately impressed him - it was pure Greek Doric, and it contrasted markedly with the general dilapidation of its surroundings in Southwark. The interior of the church was lofty, light and unadorned. Most of the pews were well filled and Collyer took a place towards the back. He felt pleased to be attending, rather than conducting, a church service. Robert Spears's preaching was lively, enthusiastic, and bible-based; there was 'light and shade' where anecdote and humor contrasted with his stirring call for commitment and service. Here was no mealy-mouthed ambiguity or denial of

---

[1] The Metropolitan Railway's first line (Paddington to Farringdon Street) opened in 1863. The extension to Moorgate opened in December 1865. Jerry White, *London in the Nineteenth Century* (London: Jonathan Cape, 2007) 45.

[2] The location of *The Crown* (7, Essex Street) and the headquarters of the British and Foreign Unitarian Association are given in Mortimer Rowe, *The Story of Essex Hall* (London: The Lindsey Press, 1959), 29. There is no mention in Collyer's writings of his accommodation during the week's stay in London. His use of *The Crown* is conjecture.

[3] By the 1850s, over 60 major sewers and polluted tributaries, like the River Fleet, flowed into the Thames. In the hot summer of 1858, Londoners had to contend with the 'Great Stink' when MPs could not stand the smell in the committee rooms of the Houses of Parliament and were forced to abandon their work. White, 'Stream of Death: The Thames, 1855-1875', in *London in the Nineteenth Century*, 51.

Christian beliefs. He preached without the constraints of institutional traditions and his message was clear and unequivocal. Many years later, Collyer was talking to Oliver Wendell Holmes about churches and ministers. Holmes said "Brother Collyer, I love to hear a man preach who believes more than I do, and I need to hear those men; they are a great help to me." Collyer remembered that he needed help in his early years and found it in Robert Spears.[4]

At the end of the service, Collyer waited until the queue of people in line for a handshake and a few words with the minister had been satisfied. Collyer approached Mr. Spears and offered him warm thanks for his 'word' and handed him a letter from Edward Hale. Collyer relates that, after reading this 'voucher'; 'He gave me as warm a welcome as my heart could desire, and asked me promptly to take the evening service. He insisted on my going home to break bread, and would fain have made me his guest during my stay in London. And I still remember my hearty welcome in the church that evening. The Stamford Street congregation seemed close of kin in their hearts' turn to my Church in Chicago, and what Abraham Lincoln used to call the plain people. They received the word gladly – such as it was – and shook hands with the stranger as if they meant it.'[5]

Over lunch at Robert Spears's house, Collyer felt that he had met a kinsman – a true brother minister. He became aware of their shared origins and experiences and a remarkable convergence that was to bring them into lasting friendship. The similarities between the two men were uncanny.

Spears was just two years younger than Collyer. He was born in Lemington, near Newcastle, the fifth son of John Spears, an ironworker.[6] His father was a Scottish Calvinist Presbyterian, his mother a Methodist. Early in life, Spears followed his mother's faith. Like Collyer, Spears came from a poor family and his time at school was short. In the 1830's he was apprenticed as an industrial blacksmith, while his mother encouraged her bright son to educate himself. In the Methodist church Spears discovered a gift for teaching and preaching, and in the 1840s he became a Local Preacher.

In 1845, Spears attended a public debate at which Joseph Barker, a former Methodist turned Unitarian, spoke. Barker's words struck a chord with the

---

[4] Robert Collyer, 'Prefatory Sketch' in *Memorials of Robert Spears: 1825-1899,* (Belfast: Ulster Unitarian Christian Association, 1908), 2.

[5] Collyer, 'Prefatory Sketch' in *Memorials of Robert Spears,* 1.

[6] Samuel Charlesworth, 'Biographical Sketch' in *Memorials of Robert Spears,* 4-16.

young Spears, and he sought out George Harris, the Unitarian minister at Newcastle, to continue his instruction in the Unitarian way. Later in life Spears acknowledged that he began his career, with 'no college or ministerial training, no family prestige, and had the disadvantage of a northern dialect.'

In 1852 he became a Unitarian minister at Sunderland with a near-defunct church. There was no stipend from the church, and he supported himself through teaching at a local school and taking private pupils in the evening. Overflowing with zeal and commitment, Spears soon drew large numbers of people to his church. In 1856 he moved to nearby Stockton-on-Tees to take charge of a Unitarian congregation founded in the 17th century but that had fallen on hard times. Again, he soon had the pews filled with hearers drawn by his oratory, energy and willingness to argue a Unitarian understanding of the scriptures with anyone. His ministry extended into journalism and in 1859 he founded and edited a weekly newspaper, the *Stockton Gazette*, in which he upheld the principles of the Liberal Party and free trade.

Spears's reputation spread to London. Biblically-based Unitarians saw in him a new champion, one who would proclaim their beliefs and counter the 'new thought' advanced by James Martineau and John James Tayler, English Unitarians who asserted that reason was to be preferred above scripture. In 1861, despite his lack of formal ministerial training, Spears was appointed to a London church. He became minister to a tiny congregation who continued to meet at the Stamford Street Chapel in Southwark, and he soon restored the fortunes of this ailing church. When Collyer visited four years later, it was already on the way to becoming the largest Unitarian congregation in London.

After several hours in conversation, Collyer departed, greatly uplifted by Spears's message, and delighted to meet someone who had so closely trodden the same path as himself.

Collyer spent his time in London visiting the great sights and exploring churches, museums and galleries. Some hours were spent in simply walking the streets, observing London life. The diversity of its buildings and people fascinated him. He had never seen a place quite like it and he was most struck by the stark contrasts between poverty and plenty. The quiet solemnity of Westminster Abbey cheek-by-jowl with 'Devil's Acre', a vile slum centered on the Almonry.[7] Similarly, the historic and austere Tower of London lay close to the district of St. Katharine's, a dank area of hovels filled with river plunderers

---

[7] The Almonry was the place where the alms collected in the Abbey Church at Westminster were distributed to poor persons.

and all kinds of ruffian. At the eastern end of fashionable Oxford Street lay the 'Rookery' of St. Giles, full of thieves', prostitutes' and cadgers' lodging houses.[8] Everywhere, the pavements were thronged with hawkers, costermongers, and flower-girls.[9]

On Collyer's last day in London, Sunday 26 August, he preached at the Stamford Street Chapel in the morning and enjoyed another meal at the Spears's home. He returned to Leeds by train the next day. On the following Saturday (September 2) Collyer made his way to Manchester for an eagerly anticipated visit, expressly to preach at the Cross Street Unitarian Chapel and, more appealingly to him, to spend some time with the minister's wife, Mrs. Elizabeth Gaskell.

The old Cross Street Unitarian Chapel, Manchester. Author's collection.

[8] White, *London in Nineteenth Century,* 10-14.

[9] Hawkers sold their wares – trinkets, toys, cheap handicrafts and the like, from baskets. Costermongers sold fruit and vegetables from handcarts. The term *coster* is a corruption of *costard,* an old variety of apple. 'Flower-girls' also included young women who used the selling of flowers as a cover for prostitution.

Collyer's offer to preach at William Gaskell's Cross Street Chapel in Manchester would have been warmly received by the minister. Gaskell had planned to spend a month on holiday with friends in Scotland and had to fill his pulpit while he was away. On his part, Robert would appreciate the visiting preachers' fee, but he was much more interested in the chance it presented to meet the minister's wife, the author, Mrs. Elizabeth Gaskell. Collyer preached at Cross Street on Sunday September 3.[10] Unfortunately, he was unable to meet Mrs. Gaskell after the service for on that day she was returning from an excursion to London to buy furnishings for her new house in Kent. He chose to remedy this disappointment by an unannounced visit to the Gaskells' house the next morning.

Mrs. Gaskell's works were well known to Collyer. Indeed by 1865, Elizabeth Gaskell (born in 1810) was established as one of England's leading literary figures. High-spirited, witty, a shrewd observer, quick to laugh and easily moved, Gaskell wrote fiction of great variety. Her first book, *Mary Barton,* a tale of love, murder and industrial misery, took Britain by storm. It was followed by the social protest of *Ruth* and *North and South,* comedy in *Cranford,* historical romance in *Sylvia's Lovers,* and personal insights and family tensions in *Wives and Daughters,* as well as the impassioned biography of her friend Charlotte Brontë.[11] Despite her celebrity, Elizabeth Gaskell remained warm and approachable. Fortunately, regarding Robert Collyer's unexpected visit, she had a liking for Americans, and Collyer's sponsor, the Rev. Edward Hale, was a particular friend.

Edward Hale visited the Gaskells over Christmas 1859. Despite the potentially awkward timing, the visitor was warmly welcomed. Some measure of Gaskell's appreciation of Hale's visit is given in a letter written the following December: "....And now Xmas is coming round again, and we do wish you were likely to turn up again, 'all promiscuous' as our English servants say, & share our turkey, and have a merry round game at cards, and altogether make us young and happy again."[12] Gaskell wrote again to Hale in April 1861 following receipt of his book *Ninety Days Worth of Europe,* an account of his 1859

---

[10] The date of the preaching engagement has been ascertained from Mrs Gaskell's subsequent letters although I have not been able confirm this through the Cross Street Chapel archives; the relevant records are missing. (Geoffrey Head, curator - personal communication.)

[11] Jenny Uglow, *Elizabeth Gaskell: A Habit of Stories* (London, Faber and Faber, 1999), i.

[12] Uglow, *Elizabeth Gaskell,* 216.

tour of Europe, including his visit to the Gaskells.[13] It is apparent from the tone of these letters that Hale has become an 'honorary member' of the family.[14] This relationship is important with regard to the appearance of another American visitor on the doorstep of her house at 42 Plymouth Grove, Manchester.

Although an unexpected guest, Collyer spent several hours in Mrs. Gaskell's company and enjoyed a vigorous and well-informed conversation. His Yorkshire roots were soon to emerge in their discussion but were not a particular hindrance to its continuation even though Gaskell's unfavorable views on Yorkshiremen were well known to Collyer. Following his reading of *The Life of Charlotte Brontë,* he was no doubt annoyed by Gaskell's characterization of Yorkshire folk as a; '...wild, rough population. Their accost is curt; their accent and tone of speech blunt and harsh ... a stranger can hardly ask a question without receiving some crusty reply, if, indeed, he receive any at all. Sometimes the sour rudeness amounts to positive insult.'[15]

Besides eliciting news of American friends, there is little doubt that Gaskell would have sought Collyer's views on the aftermath of the Civil War. The blockade of southern ports that led to a virtual cessation of cotton exports to England, brought terrible consequences for the textile mills of Lancashire. A few mills maintained a low level of production using Indian or Egyptian cotton, but most closed down. The vast workforce was thrown onto charity, and by the summer of 1862 there was widespread famine.[16] Manchester was particularly hard hit, and Gaskell threw herself into relief work.[17] "I wish," she wrote to George Smith, her publisher, in reference to the American conflict, "North and South would make friends & let us have cotton, & then our poor people would get work, and then you should have as many novels as you like to take, and we should not be killed with 'Poor on the Brain', as I expect we shall before the winter is over."[18] The progress of the war, with its profound consequences for Manchester life, became a subject of concern that permeates

---

[13] Uglow, 222.

[14] Alan Shelston, 'Alligators infesting the stream: Elizabeth Gaskell and the USA', *Gaskell Society Journal,* 2001, 15: 60.

[15] Elizabeth Gaskell, *The Life of Charlotte Brontë* (Oxford: Oxford University Press, Oxford World's Classics, Angus Easson, ed., 1996), 15, 18.

[16] 'The Distress in the Cotton Districts'. *The Times,* August 25, 1862.

[17] letter to Vernon Lushington written April 1862, John Chapple and Alan Shelston, *Further Letters of Mrs. Gaskell* (Manchester: Manchester University Press, 2000), 237.

[18] John A.V. Chapple and Arthur Pollard, *The letters of Mrs. Gaskell* (Manchester: Manchester University Press, 1966), 698.

Elizabeth Gaskell's letters to friends in the United States. With the war ended, information concerning the prospects for the cotton trade would probably have been part of a 'squeezing dry about America' that Gaskell attempted in her conversation with Collyer. Several hours later, their meeting ended. Collyer later described it (in a letter to Edward Hale) as "the most pleasant visit at her house I think I ever had anywhere", while Mrs. Gaskell evidently enjoyed it too.[19]

The following day (September 5, 1865), Gaskell wrote to her daughter Marianne; 'Yesterday morning Selina Collie came; about 11 & presently afterwards came a very nice American (Yorkshire man) & the two staid till 5 o'clk. This was pleasant but sadly interrupted my writing.'[20] On September 8 she wrote two letters, and both made mention of American visitors. In the first, Gaskell wrote to James R. Lowell thanking him for his gift of *Fireside Travels,* and relating that: 'We have had two Americans here this week ... We tried hard to squeeze them dry about America; but though we talked five or six hours consecutively we could not do it, — But we were glad to see them, as the swallows are to make our summer.'[21] In the second letter, Gaskell tells another American friend: 'I tried to hear something of you from two (separate) Americans — at least one was a ci-devant Yorkshire blacksmith from Chicago, — who turned up unexpectedly — the one on Monday, the other on Tuesday — but they neither could say anything particular about you. The American Yorkshireman was a Mr. Collier (sic) Unitarian Minister at Chicago, — who had been a nurse and Captain of nurses under the Sanitary Commission; the Tuesday man was introduced by our dear Mr. Field; a Mr. Phillips Brooks, Episcopalian clergyman of Philadelphia and formerly a student at Cambridge [USA]. He had been among the free negroes. Indeed, both told us most interesting things. I don't know which was the most interesting.'[22]

---

[19] In early December 1865 Collyer learnt of Gaskell's sudden death and wrote to Edward Hale (December 13) to express his sadness; 'I am sorrowing with you for the death of dear Mrs. Gaskell. I had the most pleasant visit at her house I think I ever had anywhere. She spoke of you with the greatest affection. It is a sad loss to the world as well as to us, if death in the divine order ever can be a loss.' Holmes, *Life and Letters of Robert Collyer,* 2: 60.

[20] Chapple and Pollard, *Letters of Mrs. Gaskell,* 941.

[21] Chapple and Pollard, *Letters of Mrs. Gaskell,* 776.

[22] Chapple and Pollard, 774. An expanded account of Collyer's meeting with Mrs. Gaskell can be found in Michael F. Dixon, '*A very nice American – Gaskell's enigmatic Mr. Collier,*'(*sic*), The Gaskell Society Journal, 2008, 20: 86-95.

Collyer returned from Manchester to Leeds and stayed the night at his sister's house. The next morning after tearful farewells with his sister and mother, Collyer set off for three weeks of pure holiday on the Continent before sailing for home. He had arranged the holiday specifically to see the mountains of Switzerland. Robert had never walked among genuinely great mountains. 'The sweet, heathery hills of the North of England, with their grey crags and purple bloom, their free-blowing winds and rippling sunshine' had, in his mind's eye, assumed a magnificence unrelated to their size, but he knew they were not mountains.[23] There were great mountains in Switzerland and now he had the opportunity to go there, but first there were places in France and Germany he wished to explore.

Collyer caught a train at Blackfriars Bridge Station that took him to Dover, and thence via a cross-Channel ferry, the '*Empress*', to Calais. Another train then took him to the Gare du Nord in Paris. After a couple of days exploring Paris, he headed for Rouen, expressly to visit the cathedral and the archbishop's palace. Then back to Paris and an onward train to Cologne to add the magnificent cathedral there to his memory store of wonderful cathedrals.[24] From Cologne he journeyed to Frankfurt where he caught a train bound for Zurich. Darkness fell long before he reached his accommodation in Zurich and he went to bed that night eagerly anticipating the sunrise. Early next morning as the day dawned bright and clear, he dressed and went out. The manager of the Inn had told him that if he went to the cathedral, the Grossmünster, and climbed the tower, he would see the mountains. He found the cathedral without difficulty, climbed the tower and looked out. It was an emotional moment. He saw them, 'white and still ... looking as if they belonged to a world I had never seen before, flashing white against the green of summer from their eternal snows. Then I said in my heart, now I know what they mean by mountains, and what Ruskin means when he likens them to the shadow of God.'[25]

Collyer was determined to confront the mountains. He did not have the daring, or desire, to climb Mont Blanc, but he did want to see it close-up, face to face in all its glory. Thus, the next day he travelled to Lucerne and from there

---

[23] Holmes, *Life and Letters*, 2: 61.

[24] Collyer developed his recollections of famous cathedrals into a full lecture that became a popular item in his repertoire. See 'Cathedrals' in John Haynes Holmes, ed., *Clear Grit: A collection of lectures, addresses and poems by Robert Collyer* (Boston: American Unitarian Association, 1913), 40.

[25] Holmes, *Life and Letters*, 2: 63.

set out; 'winding among the valleys in the most curious fashion, catching glimpses of queer little towns and villages that seem as if they had been made on purpose to delight Americans, and especially those who, as I was then, are tired and sick of the everlasting sameness of the western plains.' The carriage took him to Martigny, and from there he chose to undertake the nine hours walk to the foot of Mont Blanc. He could have gone by horse, but he did not trust the horse to be of the same mind as himself and preferred to use Shanks' pony on this occasion. He did not regret it. 'The walk over the Tête Noire is one of the events of a lifetime – so full of wonder and delight that I only remember the most of it as a fine ethereal intoxication. Every mile of it was a new surprise – little green valleys far down on one side of us, great grim scars far up on the other. At the end of seven hours' walk you came to a sharp turn by a little town, and then the mountains that have hidden away the sight you came to see, stand back, and there is Mont Blanc. It was a disappointment, for a few minutes, as Niagara is. You have been expecting that Nature will do something melodramatic and send some peak, sharp and clear, into the sky, as they would on the stage. Nature knows better; her work is for the ages, and so she lays vast foundations, and builds to her base, and then just raises the great summit over all. At last, I think I did see it as she intended we should, for when we got to Chamonix and had rested, we went across the valley, in among the vines and roses, and there we sat down.'

'It was evening, the sun had set to us, and the night drew on, but up there he was shining still, transfiguring all the white with his gold, lingering as if he loved it and was loath to leave it, kissing the snow with fire. And then the gold changed to rosy splendors that seemed like the light through stained glass windows. The stars came out as the Alpen glow, as they called it, deepened, and starlight and sunlight lay together on the lovely desolation. They told me travelers would spend weeks, sometimes, in the valley and not see this sight more than once, and it is reckoned the supreme glory of Mont Blanc. It is to me, one of the wonders of my life – it stands alone.'[26]

Collyer returned from Switzerland by train to Bremen where he embarked on a Norddeutscher Lloyd ship bound for New York. After returning to Chicago, he wrote to an American friend; 'Nothing ever did so much good as my journey to England.....It fulfilled a score of old dreams in a way that seemed perfectly wonderful.'[27]

---

[26] Holmes, *Life and Letters*, 2: 66.

[27] Holmes, 2: 69

23: A new Unity

During Collyer's absence in Europe, the elders of the Unity Church had decided to tackle the problem of overcrowded services head on. They would build a bigger church. The North Side was increasing in population and prosperity and there was an air of confidence among the congregation. Other denominations were involved in ambitious building schemes, and the Unitarians were not to be left behind.

Collyer, reinvigorated by his trip to Europe, was soon caught up by the ambition and enthusiasm of his people to build a new church. Indeed, the renewed energy and power he brought to the Unity pulpit soon exacerbated the problem of overcrowding as more and more people felt the call to 'hear Collyer' and were prepared even to stand in the aisles to listen to him. The appeal of Collyer's preaching is difficult to explain; he continued to read his sermons, and there were occasions when in his haste and enthusiasm he would stumble over the written words, or in endeavoring to make eye-contact with his listeners, he momentarily lost his place.[1] Nevertheless, Collyer had the capacity to write in simple, plain language which moved easily from manuscript to speech. It was clear to his congregation that they were listening to a man who lived out his message. Whether it was a statement of faith, or some moral, social or political point that Collyer was making from the pulpit, they knew he spoke with complete sincerity.

---

[1] John Haynes Holmes, *Life and Letters of Robert Collyer,* (New York, Dodd Mead and Company, 1917), 2: 127, – part of a surprisingly critical analysis of Collyer's preaching style by a 'Brother' minister.

Collyer had a warm and hearty personality and a great 'presence'. He was a big, handsome man with a voice that could fill the sanctuary and transmit his vitality and zest for life, but also, in quieter passages, conveyed empathy and concern. When it came to the prayers, he needed no script. He would hold the open bible in his left hand and grip the rim of the pulpit with his right, then turning his face upwards, he began a public conversation with God, a conversation that touched on the sorrows, the anxieties, the hopes and dreams of every man and woman that heard him. It was no doubt this ability to convey personal feelings and speak to the predicament of many in his congregation that forged the strong bond between preacher and listener, a bond which encouraged them to tell others that they must 'come and hear Collyer'. There is no doubt that through his preaching, his public speaking and his articles in the *Tribune,* Robert Collyer was already a 'celebrity'.

The frequent speaking engagements Collyer had undertaken during the War had prepared him for a new venture, the public lecture. Initially, his love of literature was the driving force behind a series of lectures on the great writers of his day given at Sunday evening gatherings at the church. Success in his own pulpit gave him the confidence to accept 'outside' engagements and he was soon lecturing on a variety of subjects on platforms throughout Chicago. Likewise, authorship now made regular demands on his time. His earliest published works were sermons in pamphlet form, but he soon began regular contributions to newspapers and religious journals with articles that focused on travel, churches, literature, and homely personal reminiscences such as 'Thoughts in an iron mill' and 'Life and Labor of the working classes in Yorkshire'.[2] Finally, in 1867, he published his first book, a collection of sermons entitled 'Nature and Life'.[3] The preface neatly sums up his basic humanity, and humility; 'I let this little book go out into the world, feeling almost as if it were one of my children. I cannot be indifferent to its reception because I love it. So I trust it will be welcome wherever it goes, - that friends will be glad to see it for my sake, and strangers for its own. If it should be blessed with a long life, I shall rejoice greatly; but, if it die early, I shall still be glad it was born.' The 'child' quickly flourished. The book enjoyed huge sales and ran to eight editions in 18 months, a remarkable achievement for a humble collection of sermons. Copies of the book soon reached England. Collyer tells Flesher Bland; 'I sent a dozen copies by a young gentleman from Burnley in Lancashire, seven

---

[2] Holmes, *Life and Letters,* 2: 86.

[3] Robert Collyer, *Nature and Life* (Chicago: Horace B. Fuller, 1867).

to be given to John Dobson for himself and other friends I have named, and four to Manchester, one of these to Meta Gaskell' (Elizabeth Gaskell's daughter).[4]

Collyer's income from lecturing and publications gradually increased and provided a welcome supplement to his regular stipend from Unity. Not that he was poorly remunerated, but he had decided to forego increases in his stipend so that the church could use more of its resources towards the building scheme. He explained to his friend, Edward Everett Hale: 'I have refused a big salary — take only $3,000 a year, and of that this year have subscribed and paid in spite of their protests ... $500 toward the new building. Meanwhile I have a big rampaging family, am a trifle extravagant as to books, and am clearing off a debt on our homestead at the rate of about $500 a year... To do this I have to skin it. I lecture, and that is a great lift. Then I write, and that helps. I pull up by all means to about $5,000.'[5]

The first step of faith by the Unity fellowship towards their goal of a new building was the purchase of a vacant lot on the corner of Walton Place and Dearborn Avenue across from the existing church. A building committee was appointed, and plans drawn up for a substantial stone church 'to cost no more than $60,000', but this proved to be a serious under-estimate. Their plans were ambitious. They retained a leading architect, Theodore Wadskier, and told him 'to measure the largest Protestant church in Chicago and build ours a foot longer and a foot wider'.[6] In May 1867 the ground was broken and in August, the corner-stone was laid.

As the foundations rose into walls, and the walls were crowned with roofing, so the costs rose with them. The original estimate was soon exceeded. Subscriptions and loans were solicited from the congregation to maintain building work, and the people responded to the utmost. The principal building contractor and a member of Unity, George Chambers, waived his bill amounting to $5,000 declaring 'this is my subscription'. Another boost was given by the sale in October 1867 of the original wooden church to the Baptists for $16,662. By then the basement of the new building was available for Sunday morning services, while the work went on above their heads.

---

[4] Holmes, *Life and Letters,* 2: 89.

[5] Holmes, *Life and Letters,* 2: 104.

[6] Robert Collyer, *Some Memories,* (Boston: American Unitarian Association, 1908) 177.

The design of the church was in the decorated Gothic style with towers at the front corners each with an octagonal spire rising to a height of 170 feet. The church was built with dolomite from the Athens quarry in Illinois, and the walls were finished in rock-faced ashlar, but one building material gained special recognition. Collyer was aware that a new church built by the Congregationalists on the next-door plot had a stone placed over the main doorway taken from the Plymouth Rock. Not to be outdone, he wrote to a lady member of Unity who was staying in Geneva in Switzerland and asked her if it was possible to obtain a stone from a hill above the city to commemorate the death of the Unitarian martyr, Michael Servetus, in 1553.[7] In response to Collyer's request, a neatly cut stone arrived from Geneva some weeks later and, after the inscription 'Champel 1553' had been carved into its face, it was lifted into place above the Unity doorway.

Gradually, the building work moved towards completion. Everything ran smoothly, there were no labor problems and only one injury – remarkable in a building project of this size. The injury was relatively minor, a laborer whose shoulder was bruised by a stone. The chairman of the building committee sent him home and told him to stay there until he was well, and his wages would be paid. Many weeks passed before the chairman thought it was time to look him up and sent a man to see how he fared. He reported back that the injured man had been well for some weeks but had not felt like reporting for work, only well enough to draw his wages, for which he sent his wife.[8]

By May 1869, the church was finished and furnished. Collyer viewed the result with immense satisfaction. The largest preaching auditorium of any Protestant church in Chicago, ample meeting rooms, a large lecture room, which also accommodated the flourishing Sunday School, and Collyer's own study cum vestry. This room had two large bookcases, one filled with theological treatises and the second with lighter books of history, travels and poetry. 'A few pictures of the learned and the great are on the mantelpiece. The large desk in the center of the room is devoid of littered papers and books' — possibly tidied away for the visit of the Chicago Tribune reporter who concludes that 'this shows the methodical mind of its user.' The report continues; 'From a little room opening off from this (study) which is used as a

---

[7] Servetus, a theologian who promoted a non-trinitarian Christology, was arrested in Champel, Geneva, and burnt at the stake as a heretic by order of the Protestant Governing Council.

[8] Collyer, *Some Memories,* 178

wash and dressing-room, a flight of steps leads directly to the pulpit on the floor above.'[9] The hidden ascent from the study and Collyer's sudden appearance in the pulpit must have provided a dramatic entrance. Collyer's study, however, also had a unique piece of furniture. Set against one wall and mounted on a large wooden block was the battered anvil on which Collyer had fashioned horse-shoes in former days in Yorkshire. A member of his congregation, William G. Lewis, was on holiday in England when he decided to visit some of the 'old haunts' of his pastor in Yorkshire. In Ilkley he found the old smithy on the point of demolition and offered to buy the anvil. His payment was accepted, and he subsequently had the anvil and a hammer shipped over to Chicago as a gift for Collyer.[10] Its place of honor in his study not only underlined Collyer's humble origins but gave substance to his rise from anvil to pulpit.

The new Unity Church opened in June 1869.

[9] 'Unity Church: Description of the Building', *Chicago Tribune,* August 4, 1866.
[10] Holmes, *Life and Letters* 2: 339.

While Collyer and the congregation drew great satisfaction from seeing the new church completed, this had been achieved at great expense, an expense that the church could not meet. Subscription income amounted to around $80,000 to which was added the money raised from the sale of the old church, but the total cost of the building was $201,330 and the organ cost $10,550 which left a deficit of more than $110,000. This was a huge amount and there was some talk of needing to reduce it before opening the church, but a contrary view which sought to open without delay, held sway and the date for the dedication service was set for June 20, 1869.[11]

Collyer persuaded the great Dr. Bellows of New York to preach the sermon and invited other notables to take part in the service. Collyer himself was asked to write a dedication hymn for the occasion, not something he had done before, and a challenge undertaken with some trepidation. Nevertheless, the result was a great success. The hymn, '*Unto thy Temple , Lord, we come*', proceeded to enter the hymnal of every major denomination of the church.[12] Collyer had briefed Dr Bellows on the precarious financial state of the church and following instructions he ended his address with an impassioned plea that the debt should be cleared; 'We will free this beautiful temple from every blemish.' Immediately he finished, and with the challenge still ringing in his listeners' ears, Collyer moved into the pulpit, his voice at once jubilant and pleading; "Brethren and sisters, we must have this money." The congregation responded with a great outpouring of generosity. Collyer held his place in the pulpit as subscriptions, cheques and money were handed over to the stewards below. He announced, in a voice choked with emotion, the sums pledged; thanking, urging, exhorting, calling out the running total and thanking again. And when the last pledge had been received, and the last coin dropped in the plate, it was found that the whole grand offering amounted to very nearly $60,000 (about $1.2 million in today's value), 'according to contemporary newspapers the largest church collection of its kind ever made in the United States.'[13] Within a year of the opening, the debt had been cleared. In the next Annual Report published in April, 1870, the Trustees declared; 'In reviewing the history of its success, we believe the society will consider it eminently just and proper that we should place upon its records our testimony and belief, that, first among the agencies which have contributed to this great result, are the influence and

[11] Holmes, 2: 106.

[12] Holmes, 2: 110.

[13] Holmes, 2: 114.

example of our first and only pastor, and the beloved friend of us all, Robert Collyer.'[14]

Over the next few years, Collyer was at his zenith. He was in the full vigor of his mature years, his stature in the pulpit and on the Lyceum platforms was unparalleled, and he held sway over some of the highest offices in Chicago society. In 1869-70, Collyer was President of the influential Young Men's Association, an office through which he brought great pressure to bear on the administration for the establishment of a Free Public Library in Chicago.[15]

Perhaps the strangest of Collyer's extra-mural activities was his Presidency of the 'Chicago Colorado Colony'.[16] This organization was formed with the aim of establishing towns free from the vices that pervaded the new settlements of the 'Wild West'. To achieve their aim the Committee recruited 'colonists' who practiced temperance, were in stable partnerships, had good work records and solid references, in short, people who would make commendable citizens. Membership of the colony was given to worthy candidates who made a token payment for which they would be allocated land on which to build their homesteads. The Chicago Committee determined that the colony was to occupy a site in Boulder County, Colorado, near the St. Vrain river. At an early stage in the deliberations the name proposed for the settlement was that of the Committee's President – 'Collyer', but this suggestion appears to have aroused jealousies that were only calmed when the neutral name 'Longmont' emerged.[17] Collyer's name was, however, attached to a second settlement when, some years later, he saw that land was to be made available for homesteads in Trego County, Kansas.[18] He advertised for potential colonists and, having identified a group comprising mainly ex-soldiers and sailors

---

[14] *Constitution and By Laws of Unity Church and Reports of Trustees, Building and Organ Committees, 1870* (Chicago: Press of James & Morse, La Salle Street, 1870), 8-10.

[15] Gwladys Spencer, *The Chicago Public Library: Origins and Backgrounds* (Chicago, The University of Chicago Press, 1943), 67-69.

[16] James F. Willard and Colin B. Goodykoontz, eds., *Experiments in Colorado Colonization 1869-1872* (Boulder: The University of Colorado, 1926), 137.

[17] Willard and Goodykoontz, eds., *Experiments in Colorado Colonization 1869-1872*, 243. Collyer's association with the city is remembered, however, in the names Collyer Park and Collyer Street.

[18] Ray Purinton, *History of Collyer, Kansas.* http://www.ksgenweb.org/trego/collyer.html

willing to pay a $2 deposit, filed on pieces of land for them. Thus, a new settlement, "Collyer, Kansas", came into being.[19]

A photograph of Collyer Park, Longmont, taken by an unknown photographer in the early 1900's. Courtesy of the Longmont Museum and Cultural Center (2002).

No doubt influenced by his friendship with Lucretia Mott, Collyer was a strong advocate of Women's Rights. He publicly criticized prevailing attitudes to women's wages which never achieved parity with male colleagues even when they did the same work.[20] When the celebrated champion of Women's Rights, Susan Anthony, came to Chicago to address the Cook County annual suffrage convention at the Farwell Hall in May 1870, it was Robert Collyer who

[19] The two settlements had widely divergent outcomes; Longmont is a thriving city with a population of 86,270 in the 2010 census while Collyer, Kansas, had a population of 109 in the same census. Its population has decreased by 61% since 1950 and has been described as a 'ghost town' - www.ghosttowns.com/states/ks/collyer.html

[20] 'Womans Wages', *Chicago Tribune,* Dec 6, 1868.

acted as host for the meal that followed.[21] Indeed, being the host was a regular occupation for the Rev. and Mrs. Collyer. Almost every Sunday, one or two guests would come to the service and be entertained afterwards at the Collyer home. Their hospitality was extended to distinguished Americans such as Ralph Waldo Emerson, Henry Thoreau, John Greenleaf Whittier, Edward Everett Hale, and the actor Lawrence Barrett, friends such as Flesher Bland and his wife, a succession of travelling Englishmen, some curious or admiring strangers, Unitarian ministers on the move, clergymen of other faiths and theological students requiring counsel; all were welcome alike to bed and board. It was said that for fully 300 days in the year, the house gave hospitality to passing friends, and good hospitality at that. It was Lawrence Barrett who declared; 'I'd rather be guest to Collyer than to the king.'[22]

Inevitably, Collyer's family were a part of that hospitality. His son Samuel was now in his early twenties and worked at Mears, Bates & Co., timber merchants. Eli Bates, a powerful figure in the Unity Church, was no doubt glad to be able to offer the minister's son a position in his company. Emma was by now a young woman, and Hattie was lost in writing adolescent poetry. Annie was the eager schoolgirl, hugging her father each morning before she left for the Ogden School nearby, while young Robert 'beats the world for mischief and beauty'.[23]

News of Collyer's standing as a major pulpit figure in the United States reached the Unitarian Church in England and he was invited to deliver the sermon at the annual meeting of the British and Foreign Unitarian Association in London in the spring of 1871. This prestigious invitation, and the prospect of an expenses-paid trip to England, could not be resisted. The church officers gave him leave of absence and at the beginning of April 1871, in the company of his wife and youngest daughter, Annie, Collyer set sail for Liverpool.

Naturally, their first destination was Leeds and a visit to his mother. She was now seventy-five years old and lived with her daughter, Maria, and her husband, John Shires.[24] Collyer recalled that; 'As we sat about the table, she (Mother) said, "Children, did you know it was twenty-one years ago this

---

[21] Ida Husted Harper, *The Life and Work of Susan B. Anthony* (Indianapolis and Kansas City: Bowen Merrill Co., 1899), 380. see https://www.gutenberg.org/files/15220/15220-h/15220-h.htm

[22] Holmes, *Life and Letters,* 2: 139.

[23] Holmes, 2: 138.

[24] Collyer's mother lived with his sister Maria Shires in Greenmount Street, Coupland Road, Hunslet, Leeds.

morning since you started on your way to America, the day after your wedding?" We had not remembered but mother had kept true time: our wedding journey had taken in twenty-one years.'[25]

Early photographs of Collyer, Kansas, from Special Collections, Wichita State Library

[25] Holmes, 2: 143.

24: London and Paris

While the family were staying in Leeds, Collyer left his wife and daughter at sister Maria's and went on his own to Ilkley. Even though he had been there six years before, new buildings had appeared, and old ones removed. The blacksmith's forge had gone, replaced by shops with apartments above, but at least he had the precious anvil back in Chicago. However, it was not buildings and once familiar Yorkshire Dales scenery that he had come to see, it was his old friend John Dobson, a reunion that filled several hours with animated conversation. The meeting over, he returned to Leeds where, next morning, the family boarded a train to London and made their way to the home of Robert and Mrs. Spears. It was the Rev. Spears, now Secretary of the British and Foreign Unitarian Association, who had issued the invitation for Collyer to address the Annual Conference, and on this occasion Spears insisted that they should stay at the manse in Southwark. The sermon at the conference was Collyer's prime concern. He felt that once he had delivered this address he could look forward to a few weeks of relaxation, albeit followed by several more preaching engagements. The Conference was held in the Essex Street Chapel just off the Strand, the headquarters of the British Unitarian movement. Given the prior publicity and Collyer's high standing as a preacher, the Hall was full to overflowing. Collyer was unusually nervous; this was one of the most prestigious appointments he had had as a preacher, but a more pressing cause for concern was the highly contentious subject of his sermon.

His sermon was titled 'The Cleft in the Rock' and the biblical text was two verses from Exodus 33, but these gave no clue as to his subject matter.

"and the Lord said unto Moses....

22 And it shall come to pass, while my glory passeth by, that I will put thee in a cleft of the rock, and will cover thee with my hand while I pass by:
23 And I will take away mine hand, and thou shalt see my back parts: but my face shall not be seen."

The subject matter, however, soon became apparent. Collyer began; "We are beginning to hear the mutterings of such a storm in the churches about Darwin's book, '*The Descent of Man*', as the fathers heard when geology came into court to testify concerning the creation of the world,".[1]

Evolution was a remarkably topical subject on which to base his address; '*The Descent of Man and Selection in Relation to Sex*' was published on February 24, 1871, just three months before the Conference. In his seminal work, '*The Origin of Species by Means of Natural Selection*', published in 1859 while Darwin was undergoing hydrotherapy in Ilkley, he explicitly omitted any mention of the evolution of mankind.[2] In '*The Descent*', however, he asserts that man did indeed originate from more primitive precursors. '*The Origin*' had been met with scorn and anger by most of the Christian establishment, now a second furor was unleashed by this new work exploring man's likely origins.[3] Certainly, the reaction among conservative evangelical sections of the Church was one of disdain and rejection, but the brand of liberal Christianity followed by many Unitarians could lead to a more favorable response. Nevertheless, this was uncharted territory for Collyer, and he risked touching on some raw nerves among his listeners. He continued; "I have no doubt in my own mind that it will end in the same way, by the churches coming to the scientific conclusion, whatever that shall be, when the investigation is complete. And just

---

1 *The Cleft in the Rock.* A sermon preached at the Annual Meeting of the British and Foreign Unitarian Association in Essex Street Chapel, Strand, May 31, 1871. Published at the Request of the Committee, Unitarian Association Rooms, 178 Strand, London, 1871.

2 See Mike Dixon and Gregory Radick, *Darwin in Ilkley* (Stroud, Gloucester: The History Press, 2009).

3 Notable opposition came from the Baptist preacher Charles Haddon Spurgeon. On October 1, 1861, he gave a lecture entitled 'The Gorilla and the Land he Inhabits'. During his discourse, in which he had a stuffed gorilla on stage, Spurgeon said; 'there is Mr Darwin, who at once is prepared to prove that our great-grandfather's grandfather's father – keep on for a millennium or two – was a guinea-pig, and that we ourselves originally descended from oysters, or seaweeds, or starfishes.' From Nigel Scotland, 'Darwin and Doubt and the Response of the Victorian Churches', in *Churchman* (London: Church Society, 1986), 100: 293-308.

as now there is only one man to be heard of in England or America who questions the conclusion of Galileo about the motion of the earth, and he is suspected of being a fool ..... so I think the day must dawn when this new truth, now considered such gross infidelity, will be accepted as the truth of God. We shall have to see..... that this (natural) selection of species and of sex, with all its consequent struggles, was a divine thing of the same order as this that built up the world from the fogs and fires of the first day to the apples and corn of this new summer, from the primitive granite to the June roses, and from the hideous monsters of the prime to the orioles and humming birds. ... Darwin's grand book is not only retrospect, but a prophesy. Humanity is not on the top of the stairs; it is only a very little way from the bottom. But it is climbing..."

There was much else in the sermon touching on humanity's view of God. Collyer's position was that the view is always partial, as looking from a cleft in the rock with God half-hidden. "Science may sometimes further obscure the view, but we can know God through divine inspiration in nature and life, and in time we shall see Him face to face."

The reaction to his daring address was positive and immediate. As he was speaking, Collyer had noticed a man sitting near the pulpit with snow-white hair looking up intently through a pair of formidable spectacles. These would be thrown back on his forehead when something was said that he may have liked or disliked, it was impossible to guess which. As soon as Robert was down from the pulpit, the man came forward, clasped his hand warmly and mentioned his name, John Bowring[4]. Collyer explains; "It was the good knight Sir John and I bowed my head in reverence, not to the knight, but to the man; for he was known to me through my reading and common fame." Bowring was not the only knight present that morning. Sir James Lawrence introduced himself to Robert and after a brief exchange offered to show him some of the sights of London, an offer that Collyer took up some days later.[5] Lawrence was well qualified to act as a guide, he had been the Lord Mayor of London in 1868

---

[4] Sir John Bowring (1792 – 1872), was a political economist, traveler, polyglot, writer, literary translator, England's ambassador to China and the fourth Governor of Hong Kong. *Memorable Unitarians: being a series of brief biographical sketches* (London: British and Foreign Unitarian Association, Essex Hall, Strand, 1906), 289.

[5] Sir James Clarke Lawrence (1820 - 1897), principal with his brother Edwin in the family building firm, he was Lord Mayor of London and a Liberal politician who sat in the House of Commons from 1868 to 1885. *Memorable Unitarians,* British and Foreign Unitarian Association, 419.

and by this office, he was able to show Collyer the Guildhall and its treasures and Newgate prison and its horrors.[6]

Collyer's own assessment of the service was a positive one based on "how they spoke to me and clasped my hand." Writing for an American audience he said; "They are by no means so clever … in England as they are on this side of the water; they need to be thawed out ... But there was no ice that morning or down to zero, in the good old chapel, and I felt I was at home in London, and in England also; for from that day, as it seems to me, all the churches of our faith and order gave me the freedom of their pulpit."[7]

An 1871 portrait of Robert Collyer taken by C.D. Mosher, 951 Wabash Avenue, Chicago, Ill. Author's collection.

News of his preaching success soon reached Chicago. The managing editor of the London *Daily News,* John Robinson, was in the congregation and, after shaking Collyer's hand warmly, said he would write something about the service for the *Chicago Evening Journal.* The London correspondent of the *Chicago Tribune* reported that; "the Rev. Robert Collyer preached yesterday

---

[6] Collyer, *Some Memories,* 212.

[7] Collyer, 204.

(May 31) to a distinguished congregation assembled in a church of historic note. The Unitarian denomination includes men of mark in literature and the sciences, and several of these were among Mr. Collyer's listeners. ...Mr. Collyer's style of address was new to nearly everyone present. His accent, his peculiar emphasis, his freedom from conventionality, and his dramatic power created a lively sensation. I heard many say afterwards that he was the most striking pulpit orator they had ever heard. He enchained the attention from first to last. It was a treat to escape from metaphysical subtleties, as from dogmatic definitions, and to get instead, the topics in which civilization is at this hour intimately concerned. I had never seen Mr. Collyer before, but he appeared to me to possess a large amount of intellectual and oratorical power in reserve. The average English preacher, of whatever sect, is much his inferior. If there are many such men growing up in Chicago, the fame of your city will be great."[8]

The initially daunting, but then exhilarating, experience of preaching to the Unitarian Conference behind him, Collyer with his wife and daughter embarked on a short Continental holiday. Travelling by train, they visited Antwerp and journeyed through the Rhineland to Switzerland. From Geneva they travelled to Lyon, changed trains, and from there went north-westwards to Dijon and Paris.

Events over the past year had stimulated in Collyer a deep interest in Paris and a sympathetic concern for its people. In February 1871, he used his status as a preacher (and the columns of the *Chicago Tribune*) to mount an appeal to send financial aid to France to alleviate the widespread suffering consequent upon the Franco-Prussian War and the Siege of Paris.[9] He shared the platform at the Opera House with several persons of influence in Chicago society including William Coolbaugh, founder of the National Union Bank, property developer James H. Bowen, politician and lawyer James R. Doolittle, and the French writer Adolphe Pineton, the Marquis de Chambrun. The 'special relationship' that existed between the United States and France meant that the plight of the French people, many living in poverty and starvation, struck a sympathetic note that prompted around 1200 people to attend the meeting. The audience responded to the pleas for financial assistance with enthusiasm and generosity pledging cash and goods for the relief effort.

---

[8] *Chicago Tribune.* June 19, 1871.

[9] 'Prostrate France: Chicago sympathizes with the Suffering People.' *Chicago Tribune,* February 5, 1871.

In the months that followed Collyer read increasingly alarmist reports in the American newspapers of a left-wing insurrection in Paris, the so-called Paris Commune, and its subsequent violent suppression by the French Army leading to the death of thousands of 'Communards'.[10] Thus, Collyer felt compelled to visit Paris and see for himself the devastation caused by the Prussian siege and the destruction of the Commune so vividly reported by the American press.[11]

Collyer's visit to Paris was less than three months after the 'Bloody Week' of May 21-27, when an estimated 20,000 'insurrectionists' were killed. In defending the city, the Communards had set fire to public buildings and built barricades from demolished houses. Signs of destruction were all about; the Tuileries Palace and the Hôtel de Ville were charred ruins, the once fashionable shops and apartments along the Rue de Rivoli were fire-scorched shells, and many of the houses had been reduced to piles of rubble. With the city pitifully scarred and the people cowed from an excess of fighting and bloodshed, Collyer cut short his planned stay and headed for Calais and England.

On his return to London he preached at James Martineau's chapel in Little Portland Street, although he did not have an opportunity to hear the great theologian and philosopher preach himself.[12] Heading north to join the Cunard Line's *S.S. Batavia* in Liverpool, Collyer preached at Mill Hill Chapel in Leeds where he also paid a final visit to his mother — this would be the last time that he saw her.[13] He broke the journey again in Manchester where he preached at William Gaskell's church, and finally gave the sermon for Charles Beard at Renshaw Street Chapel in Liverpool. While these preaching appointments were not without their stresses, each came with a handsome fee and the total received more than met Collyer's holiday expenses. Thus, tired with travel and the pressures of preaching, Collyer was relieved to board the *Batavia* and relax for ten days before the welcoming sight of the New York waterfront signaled the return to his adopted homeland.

---

[10] Samuel Bernstein, *The impact of the Paris Commune in the United States.* The Massachusetts Review, 12: 1971, 435-446. see https://www.jstor.org/stable/25088137

[11] For example, 'The Struggle for Paris', *New York Times,* 1871, May 25.

[12] *Clear Grit: A collection of Lectures, Addresses and Poems by Robert Collyer* (Boston: American Unitarian Association, 1913), 187.

[13] Collyer's mother lived with his sister Maria (Mrs John Shires) in Green Mount Street, off Coupland Road, Hunslet, Leeds.

25: Conflagration

The tonic effect of Collyer's holiday had disappeared within days of his return to Chicago. Starting with a rousing speech at the 'Welcome Home' reception on Saturday, September 9, and two sermons to congregations of over a thousand the next day, he embarked on a demanding schedule of sermon preparation, church services and meetings.[1] By the evening of Sunday, October 8, 1871, Collyer was exhausted. It was after nine o'clock when he finally left the church. He had substituted the evening service with a talk on the destruction of Paris – the Commune and its aftermath – and the subsequent questions and discussion were difficult to curtail. As he trudged home, he became aware of a red glow in the sky to the south, the glow of a fire. He was not particularly alarmed as there had been a large fire the evening before which had been successfully extinguished. Despite knowing that another fire had broken out, Robert went straight to bed.

Just before midnight his wife woke him up, such was her anxiety about the fire. Robert hurriedly dressed and decided to walk down to the river to assess the fire's progress. With two of the children, Hattie and Robert Jnr, they headed for the Rust Street Bridge, but quickly realized that they were going against a steady flow of people hurrying north to escape the flames. At the bridge, they stopped. There was a strong wind carrying smoke and sparks high above them and they could see flames rising into the night sky not far from the bridge. Swirling vortices of sparks and embers rose into the air and burning fragments of wood were borne northwards by the gale-force wind. The fire spread from

[1] 'Robert Collyer: His Reception Last Night at Unity Church', *Chicago Tribune,* Sept 9, 1871.

building to building along an advancing front that approached the river. Ahead of the main front, wind-borne firebrands landed on the tar-covered roofs of warehouses, on wooden pavements and on the shingle roofs of timber houses, all rendered tinder dry by the long summer drought, and started 'new' fires. Collyer, along with the other North Side residents, had hoped that the river would block the fire's northern progress but from the bridge he saw that the roof of a warehouse on their side of the river was in flames. It was time to retreat.

The exodus of people crossing the Randolph Street bridge. From an original Currier and Ives colored lithograph (1871). Chicago Historical Society via Wikimedia Commons.

Collyer and the children rushed home to begin a hurried evacuation of their house. His immediate thought was to carry what they could over to the church. Surely a masonry building would be a haven against the fire? The family rushed around gathering all the 'treasures' that they could carry; young Robert took down a favorite painting, a landscape by William Hart, and looped the cord around his neck. Collyer began to bring out piles of his treasured books. He hailed a passing 'express man' and offered him all the ready cash he had if he would take a load of books on his cart and leave them in the garden of a friend's house further north. He was relieved when the man agreed, thinking his 'treasures' were now safe, only to discover later that the books had been consumed by the fire. With flames now approaching the front of the house, Collyer sent the family, laden with bags and boxes filled to overflowing, off to the church. He lingered a while longer to pocket a few more items and escaped via the rear door, pausing at the kitchen stove to pat the kettle as a farewell gesture to an old friend. He caught up with the family as they walked the four blocks from their home in Chicago Avenue across to the church on North Dearborn Street. By the time they arrived, Little Robert was crying as the picture frame had repeatedly struck his shins, but he would not abandon it. The goods were taken into the auditorium where other folk had sought shelter. Collyer went down to his church study and removed another stack of books; he took these across the road to Washington Park and left them there to take their chance with the flames. It was now early morning.

Some church members were gathered outside Unity and, despite the constant shower of firebrands, they began to tear up the wooden sidewalk around the church. Although the church, being built of stone with a slate roof, was considered 'fire-proof', some of the men had heard that when stone buildings are surrounded by fire, the intense heat can cause their wooden interiors to burn spontaneously. Perhaps if the outside was doused with water, that might prevent such spontaneous combustion? A neighbor, Mr Mahlon Ogden, whose home had been spared by the fire, had a large cistern full of water which he offered to the church folk. Buckets were brought from nearby homes. Soon a chain of people passing buckets was established, and water thrown over the lower part of the church, but this had barely started before someone shouted that a wooden slatted ventilator in one of the spires was alight. Now, nothing could prevent the fire spreading into the roof timbers and the building would be consumed. Collyer ran inside and helped the family move out with their belongings. Once they were safely outside, he went back in, climbed into the pulpit and picked up the bible, still open at the passage he had read the previous day and, with tears streaming down his face, he headed outside.

At this point, a combination of smoke, heat and panic caused Collyer to cry out that he could not see, and his hands went into a claw-like spasm. His wife led him away from the church, shortly to become a funeral pyre so soon after its birth.[2] She took the bag containing their silver and buried it in a nearby celery patch and told the children to abandon all but the most precious items that they could carry.[3] Collyer suggested that they should walk to the home of a parishioner, Mrs. Price, who lived several blocks to the north where they hoped to be safe. They found a ready welcome from Mrs. Price and her sons; Collyer's swollen eyes were bathed, his taut hands were gradually loosened, and they were given food. Before long, however, the Price property was threatened by the pursuing fire. The Collyer family helped to bury some of the Prices' possessions in the sandy soil of their garden, but by mid-afternoon they resumed their northward flight.

The northward rush of people through the Potter's Field cemetery making for Lincoln Park. Harper's Weekly, November 4, 1871, via Wikimedia Commons.

This time they were without a plan; they simply joined the stream of people moving away from danger. Then a remarkable thing happened, a man with a wagon pulled up alongside the family and helped them get aboard. This was

---

[2] Robert Cromie, *The Great Chicago Fire* (New York: McGraw-Hill Book Company,1958), 197.

[3] Collyer, *Some Memories*, 225.

no chance encounter, however. Another member of the Unity congregation, a Thomas Moulding, had seen the exodus from the city, and enquired whether the Unity Church had burnt. On hearing that it had been destroyed and that the Rev Collyer had been seen heading north, he yoked up his horses to the wagon and set out to find him and his family. Mr. Moulding, a widower who lived with his son and family, had moved from their home in Lakeview to their vacation retreat fifteen miles to the north of the city. There in the lee of a small lake they were safe from the fire.[4] How he subsequently found the Collyer family among the crowd of refugees is not apparent, but two hours later they were safely ensconced in Mr. Moulding's lakeside home.

Collyer remembers his reaction once he was alone with Ann; "I quite broke down, for the pity of it and the pain. The church was burnt, and the home we owned, with nearly all the homes in our parish, while we feared also that dear friends had been caught as in a trap when the great volumes of fire ... barred their escape by the avenues northwards ... we feared the worst."[5]

And then it rained. About 11pm a fine drizzle was felt in the air. This did little to counter the flames but after weeks of drought, many people saw this as a miracle and began shouting with joy. The drizzle intensified and by three in the morning a steady rain was falling which halted the fire. While hundreds of fires were still burning on Tuesday morning, most were under control. Small pockets of fire flared up from time to time, and would do so for several days more, but the Great Fire was done. The burnt district was over four miles long and one mile wide; 17,500 buildings and seventy-five miles of streets had been destroyed and almost 100,000 citizens had been left homeless by the fire.[6] In view of the densely populated area affected, the death toll was relatively low being estimated at 300, an estimate because only 120 bodies were recovered, and 'relatively low' compared to a fire the same night in Wisconsin.[7]

For Collyer, a semblance of normal life had to resume; there was his son's wedding to consider. Samuel, who was now twenty-four years old, was not at home when the fire struck. He was staying at a small cottage he had built the summer before on a lot in Orchard Street purchased from Mr. Chapman, a fellow Unitarian. Fortunately, the cottage was outside the fire zone.

---

[4] Probably one of the Skokie Lagoons near Winnetka

[5] Collyer, 228.

[6] Jim Murray, *The Great Fire* (New York: Scholastic Inc., 1995), 95-100.

[7] The fire which afflicted Peshtigo, Wisconsin, on October 8, 1871, killed between 1,200 and 2,500 people.

Smoldering ruins in the immediate aftermath of the Fire. (from Wikimedia Commons)

Samuel quickly discovered the whereabouts of his parents through a remarkably effective word-of-mouth network established by the now dispersed Unity members. On Wednesday he was glad to be re-united with his family but distressed that the wedding arranged for the following day could not now take place. Collyer, however, would not hear of postponement. He reminded Samuel that he didn't need a church in which to be married and advised him to go ahead anyway; "go right away, after he had seen his sweetheart, to hunt up the man who would issue the license." Samuel found his fiancée – her family had escaped by taking to the lake in a boat, and he found the city clerk, but his official forms had all been burnt.[8] Nevertheless, he wrote out a license on a sheet of paper and all was set for the marriage - apart from a venue for the wedding, the loss of the bride's trousseau in the fire, and the absence of a wedding feast.

---

[8] Samuel married Miss Rebecca Moore of Odell, Illinois.

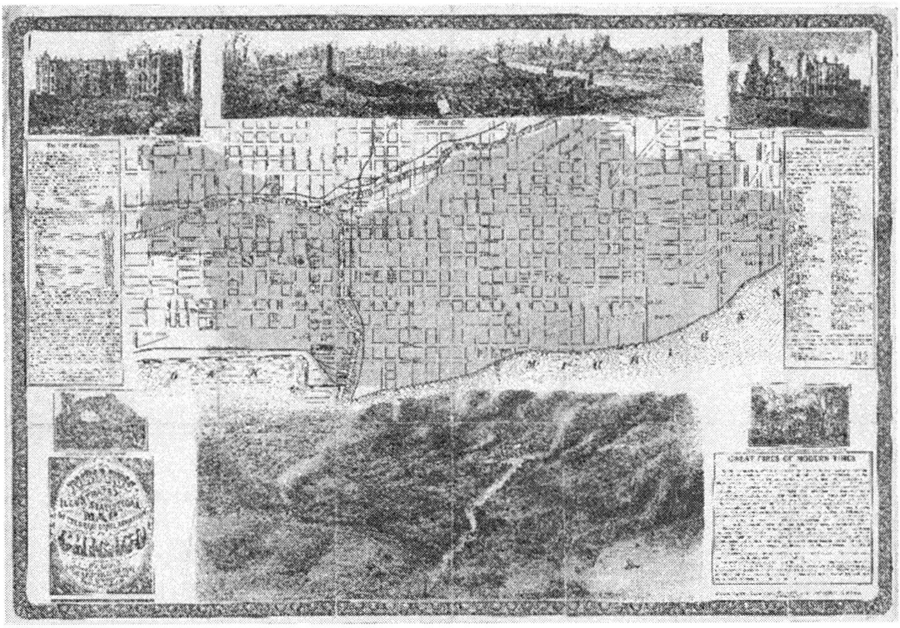

Richard's Map showing the area consumed by the Great Fire (from Wikimedia Commons)

All these problems were resolved; the wedding was held at the home of a friend on the West Side, the bride recovered some clothes from a trunk she had left at the cottage and was married in a simple calico dress, and food was sent in by friends who had not been burnt out. Importantly, Collyer hitched a ride over to the West Side and was able to preside at the wedding ceremony. Everything went off well, if under much reduced circumstances, and after the shared 'feast', Mr. Chapman "brought the bridal couple to their home in his carriage and they began housekeeping in their cottage at once."[9]

It was apparent to Ann Collyer, if not her husband, that the Moulding family could not accommodate them and their children for very much longer. Before the situation came to a head, however, a fellow minister intervened. The Rev Charles Wendte, minister of the Third Unitarian Church on the South Side sought them out and arrived at the Mouldings' house to take the Collyer's under his care, or more precisely his mother's care. So, they moved in with the Wendtes' until they found a place to board through the impending winter.

[9] https://www.greatchicagofire.org/anthology-of-fire-narratives/chapman/

Back in the city, Robert went to view the ruined church. He could have broken down again but instead resolved to rebuild the church out of the embers of the old. He knew he had to act quickly to restore that sense of fellowship and common purpose essential to the task. Could he begin on that first Sunday? Could he assemble enough Unity members to hold a service outside the smoldering ruin? The form of service and the message had to wait, first he had to rally the Unity folk.

Collyer discovered that the *Tribune* offices and presses had escaped the fire. He went over to see his friend, the editor Horace White, and found him hard at work on the first edition since the fire. White agreed willingly to announce that a service would take place in the ruins of the Unity Church at 12 noon on Sunday, October 15.

City life resumes after the Fire. (from Wikimedia Commons)

Accordingly, Collyer arrived at the church shortly before noon to find a large crowd of Unity people together with friends, and many strangers, gathered outside the ruined façade on Dearborn Street. Carrying a bible and a hymn book borrowed from Brother Wendte, he moved between them and stood on a large fallen stone as a platform. Some members of the choir were there to lead the singing, and Collyer chose familiar hymns which he read two lines at a time for the congregation to follow, just as he had done as a preacher in the Yorkshire Dales where some of the folk didn't have a proper grasp of reading. Lessons were read from the bible and he gave an extempore address, finding words of consolation and courage, for himself as well as his listeners. Then he spoke about the situation on all their hearts. They must rebuild. He told them that he would forego his stipend for the year to come, he would take care of his family; "I could go back to the anvil at a pinch and make horseshoes, whereat they smiled and so did I."[10]

Collyer preaches among the ruins of Unity Church, after a photograph by Thomas R. Sweeney. Harper's Weekly, November 4, 1871.

When he was through, one of the elders, William Clarke, offered the resolution that; "We would go right on and rebuild our church as soon as we

[10] Collyer, *Some Memories*, 236.

were able. The resolution was passed with something like a shout of gladness, and then we closed our service with the doxology and benediction, and went wherever we had found shelter."

Collyer came away satisfied that he had stirred the congregation into immediate action. What he did not realize was that newspaper reporters and a photographer had been present at the service and his simple exhortation among the ruins would serve as a clarion call to the whole of Chicago to face the challenge of rebuilding. Furthermore, his defiant act caught the imagination of the nation as people throughout America responded with sympathy and generosity to the plight of the Chicagoans. A front-page picture of Collyer preaching among the ruins of Unity in *Harper's Weekly* became an icon of Chicago's courage, and the story was widely reported in America and abroad.[11] Now he had to practice what he preached and throw his efforts into recovery.

---

[11] *Harper's Weekly*. New York, Vol. XV, No. 775. November 4, 1871.

26: Recovery

Collyer's first step to recovery was to get some money. He had given all he had to the expressman for, what proved to be, the futile transfer of his books to another property destined to perish in the flames. He could not live on the Rev. Wendte's charity for long and his bank was burnt down. Fortunately, the day after the wedding, the Unity Church deacon, Mr. Mears, sought him out and 'emptied all his pockets one by one into his hands'.[1] But it was the recovery of the Chicago people that was his main concern.

Despite the chaos and confusion, Mayor Roswell B. Mason and other city officials, acted swiftly to secure public order by drafting in extra police, fixing the price of bread, supplying free food where needed and calling in U.S. Army troops. On October 13, the Mayor declared that the Chicago Relief and Aid Association, a well-respected organization founded 20 years before, would act as the central bureau for the receipt and disbursement of all money and supplies.[2] Collyer was appointed superintendent of the corps of visitors for the North Side district, the rest of the city being divided into four other districts.

It transpired, however, that Collyer's temperament was ill-suited to the rigid system of investigation of the claims for aid, and the keeping of records. He was a man of hands-on action, preferring to follow his own instincts and local knowledge than sit in the office in Washington Street directing others. In

1 Collyer, *Some Memories,* 232.

2 Otto M. Nelson, 'The Chicago Relief and Aid Society 1850-1874'. *Journal of the Illinois State Historical Society,* 1966, 59: 48-66.

an early letter to Rev Edward Hale, he considered the enterprise 'a vast Babel'.[3] He writes, 'Please see that only those packages are sent to my name which are meant for private distribution in and about my parish among those who are as poor as the poorest but can never muster heart enough to stand in the long ranks of applicants for aid. Let all the rest go to the great store as it only bothers me when I ought to be at my work attending these lost ones.' Unsurprisingly, within a short time he stood down as a Relief and Aid Association superintendent and concentrated on his own relief work in the parish.

As the weeks went by, it was Collyer himself who emerged as the focal point for many of the donations, particularly those from the Unitarian connection. Innumerable consignments of food, clothing and funds for the sufferers were sent to Collyer — on one day alone he received thirty-five parcels — and those he could not distribute himself were forwarded to the Relief and Aid Association. The day after the fire, Collyer received a message from Mr P. R. Sabin of Jackson, Michigan: "I send one thousand loaves of bread. What do you need most? Please answer."[4] Another letter brought a most unusual offer; this was the potential gift of $1000 from the students of Cornell University contingent on Collyer making a horseshoe. Collyer had not made one for twenty-two years, but a thousand dollars was a handsome sum and the horseshoe was a challenge. Collyer sought out a nearby farrier who had managed to restore his forge after the fire, and asked for the loan of his anvil – and some assistance with the bellows. This was agreed with some mirth, and Collyer set about the task. Always one to court publicity for his cause, Collyer invited newspaper reporters to attend at the forge while he fashioned the horseshoe. The story was widely reported and struck a sympathetic chord with the American public. Before long, framed reproductions of a painting of the 'saintly blacksmith' at his labors by the portrait painter Alvah Bradish, adorned the walls of countless homes.[5] The horseshoe was made, stamped with the name of its clerical maker, wrapped in an affidavit duly signed and sealed, and sent to the college at Ithaca. Back came a bank draft for $1050, and subsequent contributions from Cornell added up to a grand total of $2,250.[6]

---

[3] Letter to Edward Everett Hale, date obscured but sent soon after October 14, 1871. Papers, bMS 512/4 (31), Andover-Harvard Library, Harvard Divinity School.

[4] 'Unity Church report', *Chicago Daily Tribune,* Oct 28, 1872.

[5] Morris Bishop, *A History of Cornell* (Ithaca, Cornell University Press, 1962), 195.

[6] Holmes, *Life and Letters,* 169.

Unity Church after the fire. While the roof and the interior were destroyed, the towers and two of the walls were sound. (Author's collection)

Over following days and weeks, Collyer received hundreds of donations – small and large, each one acknowledged by a personal, hand-written letter of thanks. There was a gift of $16 from the newsboys, bootblacks and other homeless lads at the Rivington Street Lodging House in New York, while Mr. William Gray of Boston sent $5,000, 'for your own personal expenses instead of a salary from Unity Church during 1872'. In a letter to Flesher Bland written on October 30, Collyer declared; 'Many thousands (of dollars) have been sent me for personal distribution among those who cannot beg', that is those who cannot bring themselves to apply to the Relief and Aid Association, and 'Thirty-one hundred dollars came by the evening mail for the (same) purpose.'[7] Mr John Ritchie, Secretary of the Second Presbyterian Church, Belfast, sent £46 15s 2d, the amount of a collection made by the congregation, 'in aid of their brethren who suffered by the great calamity'. A donation of £114 was sent by Unitarians in Lancashire, England, to 'Mr. Collyer, to be used by him either for meeting the present wants of the members of his congregation, or for assisting the fund for the rebuilding of the chapel, as he may think best.' This sentiment reflects the change in emphasis by the donors as time went by, moving away from aid for destitute people towards the rebuilding of the church. In January 1872, the officers of the 'Unitarian Aid Society for the Relief of Chicago' in London agreed that 'from the residue of the fund, £1000 be contributed for the rebuilding of the Rev. Robert Collyer's church and schools, and the balance be placed at the disposal of the Committee on the spot.'

Collyer became the recipient of donations or pledges of money from Unitarian churches throughout America. In answer to numerous invitations, Collyer addressed great audiences, telling them of the devastation and misery caused by the fire and the desperate need for relief. He spoke in St. Louis, at the Church of the Messiah in New York, the Music Hall, Boston, and elsewhere, and collected during the winter the handsome sum of $15,000.[8] In March 1872, he was able to tell a meeting of Unity members that $40,000 was held by the National Association in Boston towards rebuilding the church.[9] At this meeting, Collyer was asked, "to give some account of his recent journey to the East for the purpose of raising funds." Somewhat surprisingly, he replied; "that he didn't go to New England for the purpose of raising money for Unity Church, but for himself, and to make a beginning for the church." Collyer does not appear to have disclosed the fact that his salary was being covered by a generous donor when he embarked on a busy schedule of preaching and lecturing for which he was richly rewarded. He told the meeting that Mr. William Gray of Boston (the undeclared 'generous donor'), "had advised Mr. Collyer not to waste his time and energies on public meetings on behalf of his mission", i.e. raising funds for Unity, but instead to attend a forthcoming meeting of the top men in the National Association at Mr. Gray's house when, "Mr. Collyer could make his statement of the needs of his church." In this way

[7] Holmes, 166.

[8] Holmes, 177.

[9] 'Robert Collyer's Church'. *Chicago Tribune,* March 7, 1872.

Collyer was confident that at least $50,000 could be got from the Association.[10] It also meant that the way was now clear for Collyer to concentrate on personal income generation, and he tackled this with a will.

In addition to receiving substantial fees for giving guest sermons and lectures (around $200 a time), Collyer also received many personal donations. He tells Flesher Bland, 'Our churches in London telegraph me that they have mailed £500 for my personal use. One church at the East sent me $1000, and another (sent) $1130 strictly for the same purpose, besides which I have had many hundreds more, the sum of which I have not counted.' Other donors include; Sir James Lawrence in England who gave £500 'for your family'; Mrs. S.E. Wetherell of Boston gave $50 'as a personal gift to Robert Collyer'; $150 from Harper and Brothers, 'at the request of Mr. M.D. Conway'; Richard Warren of New York sent $300 'for yourself and family', and one dollar came from a Catholic working-girl who 'wanted to help.' While it is not possible from the available records to arrive at an accurate total for Collyer's income in the year following the fire, it cannot be less than $10,000.[11]

After that first momentous service in the ruins, the congregation became dispersed. Many went to stay with relatives or boarded out of town, some were reduced to living in hastily constructed sheds and shanties. This did not bring about the end of Unitarian services, however. Services were held in houses outside the burnt zone, for instance at Mr Dow's house on Orchard Street, services which Collyer conducted when he could.[12] Other Unity members travelled to the unscathed First or Third Unitarian Churches to attend their services. Although taking time away from Chicago to fulfil his speaking engagements, when he was at home, Collyer preached three times every Sunday at venues five miles apart, often walking between appointments. Matters improved when the neighboring 'New England Church' erected a temporary wooden frame building on land behind their ruined church and generously offered its use to Unity. Thus, on Sunday afternoons most of the Unity congregation could once again assemble for worship.

---

[10] The final sum was $59,387. Holmes, *Life and Letters,* 177.

[11] This is a very large sum, having a *relative inflated worth* of at least $218,000 in today's (2020) values. Karen Sawislak, in her book *Smoldering City; Chicagoans and the Great Fire, 1871-1874* (Chicago, The University of Chicago Press, 1995), 72, uses Robert Collyer's substantial income to illustrate 'The Patchwork of Loss' where she asserts that Collyer, "ended up drawing a sizable cash profit from the Great Fire."

[12] https://www.greatchicagofire.org/anthology-of-fire-narratives/chapman/

In the meantime, the Building Committee at Unity had been re-constituted – it was only three years since they completed their work on the former building, and the group had consulted with the city's leading architect, Mr. Edward Burling, on reconstruction of the church. Mr. Burling had waived his fee for the original Unity, and he was prepared to undertake the re-build on the same terms.[13] While the fire had completely destroyed the roof and interior of the church, two of the walls remained in good condition and the towers were largely intact. Mr Burling estimated that the building would cost no more than $65,000 to restore — not including furnishings and an organ. The decision to start re-building work was taken in March 1872, and by November of that year services were resumed in the Sunday School room on the ground floor.[9] The new auditorium was practically completed by June 1873, but not occupied until December 3, when the formal service of dedication was held. 'It was a happy time, with no weeping over past gloom, ... Dr. Furness, of Philadelphia, preached the sermon; and Collyer wrote another original hymn, to match the one sung at the dedication four years ago.'[14]

The summer of 1872 also saw the start of building a new home for the Collyers'. In a letter of May 23 to Flesher Bland he tells him; 'We have sold the old lot, 29 by 110, and bought a new one on a better street, 48 by 165, and mean to make the one pay for the other. Shall put $10,000 into the house.'[15] Collyer discovers quite soon that this is a gross under-estimate. A year later he was writing to Bland; 'House building in Chicago costs like cinnamon, and so by October, I began to see my way to a load of debt.'[16] He was rescued from a heavy mortgage by his activity on the lecture circuit. He was groaning about the impending mortgage to a wise old fellow among his flock who said; "Aint you one 'er them big lecturers 'et kin make no 'ind o' money just talkin' around?' Collyer replied; "Oh, yes, but I cannot talk; I have got the church to see to."[16] The result was that the old man went around the church folk and

---

[13] It was said of Burling that he was "a splendid specimen of the best type of self-made men," the highest compliment one could offer in that enterprising age. He formed a firm with the great architect Dankmar Adler, and the pair were said to have reconstructed four linear miles' worth of streetscape in the single year after the fire, more than 100 buildings in all. http://driehausmuseum.org/blog/view/speaking-of-architecture-the-life-and-work-of-edward-j.-burling

[14] Holmes, *Life and Letters,* 182.

[15] Holmes, 173.

[16] Letter of May 14, 1873, Holmes, *Life and Letters,* 182. Cinnamon was extremely expensive in nineteenth century America.

made them see that they should offer their pastor leave of absence for the winter season while he toured the lecture circuit. At a subsequent church meeting, Collyer proposed that he would relinquish his stipend, which the church had started to pay him again, and use the money to fill the pulpit each Sunday with good men who he would nominate. The people agreed to this gladly and voted him the six months' vacation necessary.[16]

Collyer had lectured now and then over several winters using the Redpath Bureau in Boston, but he had not thought to approach them until after the church was dedicated and all things were in order.[17] Now the way was clear to accept all the engagements that they could arrange. So, from early in November 1872 to well on in May 1873, he lectured up to five nights a week criss-crossing the States from Belfast in Maine, to St. Paul, Minnesota. He offered a limited repertoire of talks which he had re-written after losing all his manuscripts in the fire; 'Clear Grit' was chief among them, but other popular offerings were 'From Anvil to Pulpit' and 'The True George Washington.'

Just as when sermonizing, Collyer relied on a manuscript to deliver a lecture. No matter how many times before he had given the talk, he required the whole speech to be written out. It is difficult to envisage how a public speaker who needs a full manuscript on the lectern can connect with an audience in the way that Collyer did. It seems more likely that the manuscript was largely a prop to his self-confidence, and not read verbatim. No matter how physically tired he was, when he rose to his feet on the platform or podium, he became transformed. 'All the gladness, kindness, goodness that this grand and wonderful face could express, glowed upon the audience, and his voice cheery and strong, rang out so that all could hear.'[18] He enjoyed the exhilaration of addressing large audiences and moving them to laughter and tears, but the travelling proved to be a great strain. He missed the church, and he longed for the company of his wife and children, but he kept doggedly at it, and so far as he could remember in later years, did not miss a single

---

[17] James Redpath and George Fall started the Redpath Bureau as the Boston Lyceum Bureau in 1868. It supplied speakers and performers for lyceums across the country charging a 10% commission for doing so. It represented figures such as Mark Twain, Henry Ward Beecher, Susan B. Anthony and Frederick Douglass. After 1874 other proprietors took over, and the "Boston Lyceum Bureau" and the "Redpath Lyceum Bureau" expanded vigorously into the 20th century, with branches throughout the United States. https://en.wikipedia.org/wiki/Boston_Lyceum_Bureau

appointment.[18] Charging between $100 to $200 dollars, the result was that after paying all his expenses he cleared about $10,000.

By the early summer of 1873, his new house was built and paid for. It was a handsome detached brownstone house located at 500 North La Salle Street, said to be worth $16,000. Once the Collyers felt that it was sufficiently 'ship-shape', they gave notice of a house-warming event open to all at Unity Church.[19] Naturally, people were just as interested in their pastor's home as in the pastor himself and a large number, old and young, turned up. Collyer was there at the door ready with a handshake and a warm welcome. After liquid refreshment served by Mrs. Collyer and the children, the visitors were free to explore the reception rooms. Later, there were speeches and an elder of the church, Mr. Wirt Dexter, presented Collyer with a handsome set of silver; the salver being engraved "Presented to Mr. and Mrs. Collyer by the friends of Unity Church, June 1873."[19] Once the formalities were concluded, a light supper was served and the evening ended with music and dancing – but not for Collyer. He stationed himself in his study, a large room with an open fireplace and a generous desk, lined by bookshelves filled with his newly acquired library, where he proudly explained to the visitors how his collection had been re-assembled after the fire.

The restoration of Collyer's library was in large measure the work of; 'a good woman, a writer, (who) saw me in the stress of trouble'.[20] She wrote a letter for publication to the New York *Tribune* emphasizing Collyer's loss, and sent letters to all the major publishing houses explaining that his valuable collection of books had gone up in flames with the rest of his possessions, and begged for replacements as an act of charity towards this notable bibliophile. Other friends negotiated with the publishers to purchase books for Collyer at cost price, bought from a fund organized by the journalist Junius Henri Browne and raised from fellow journalists and other literary people.[21] By the end of 1871, Collyer had received two hundred and three volumes from friends in New York and Providence who also advised him that they had a further $200 to spend as he directed on other works.[22]

---

[18] Holmes, *Life and Letters,* 184.

[19] 'Robert Collyer – What Occurred to Him at His New House Last Evening', *Chicago Daily Tribune,* June 12, 1873.

[20] Collyer, *Some Memories,* 247.

[21] 'Robert Collyer's Library'. *Chicago Tribune,* January 11, 1872.

[22] Holmes, *Life and Letters,* 172.

In addition to general works, over the years Collyer had accumulated a collection of mainly antiquarian books about his home county of Yorkshire that were especially precious to him. When news of his loss reached London, his friend Sir Edwin Lawrence offered to duplicate them. Collyer recalled that Sir Edwin asked him; "if I could remember the titles of those books. Well, I could not forget them; they were graven shall I say? on my heart".[20] Collyer sent him the list, and true to his word, a large consignment of Yorkshire books arrived just after he had moved into his new house. His library was complete.

Sir Edwin Lawrence, Collyer's benefactor and restorer of his Yorkshire book collection. (Wikipedia)

Collyer's theological books had been kept in his study at Unity Church. It was these books that he rescued at the eleventh hour and simply placed them in piles in the park across the road. Much to his surprise, when he went to the ruined church on October 15, the books were still where he had left them in the park. The flames had swept over them but not consumed them. The covers and spines were scorched but the pages were largely unaffected. He retrieved and stored the books until they could be reinstated in the study of the new Unity Church. Later, when visitors to his study saw the burnt covers, they often asked why he had not had them re-covered? Collyer declared that he wanted them just as they were - as an enduring metaphor; "like faith that is more precious than gold that perisheth, though it be tested with fire."[23]

---

[23] see 1 Peter 1:7, King James's Version.

27: Calls to New York

Towards the end of September 1874, a letter from New York landed on Collyer's desk. Its contents threw him completely off balance; it was an invitation to take the pastorate of the Church of the Messiah, one of the largest Unitarian churches in that city. He knew the church, it was on his itinerary of fund-raising engagements after the Fire, but he had no inkling that they were seeking a new minister. The invitation arrived at a difficult time for Collyer; he was going through one of his 'bad patches'.

The Unity Church had been re-built and he and his family had moved into a smart new house, but instead of gaining security and peace of mind, Collyer had slumped into despondency. The strain of holding his church together when the entire parish had been destroyed was a Herculean task. Many of his flock had moved away, others had the re-building of their homes and businesses put on hold by the great financial slump of 1873, and the income of the church had suffered accordingly. Collyer often had to face the disappointing and unfamiliar sight of a half-empty church. In addition, for over two years, Collyer had undertaken an exhausting schedule of fund-raising services and lectures, with its disruption to family life and a considerable toll on his physical and mental well-being. Not only that, but his mother's death on July 11 had hit him surprisingly hard. Although his rational self would excuse his absence in her dying days, he felt intensely guilty that he was not at her bedside in Leeds, and not been there to comfort his sister at the funeral. He confided in his friend Flesher Bland that; "the world is dim to me since she went away."[1]

[1] Holmes, *Life and Letters,* 2: 189.

In such periods of depression, Collyer's self-esteem always took a drastic slump. He imagined that by now the Unity congregation would be tired of his 'simple' sermons, that the novelty of his homespun philosophy would have worn off, and that his time with them was done. In contrast, the New Yorkers were begging him to come to their church and they had offered him an annual stipend of $10,000 – a king's ransom. At the Church of the Messiah he would be a 'fresh' broom sweeping the dust away, and the tired and depleted congregation would derive new motivation from his arrival. Besides which, he would be painting on a much larger canvas; New York presented unparalleled opportunities for influence and fame. The idea of a move began to take hold in Collyer's mind.

Collyer attended a meeting in New York with a committee of the Messiah church and gave them encouragement that he would accept the call, but he needed reassurance on two important points before he could make a definite commitment. The first reservation was that he had raised by his own appeals around $50,000 towards the re-building of Unity and felt that this was money donated to him and his people. Was he not obligated to the donors to continue to serve in Chicago? Collyer sought advice from Rev Rush Shippen in Washington D.C. who consulted a group of Unitarian ministers and senior laymen on the issue; they responded with an assurance that he was under no obligation, and that he was free to make up his own mind.[2]

The second potential sticking point was the financial status of the Church of the Messiah. The New York church had also had its problems with a fire. The original edifice burnt down in 1837, possibly the result of arson, and a new church was built on Broadway and opened in 1843. The migration of its parishioners out of the inner city to the suburbs and the demand for prime down-town sites by ever eager businessmen, persuaded the church to sell, and to build at a different location.[3] They bought a site at the corner of Park Avenue and 34th Street, and the foundation stone of the new church was laid with much ceremony in October 1866.[4] The architect's brief was to build a church that would cost no more than $120,000. Although this was $40,000 more than the church's cash reserves, it was thought the deficit could be raised by the sale of

---

[2] Holmes, 2: 210.

[3] The building was sold to department store magnate, A.T. Stewart, and converted it into a theatre. https://en.wikipedia.org/wiki/Church_of_the_Messiah_(Manhattan)

[4] Park Avenue and 34th Street is two blocks from the site of the Empire State Building.

pews.[5] In reality, the building cost $320,000 and the church was saddled with a debt of $165,000. By 1874, little had been achieved in reducing the debt and it was apparent that they viewed the arrival of Collyer as a God-send who would restore their fortunes.[6] Whether or not these financial problems held sway with Collyer is not known – at one point in the negotiations he did offer to receive a reduced stipend of $7,500, but in the final analysis it was Chicago, not New York, who determined his future.

When the members at Unity became aware that an approach had been made to *their* Minister, *their* beloved pastor, to move to a church in New York, they were alarmed, affronted, and angry. An urgent meeting was called for October 15 to discuss the situation. About two hundred people attended the meeting, not only church members but people from the wider community who were equally shocked to think that Collyer could be leaving Chicago. Towards the close of the meeting (not attended by Collyer), a whole raft of resolutions was passed that captured the depth of feeling, the widely held and deep affection for him, and the hurt at his possible departure. There was a unanimous declaration that he must not leave Chicago.[7] When, at a meeting with Collyer next morning, the resolutions and other representations were conveyed to him by the elders, he became fully aware of the vote of confidence from the congregation that his floundering self-esteem so desperately needed. His mind was made up, he would stay.[8]

An unusually large congregation greeted him on that first Sunday morning after his decision. The pulpit was decorated with wreaths and bunches of flowers surmounted by two sheaves of corn. These adornments were placed in memory of his mother but evoked in Collyer remembrances of the Harvest Festival decorations in the churches of his beloved Yorkshire Dales. In underlining the friendship and esteem of his congregation, Collyer was visibly moved by this display of affection, and he took some time to compose himself before beginning the service. He started with an explanation of recent events and why he had resolved to stay in Chicago. Eventually, with uplifted eyes and obvious emotion in his voice, he declared; "And so nought but death shall ever

---

5 In former times churches raised funds by 'selling' pews. This gave the purchaser reserved seating, i.e. a pew, for perpetuity. In most churches, however, pews were rented out on an annual or quarterly basis.

6 Holmes, 2: 212.

7 'Robert Collyer. The meeting at Unity last night', *Chicago Tribune,* Oct 16, 1874.

8 'Robert Collyer. He has decided not to leave Chicago', *Chicago Tribune,* Oct 17, 1874.

part ye and me, and we will work together to the end for the goodness and grace of God."[9] While sincerely meant, this did not come to pass.

Although Collyer's church work went steadily forward, Unity failed to recover its former status. In March 1875, the Treasurer reported that the income derived from pew-rents showed a quarterly deficit of about $1500 and that "on the main floor of the church there are still many pews not taken."[10]

Over the next two years, Robert and Ann Collyer became concerned over the health of their son, Robert Junior, and they feared for his life at one time. Fortunately, he made a slow recovery from this episode. Further concern surrounded their daughter Annie, a delicate child who 'took music' rather than having a regular education, and Ann herself had occasional episodes of ill health.[11] By the end of 1877, however, Collyer was able to declare; "Rob mending slowly, goes on his crutches nicely now .... all the children good as gold, sturdy and steady..... Wife and self, evidently older and somewhat stout."[12]

In the summer of 1878, he felt sufficiently confident over the family's health to accept a long-standing invitation to travel to England where, in return for his travel expenses and one hundred guineas spending money, he would give twenty-six sermons at Unitarian churches throughout the country. On July 10, he sailed from New York on the S.S. *Scythia.* After landing in Liverpool, he headed for Leeds to see his sister and then stayed for some time in Ilkley. Thereafter he combined his widely separated preaching engagements with occasional, remunerative, lectures and plenty of sight-seeing. He had a pleasant ten days in France with his brother Tom, staying in Brittany, and returned home on September 20; "after the most delightful journey I ever made in my life."[13]

The tonic effect of this working holiday quickly evaporated. The health of his family, and particularly that of his wife became an over-riding concern. Over the next six months her health deteriorated, and young Robert required surgery. On March 24, 1879, Collyer wrote a very telling letter to his friend Miss Alice Baker; "We are in dolor ..... Mother (his wife) has been *very* sick, and Rob

---

[9] 'Robert Collyer. Statement to his Church', *Chicago Tribune,* Oct 19, 1874.

[10] 'Unity Church. The Annual Meeting', *Chicago Tribune,* Mar 31, 1875.

[11] Holmes, *Life and Letters,* 2: 191.

[12] Holmes, 2: 195.

[13] Holmes, 2: 196.

so weak and ill after a very severe operation that I began to despair.[14] But they are now at Hot Springs 700 miles in the wilderness, and amending nicely...[15] If you and Sue can keep a dead secret, I really think I shall have to pull up stakes and bring Mother East to live, or she will die. She is always well when she sniffs the salt air; grows very feeble now staying here and trying to fight it out. My heart aches for her forever and ever, and I think a thorough change might build up the boy also ..."[16] Collyer's reference to 'pulling up stakes' and moving East does not appear to be a vague aspiration. He specifically asks them to keep it secret as though he was already making moves in this direction. No doubt through his Unitarian connections he was keeping a close watch on developments at the Church of the Messiah. Indeed, he may have already indicated that a second invitation to New York would be accepted.

Possibly as a result of Collyer's soundings, he was invited to New York at the beginning of June and preached twice in the vacant pulpit at the Church of the Messiah.[17] On June 10, 1879, he received a letter from the Chairman and Secretary of the Messiah Church inviting him to become their pastor. The position would commence in September and the salary was $5000 per annum, that is half what was on offer five years before. This time, however, the money was not a necessary inducement, Collyer wanted the move.[18] Furthermore, he had been reassured by fellow ministers that the financial situation at Messiah was sound.

When in October 1878 the then minister, William Alger, retired, the whole future of the Messiah Church was in the balance. The church had staggered from crisis to crisis carrying a debt that amounted to $125,000, and now a judgement of foreclosure on the mortgage was entered and the property ordered to be sold. At this point, a group of women in the church took matters into their own hands. The women divided up Manhattan into separate areas and, armed with lists to enter subscriptions, they each trudged around their area calling at stores and offices, shops and parlors, urging and cajoling people

[14] C. Alice Baker (1833-1909) was a teacher, historian and writer. Together with her life companion, Susan Minot Lane, she opened a school in Chicago in 1856. The women ran their school until 1864 when they moved to Cambridge, Mass., to be with Miss Baker's sickly mother. Collyer maintained a regular correspondence with her thereafter.

[15] Hot Springs – a health resort in Arkansas.

[16] Holmes, 2: 223.

[17] 'Robert Collyer. Some chance of this preacher leaving Chicago', *Chicago Tribune,* Jun 2, 1879.

[18] 'Our Robert. He will probably go to New York', *Chicago Tribune,* Jun 12, 1879.

into contributing. Their remarkable efforts resulted in a final total of over $72,000 being raised. This emboldened the church authorities to approach the Unitarian Association and other bodies for contributions and a further $57,000 was pledged. The church was free from debt.

As Collyer's impending departure for New York had played out in the columns of the *Tribune,* his resignation came as no surprise to the Unity congregation. It had lost something of its suddenness but none of its force. "For more than twenty years he had been their pastor and friend; one who has married the living and buried the dead; one whose great, manly, loving heart has beaten in unison with the heart of the people to whom he ministered."[19] On September 28, 1879, he began a new phase of his ministry at the Church of the Messiah in New York, a phase that would occupy the rest of his life.

[19] 'Robert Collyer. He accepts the call to New York'. *Chicago Tribune,* Jun 16, 1879.

28: Turbulence and Tragedy

After Collyer's arrival in New York he embarked on calmer years of steady, if unadventurous, church work; a succession of joyful, and sad family happenings; contacts with friends, old and new; and occasional voyages of discovery to Europe. These were the years of consolidation and contentment that characterized his time at the Church of the Messiah, years that should have led to a well-deserved retirement but instead became an unswerving attachment which only ended with his death thirty-three years later.

The first two years in New York, however, were not without their turbulence, and any minor disturbance was amplified through the echo chamber of the *Chicago Tribune.* The first mischievous bulletin came after just two Sundays in the new pulpit.[1] At the first evening service, Collyer had no sooner finished the sermon than a sizable proportion of the congregation got up and walked out of the church – before the closing prayers and final hymn. The reporter claimed that Collyer was too taken aback by this display of bad manners to pass any comment, but when the same thing happened the next Sunday evening, he delivered a stinging rebuke and asked those remaining in the pews to pass on the strength of his feelings to those who had left early. The *Tribune* seemed pleased to report that his demonstration of Mid-Western 'grit' resulted in several apologies and, hopefully, a stop to any further walk-outs.

After just two month's absence in New York, Collyer was back in Chicago on December 7, 1879, and preaching at the Unity Church. While this

[1] 'Robert Collyer's First Collision'. *Chicago Tribune,* Oct 14, 1879.

early return gave more grist to the rumor mill, the explanation was totally innocent; he was there to perform the marriage ceremony for his son, Samuel. Tragically, Samuel's first wife Rebecca had died just five years after their wedding and three years after the birth of their daughter, Louisa.[2] Now at the age of thirty-two, he was to marry Louisa Mary Dewey, in Chicago on Tuesday, December 9.

Collyer's former house in North La Salle had been rented out, so he and his wife stayed at the home of a Mrs. Tilden, one of his old parishioners. As if to underline the regret at his departure, there was a huge congregation for the morning service at Unity, but Collyer emphasized that he was confident in his decision to go to New York and full of hope and encouragement for the future.[3] During their stay, the Collyers' spent as much time as they could with their daughter Emma, her husband Frank Hosmer, and their son, eighteen months old Robert Collyer Hosmer.[4] On Thursday 11, and with much reluctance on Ann's part, the Collyers left Chicago to go back to New York.

Ann's homesickness for Chicago, and the pull of family ties, took a turn for the worse when early in 1880, Samuel decided to leave Chicago for a new job in Colorado. The strength of their distress is conveyed in a letter to Samuel; 'We are just heart-broken. We look at each other with tears in our eyes. .... Mother is especially cut-up.'[5] Colorado Springs must have seemed like the other side of the world from New York, and the opportunities to see each other would be rare, if not impossible. Their separation became even harder to bear later in the year when Samuel and Louisa had a child, Norman.[6]

1881 saw a significant milestone for the family when daughter Hattie married a New Yorker, Joseph Eastman, at the Church of the Messiah on June 23. Naturally, her father Robert presided, and the reception was held at the Collyers' new home at 137 East 39th Street - sometime in the past year they had moved next door![7] The presents included an unusual gift from Mrs. Collyer, 'a

---

[2] Louisa Collyer was born on January 20,1873, Rebecca died on November 18, 1876.

[3] 'Robert Collyer. Revisiting his old home'. *Chicago Tribune,* Dec 6, 1879. p.6.

[4] The Hosmers lived near the Collyers' old house, at 470 North La Salle St.

[5] Letter written on April 1, 1880. Holmes, *Life and Letters,* 2: 237.

[6] Norman was born October 24, 1880 in Colorado Springs. The name harks back to the maiden name of Robert Collyer's mother. Norman was to be the only male grandchild with the surname 'Collyer'.

[7] In the Federal Census of June 1880, the Collyer family lived at 139 East 39th Street. Robert is fifty-six years old while Ann's age is recorded as fifty-five, but this is an error - she is two years older; Hattie is twenty, Annie is eighteen and Robert is seventeen

set of her husband's published works - four volumes in handsome bindings .... their titles printed in gold letters on the backs of the books.'[8] Of rather more utility was a set of silver tea-spoons designed and presented by Miss Lucretia Mott.[9]

The Church of the Messiah, New York, c.1880. (from Holmes, 1917)

years old. Two domestic servants, Josephine and Christine Anderson, make up the household.

[8] *'Life that now is', 'Nature and Life', 'The Man in Earnest'* and *'The Simple Truth'.*

[9] 'Weddings last night'. *New York Times,* June 24, 1881.

In April 1882, the *Chicago Tribune* gave prominent coverage to complaints received from Collyer's church in New York. Under a sub-heading; '*Withering of the Roses strewn in the Good Old Preacher's Path*', the article, submitted by an anonymous member of the Messiah church, raised several problems that had arisen with Collyer's ministry and concluded that he was not worth the annual stipend of $7500 which the Trustees had recently awarded him.[10] While the complaints could not be taken as representative of Collyer's congregation, the prominence given by the Chicago newspaper warranted a strong rebuttal. It was duly delivered and one week later the paper published a letter from the Trustees of the Church of the Messiah refuting all the complaints in unambiguous terms.[11] When Collyer was asked by a reporter in New York if he would accept a call back to Unity; 'if you had received one'. He replied; "No; the work I am doing in my church here is such that I wouldn't possibly leave it even if I thought it would be of advantage to my old church to do so."[7] All this goes to support the old adage that there's no row like a church row.

After this episode of internecine strife, any disputes, such as they were, did not reach the columns of the newspapers. Indeed, the outlook for Collyer's church work was strongly positive; three quarters of the congregation had joined since Collyer's arrival, his services were well attended by members and visitors, and the finances were strong. His appointment had been hugely successful, and it was hoped that he would be given many years more to complete the work he has begun.

In the summer of 1883 Collyer took the first trans-Atlantic trip of his time in New York. On this occasion he confined his travels to England. He sailed on June 30 in the *Furnessia,* which for the first nine months after its maiden voyage in 1881 was the largest liner in service on the North Atlantic. He returned to New York on the elegant *City of Rome,* on September 13. In a letter to an unidentified Boston friend, he says of this trip; 'I had a delightful journey, wandered round and round by moor and dale to my heart's content. ... Found hosts of friends of my own age, and wondered how they could look so very old but did not say so, and saw the same wonder in their eyes about my looks but they did not say so, for we were all on our guard. Drank tea and chatted by bright cottage fires, found the burdens the poor have to bear far

[10] 'News from New York. The Voice of the Kicker Echoing in Robert Collyer's Church'. *Chicago Tribune,* April 2, 1882.

[11] 'Robert Collyer: The Trustees of the Church of the Messiah Absolutely Deny the Correctness of Certain Recent Statements Regarding Him'. *Chicago Tribune,* April 9, 1882.

lighter than they were fifty years ago, and thanked God for that, and for the brighter and better life that is slowly stealing over my good old England. Preached and lectured where I happened to be. Preached indeed every Sunday but one, when I went to the old Methodist meeting-house among the moors;[12] they invited me to preach there also, but I said, 'No it will get you into trouble with the Methodist Conference.' And then they said, `We will risk the Conference if you will take the service.' Still, I had the grace to hear the good fellow, a working mason, I think, who had walked ever so many miles with a sweet little sermon in his heart, and was not sorry that I did not preach that day.'

Further details of his trip were contained in a letter to his old friend from Addingham preaching days, Rev. Flesher Bland. Collyer writes; 'I had ever such a pleasant visit to the old home... Preached three times in London, twice in Leeds, twice in Birmingham, once at King's Ride in Berkshire, and in Liverpool the night before we sailed.[13] Lectured and preached in Ilkley, lectured in Skipton and Burnsall, and so got through a good deal of work... Took the Chair at the annual excursion of the Yorkshire Archeological Society and made the address.[14] Dined with John Bright[15], breakfasted with Forster[16], and saw a sight of nice good folk in London... I did no end of wandering round in pleasant lanes—got my very fill of it all, so that I should not fret if I never went again. You have no idea how I drank it all in and was satisfied as never before. The sun lay on the hills and filled the valleys, and the storms swept over them, the heather came out as I watched it, and I sat by lots of old friends far and wide and talked of the old times. . . . They wanted to know if I would come

---

[12] In the hamlet of Addingham Moorside.

[13] On Sunday September 2, 1883, Collyer delivered two sermons at the Newhall Hill Church in Birmingham and engaged Miss Marie Beauclerc to transcribe and edit them for publication. Beauclerc was the first woman newspaper reporter in England, the first teacher of shorthand in Birmingham and the first woman teacher at a boys' public school (Rugby).

[14] Yorkshire Archaeological and Topographical Association. Excursion to Hedon and Patrington. Wednesday August 29, 1883. *Programme and Arrangements.* Printed by Robert White, Park Street, Worksop. 1883.

[15] John Bright, a reforming Parliamentarian, was widely recognized in the U.K. as the foremost orator of his day.

[16] W. E. Forster M.P., owned a textile mill in Burley-in-Wharfedale, the next village to Ilkley, and was a pioneering educational reformer. The meetings with Forster and Bright probably took place in London.

back and settle in London, and I said, Nooooo! So I am home again and full of content. Love this new world better than ever."[17]

His contentment took a bitter blow in 1886 when his beloved daughter Annie died.[18] Her death was the first loss of a close family member since Collyer's mother died. They were grief stricken. Annie had always been a delicate child, pale and thin, and always close to her father's heart. Now he was heart-broken, and he never fully recovered. She was buried in Woodlawn Cemetery; "It is a lovely bit of land with a gentle slope and looks westward ... We shall be laid, please God on her right and left… Mother will go this summer to Chicago ... and I may go to England and Switzerland. It will help me to get well again, perhaps, for the springs of life have been badly tried, and the old hurt I got at the Great Fire of '71, turns up in the old shape of not being quite myself."[19]

On June 29, Collyer sailed on the White Star liner *Germanic* for his fifth trip to Europe. He began with an extended stay on the Continent visiting Belgium, Holland, Prussia, Switzerland and Austria. Arriving in England in early August, he visited friends in London and Exeter before venturing North. He was staying with an old friend in Surrey when his host informed him that Squire Ellis, a neighbor and a good Unitarian, had invited them over for afternoon tea; "He is far on in years and lives in a fine old Manor House. You will like to see where, as tradition runs, Queen Elizabeth stayed once overnight." Collyer told him that he would be glad to go. As they sat on the lawn taking tea, the host turned to Collyer and said; "I have been told, sir, by your friend that you emigrated from Yorkshire to the United States. My family came south from Yorkshire many years ago where my father was partner in a linen factory. The firm was Colbeck and Ellis: the factory was in Fewston. You may have heard of the place." "Yes," Collyer answered. "I worked in that factory, sir, seven years in my boyhood. My father was the smith there and worked in the factory, boy and man, thirty-two years. He was brought down from London and was bound to your father and Mr. Colbeck, I think it was in 1807." So, there they sat sipping tea together, the sons of master and apprentice, after eighty years.[20]

---

[17] Holmes, *Life and Letters,* 2: 245.

[18] Annie Kennicutt Collyer died on February 10, 1886, aged 25.

[19] Letter to Flesher Bland, April 29, 1886. Holmes, *Life and Letters,* 2: 253.

[20] Collyer, *Some Memories.* 3.

Collyer arrived in Ilkley on August 19 and stayed in Mrs. Hainsworth's apartments in West Parade, and in neighboring Middleton. He made a 'flying visit' to York, and gave his 'Clear Grit' talk in Otley on behalf of the local Ladies Sick Society. Most of his time, however, was spent in the company of old friends in and around Ilkley. A poignant moment was his visit to the site of his father's old smithy in the ruins of Colbeck and Ellis's West House mill at Blubberhouses, where he picked up a piece of cinder from the now overgrown slag heap as a souvenir. The garden of a mansion, Skaife Hall, now replaced the site of the Collyer family's' tiny cottage. The owner of the mansion, William Johnson Galloway, gave Collyer a tour of the garden where he sought out a spring which, unbeknown to Mr. Galloway, 'gurgled down in the dark' and as a child was Collyer's very own 'healing waters'.[21]

Scaife Hall, Blubberhouses, home of William Johnson Galloway M.P. (Author's collection)

Collyer left Ilkley on September 8 and had a couple of days in Leeds staying with his sister and husband in Hunslet. Leaving for Liverpool on Saturday 11, he preached at the ancient Toxteth Park Chapel the next day and sailed for home on Thursday 16, feeling refreshed and less burdened by his 'great grief'.

[21] 'Healing Waters' in *Where the Light Dwelleth* (1908), Philip Green, 5 Essex Street, Strand, London.

Writing to his daughter Emma he declared that; 'he was thinking of our darling more and more as a radiant and blessed spirit..... It was terrible and quite heart breaking while my heart was buried with her in the grave, and people say my hair has grown quite white.'[22]

By 1887, Collyer was recognized as the foremost Unitarian minister in New York and had also achieved prominence in the cultural and literary life of the city. Some measure of his status as a leading citizen is indicated by an invitation extended to him by Mrs. Frances Cleveland, wife of President Grover Cleveland. A message from the White House was delivered to Collyer's home asking him to accompany the First Lady to Bridgeport in Connecticut where she was to open the Seaside Institute. The building had been erected as an act of social betterment by the Warner brothers, two doctors whose patent corset factory across the road employed around 1,200 women, mostly immigrants. The brothers' objective was to provide an educational and recreational amenity where their workers could learn English, be taught civics, and become good Americans. Naturally, these were sentiments shared by Mrs. Cleveland. When asked who she would like to accompany her, she responded 'Robert Collyer'. Well, that's how Collyer told the story to Flesher Bland. 'She could have any man, and she said, 'Only Robert Collyer.' Think of that now, and I had never seen her, bless her, and we had such a good time'.[23]

Mrs. Frances Folsom Cleveland c. 1886. (photo from Library of Congress via Wikipedia)

[22] Holmes, *Life and Letters.* 2: 254.

[23] Holmes, 2: 256.

In January 1889, Collyer dispatched the old Fewston bell up to Cornell.[24] The association with Cornell began after the Great Fire and the presentation of the much-vaunted horseshoe took place in June 1872. After the opening of the Sage Chapel in 1875, Collyer went up to Ithaca every springtime to take one of the weekly services. Now he was relying on his brother John to deliver the bell to the University – he would formally inaugurate it on his next springtime visit. But when Spring arrived it brought distress. Collyer's wife suffered a slight stroke affecting her right side. Naturally, this caused great alarm and, although she recovered the use of her hand, they were then living under a shadow.

The shadow darkened over the next few months. Ann Collyer was crippled and weak. When summer came, they hoped a holiday would bring some relief and they headed for Sugar Hill, a village in the White Mountains of New Hampshire. Their time there, however, was saddened by news of the sudden death on August 8 of daughter Emma's husband, Frank Hosmer, at the age of forty-one. The prospect of Emma as a single parent to three young boys weighed heavily on Ann's mind. It was no surprise after returning to New York that Ann deteriorated. Over the next several weeks she slipped into a coma and died on October 21. A tender tribute was read from the Messiah pulpit and a fuller one at the Unity Church, Chicago. Collyer himself was plunged into a 'slough of despond'. With Ann's death he had lost the steadying rock, the anchor-hold on which he could fasten and haul himself up out of the bog of depression. In her absence, he had to summon help from other quarters; through prayer, through the loving support of his daughter Emma and son Robert, and through the compassion of his friends and colleagues, he slowly emerged into a semblance of normality. But he was never his former self. He held a deep-seated sorrow that could be hidden but not forgotten. Writing to Flesher Bland five years later, Collyer's words were still redolent with grief; 'We say my better half ... but we never grasp the full meaning until they are taken while we are left, and then we know it is the poorer half which lags behind tarrying, and limping, lamed ...'[25]

Collyer was back in Bridgeport in April 1891, but unlike his earlier visit with Mrs. Cleveland, this occasion lacked any shred of pleasure; he was in the town's South Congregational Church to lead the funeral tributes to Mr. Phineas

---

[24] 'A Bell for Cornell. Robert Collyer's unique present to the University'. *The New York Times,* February 1, 1889.

[25] Holmes, *Life and Letters,* 2: 261.

T. Barnum, the great showman and benefactor. As one eye-witness reported; 'It was a pathetic picture which met the eyes of the vast throng. The aged preacher, with long white hair hanging loosely on his shoulders, and an expression of keen sorrow in his kindly face, standing in a small pulpit looking down on the remains of his old and cherished friend. The speaker's voice was strong and steady throughout his sermon. Each word of that sad panegyric could be distinctly heard in all parts of the edifice, but in offering up the last prayer, he broke down. The aged preacher made a strong effort to control himself, but his voice finally became husky, and tears streamed down his wrinkled cheeks. The audience was deeply touched by this display of feeling, and many ladies among the congregation joined with the preacher and wept freely.'[26] The congregation did not realize that he was weeping for Ann Collyer, not Phineas Barnum.

[26] Joel Benton, 1891. *Life of Hon. Phineas T. Barnum.* New York: Edgewood Publishing Company. See https://www.questia.com/library/2712656/life-of-hon-phineas-t-barnum

29: Literary Connections

In response to a compelling invitation to go back to the old country, Robert Collyer set sail for Liverpool on July 6, 1892, on the *Teutonic,* accompanied by daughter Hattie, her husband Joseph Eastman and their two older children, Lucy aged nine and Thomas aged seven. The main purpose of the journey was to dedicate a library and free school in the village of Timble, near Otley, the gift of a fellow Yorkshireman and childhood friend, Robinson Gill, a stone merchant who also lived in New York. Mr. Gill formed the sixth member of the party on the *Teutonic* and shared a stateroom with Collyer. By July 15, Mr. Gill was in Otley, meeting John Dickinson of Timble, the man who had designed and built the library. Fortunately, Mr. Gill was well pleased with the library building, which was to be opened on August 2. John Dickinson writes in his diary; 'Opening of the Robinson Library and Free School. Very busy forenoon. The Rev. Robert Collyer, the eminent Unitarian Minister, came about noon and dined at our house. Carriages rolled in and by the time for commencing, 2 o'clock, a very lively scene presented itself. The large room was crowded. Mr. Collyer's address (on the subject 'Books') was a noble and eloquent discourse worthy of any occasion however exalted. Mr. Gill spoke well, all passed off brilliantly. In the evening a variety of entertainment was given. The place again crowded to excess. This has been a great day for Timble and it is to be hoped will lead on to good in many ways.'[1]

A surprising omission from John Dickinson's account was any mention of two American visitors who were in Timble at the request of Robert Collyer.

---

[1] Ronald Harker, *Timble Man: Diaries of a Dalesman* (Nelson, Lancashire: Hendon Publishing, 1988), 81.

Sarah Orne Jewett and Mrs. Annie Fields were close friends of Collyer, so much so, that they referred to him affectionately as 'Brother', or even 'Father', Collyer. The two women had taken a long detour from visits to friends in the south of England to attend the event in Yorkshire. Annie was a widow whose late husband, James Fields, had been one of the foremost book publishers in America. The Fields's had a wide circle of literary friends which included Sarah Orne Jewett, a writer who through her fiction described a New England utopia inhabited by characters who personified life in coastal Maine.[2] Following James Fields's sudden death in 1881, Annie and Sarah became companions who lived and travelled together for much of the year. Sarah shared her time between Annie's home in Boston and her summer house at Manchester-by-the-Sea, and her own home in South Berwick, Maine, where Sarah lived with her spinster sister, Mary. In South Berwick, separate from Annie, but connected by daily letters, Sarah concentrated on her writing, producing a steady stream of short stories for the leading magazines while at the same time progressing her latest novel. As a successful author her stories commanded high fees and her books sold in substantial numbers, providing her with a steady income from royalties. Annie Fields was left financially secure by her late husband's estate, but she also achieved separate distinction as a biographer and poet and devoted much time and energy to charitable work.[3]

It is intriguing to consider how Collyer became a close friend of these two talented, cultured and much younger women – Annie was eleven years, and Sarah was twenty-five years, younger than Collyer. It is likely that Collyer was introduced to Annie Fields, herself a Unitarian, by a friend and close associate in the American Unitarian Association, the Boston minister, James Freeman Clarke. Clarke was a strong supporter of Womens' Rights and worked with Annie on some of her feminist initiatives. During the holiday season, the Clarkes' summer house was close by the Fields's 'Gambrel Cottage' in Manchester-by-the Sea, and the two families became closely connected. While Collyer was visiting Boston he may, in Clarke's company, have attended one of the Saturday afternoon gatherings of literary friends at the Charles Street home of James and Annie Fields. Certainly, he and the Fields's were already friends by the early 1870s. Annie wrote to Collyer after the Fire had destroyed his house, and in most sympathetic terms she declared; '...we are reserving a

---

[2] Sarah Orne Jewett's best-known works are *A White Heron and other stories* (1886); and a novella, *The Country of the Pointed Firs* (1896).

[3] Paula Blanchard, *Sarah Orne Jewett; Her World and her work* (Cambridge MA: Perseus Publishing, 1994), 125-135.

few pleasant little things for your house when you are once more established ... which may recall perhaps the old library and the old friends.[4] I have put aside a bound Mss. of Mr. Emerson and one of Dr. (Oliver Wendell) Holmes, and we have a portrait of Hawthorne, and one or two other things of that nature to make the place look homey.'[5] The gifts indicate the strength of their friendship and their literary connections.

After the deaths of James Fields and Ann Collyer, Robert Collyer became close to both Annie Fields and Sarah Jewett, and he would spend at least one week every summer with them in Boston or Manchester-by-the-sea. Annie Fields continued to entertain an impressive circle of literary greats including Mary Ellen Chase, Harriet Beecher Stowe, Sarah Wyman Whitman, Henry James and John Greenleaf Whittier. No doubt Collyer would meet members of this elite group during his visits to Boston or Manchester. He was also reunited with his former Chicago friend, the historian Alice Baker and her companion, Susan Minot Lane, who in the intervening years had become close friends of Sarah Jewett.[6]

Collyer was no parvenu when it came to literary circles. Many years before, through his visits to Concord to stay with fellow minister and abolitionist, Moncure Conway, he had become acquainted with the writers Henry David Thoreau, Ralph Waldo Emerson, Louisa M. Alcott, James Russell Lowell, William Ellery Channing and Nathaniel Hawthorne.[7] Later, in nearby Cambridge, Collyer was introduced to Mrs. Gaskell's friend Charles Eliot Norton, and to Henry Wadsworth Longfellow. In 1875, Collyer was sent a small Samian-ware pot found in a Romano-British grave in Ilkley; he decided

---

[4] The literary gatherings at the Fields's house were held in the library, 'a room extending the full depth of the house and crammed with bookshelves, pictures hung frame to frame, plaster and marble busts, a piano, and the miscellaneous memorabilia of thirty years of personal literary history', (Blanchard, *Sarah Orne Jewett,* 148).

[5] Holmes, *Life and Letters,* 2: 165.

[6] I have employed the term 'companion' to describe these long-term, co-habiting relationships. While through modern eyes these appear to be lesbian partnerships, such close 'friendships' were viewed differently in the nineteenth century. Given the social and employment difficulties experienced by single women, it was understood that two women could live together for mutual support without the relationship necessarily being a sexual one. Such arrangements were so common in the upper echelons of Boston society that they were termed 'Boston marriages', without this being essentially a confirmation of their lesbian nature.

[7] Moncure D. Conway, 1904. *Autobiography – Memories and Experiences.* (New York: Cassell and Co., 1904), 1: 324.

to give it to Longfellow as a gift and presented it to him at his Cambridge home on his next visit to Boston. Collyer wrote that; 'he was very much pleased. I usually see him when I am East, and we are fast friends.'[8] No doubt Longfellow fellow felt some vague attachment to Ilkley through his remote ancestors.

Robert Collyer (left) and Robinson Gill on the steps of the Timble Free Library on the day of its opening and dedication, August 2, 1892. Author's collection.

After the Timble event, Collyer and his American friends went their separate ways. Robinson Gill went to Liverpool and sailed for New York on August 6. Collyer went south and visited Stonehenge, where he was touched by 'its grandeur and mystery', and Winchester to tour the cathedral and visit the Hospital of St. Cross, a beautiful Medieval almshouse where he joined the poor men living there, 'in a procession 800 years long to claim a mug of beer

[8] Holmes, *Life and Letters*. 2: 192.

and a hunk of bread provided for all hands through all time.'[9] He lunched in Canterbury with the Canon of the Cathedral, William Fremantle, and sat next to a Bishop, which impressed him greatly. He enjoyed a guided tour of the Cathedral with 'the good Canon' who told him its 'splendid story'.[10]

Church Street in Ilkley on a busy Easter Monday (1894). Author's collection.

On August 25, back in Ilkley, Collyer opened the town's first Museum, housed in the former Wesleyan Chapel on Addingham Road.[11] The following Sunday he preached in Ilkley 'to more than could get in', and then, 'stayed with a vicar north of York in whose church porch are curious grooves made where they used to sharpen their arrows before gunpowder came along.' He later told

[9] Holmes, *Life and Letters*. 2: 262.

[10] Holmes, 2: 263.

[11] 'The Historic Relics of Ilkley. Opening of a Museum'. *Yorkshire Post,* August 26, 1892.

Flesher Bland; 'what a good time I did have wandering by hill and dale, I wonder if I shall ever go again…'[12]

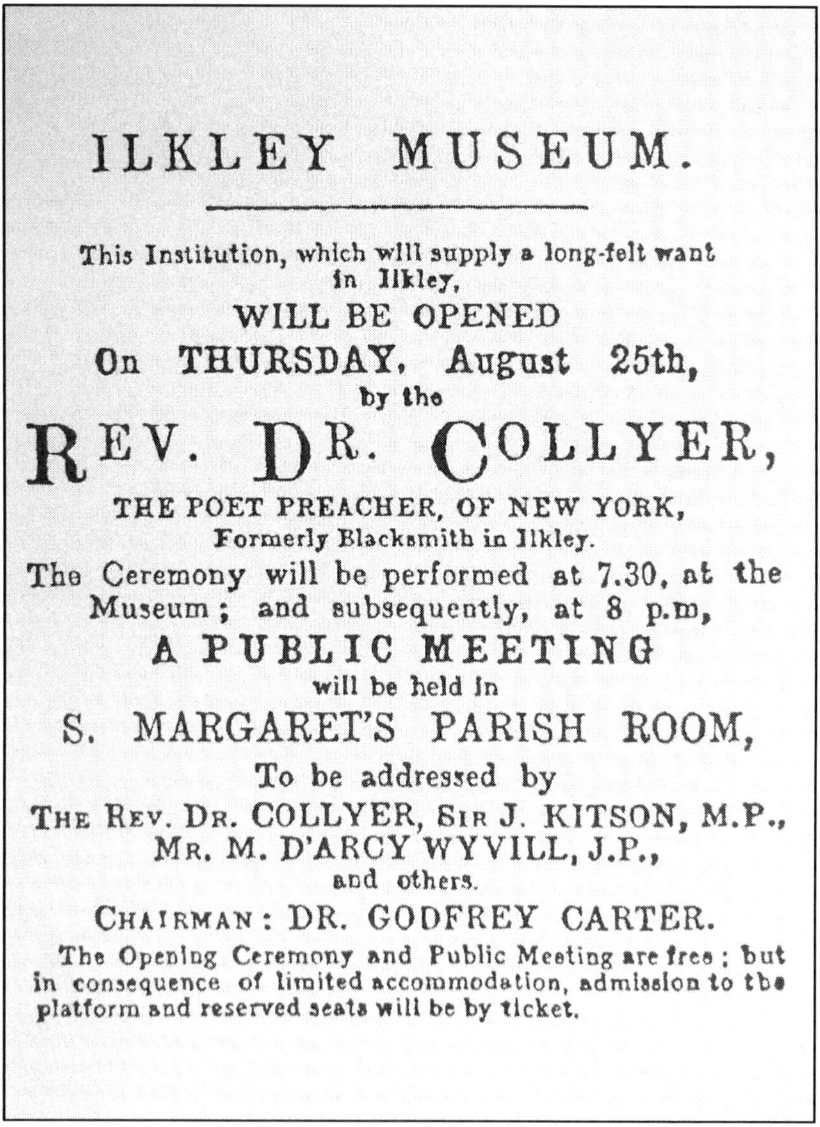

ILKLEY MUSEUM.

This Institution, which will supply a long-felt want in Ilkley,

WILL BE OPENED

On THURSDAY, August 25th,

by the

REV. DR. COLLYER,

THE POET PREACHER, OF NEW YORK,

Formerly Blacksmith in Ilkley.

The Ceremony will be performed at 7.30, at the Museum; and subsequently, at 8 p.m,

A PUBLIC MEETING

will be held in

S. MARGARET'S PARISH ROOM,

To be addressed by

THE REV. DR. COLLYER, SIR J. KITSON, M.P., MR. M. D'ARCY WYVILL, J.P., and others.

CHAIRMAN: DR. GODFREY CARTER.

The Opening Ceremony and Public Meeting are free; but in consequence of limited accommodation, admission to the platform and reserved seats will be by ticket.

[12] Holmes, 2: 263.

30: The Septuagenarian

On December 8, 1893, Collyer celebrated his seventieth birthday. The church gave him a grand reception and presented him with two baskets of roses, each containing seventy blooms, and much besides, including 'articles for use and beauty, and a stack of letters and poems I shall have bound in a volume.'[1]

Collyer appeared to view the reaching of his biblical life-span – three score years and ten, with ominous significance. While seventy was considered 'a good age' in the nineteenth century, Collyer denied to himself that he was in good health; he bemoaned his lack of drive and energy. Every annual report to the church in the ensuing years contained an *apologia* regretting that he had not done more. He explained that he was finding it difficult to sustain both his preaching commitments and pastoral work. Indeed, he began to make the case for an assistant to share the load. The plea, however, fell on deaf ears. The Trustees were content with the *status quo* and confident in Collyer's ability to serve the church to the full satisfaction of the congregation.

Despite the reluctance of the Trustees to pursue an assistant post, Collyer surveyed the field of younger pastors and began to take soundings as to their availability. In the summer of 1896, he made a strong recommendation to the Trustees which on this occasion bore fruit. The man Collyer wanted was a long-standing acquaintance, Rev. Minot J. Savage, who was persuaded out of his church in Boston to come and work at the Church of the Messiah.[2]

---

1 *Life and Letters*, 2: 263-5.

2 Minot Judson Savage (1841-1918) was pastor at the Church of the Unity in Boston, a director of the American Unitarian Association, and an author of religious books and

Thereafter, matters improved greatly; Dr Savage took on the bulk of the preaching and parish work with Collyer preaching just once a month. He had numerous invitations to preach at other churches, and initially he accepted most of them, but with the passage of time he became less inclined to travel hither and thither, even if there was a small pot of gold at the end of the journey. A few places remained in his annual schedule, however, and he was pleased to go to All Souls Church in Washington D.C., to John White Chadwick's church in Brooklyn, and without fail, at apple-blossom time, to the University at Ithaca.[3]

Robert Collyer in 1893 taken on a visit to Rowayton, Conn. (photo from Holmes, 1917)

Collyer had moved to an apartment in the Strathmore building (on the N.E. corner of Broadway and Fifty-second Street) not long before his wife died, and had rented additional space for a study and library in the Holland Building, down Broadway and opposite the Metropolitan Opera House. The Strathmore apartment was comfortable and quiet, the days of unlimited hospitality were long gone. After Ann Collyer's death in 1889, the housekeeping duties were

works on psychical research. He was widely recognized in Unitarian circles as an accomplished preacher.

[3] Holmes, *Life and Letters,* 2: 280-1.

taken over by Robert Collyer's widowed sister, Martha Merritt. Six years later, 'Aunt Martha' died 'lamented by all who knew her', but her duties were soon taken over by one of Martha's daughters, Bertha Ann, who came over from England with her husband, John Edward Roberts, to live in Manhattan with her uncle, and her cousin 'Rob', who continued to live in the family home.

Mornings were spent in the Holland Building where Collyer would write his letters, read a newspaper or magazine, revise the text of an old sermon or lecture, or take down a book from one of the floor-to-ceiling bookshelves that lined three walls of the study, and read and reflect. He might then stroll to his club, the Century in West 43rd Street, have a light lunch and get a cab back to the Strathmore. Afternoons were spent leisurely at home, or if the weather was favorable, visit one of his friends in the parish.

In the summer of 1897, Collyer took a vacation in Canada and spent almost a week with his old friend, Flesher Bland, in Smith's Falls, Ontario. He returned to Boston and went for a week's stay in West Townsend, followed by a week at Annie's house at Manchester-by-the-sea.[4] By this time, 'Collyer had become the last of Sarah and Annie's grand old men, succeeding Whittier and Holmes as a particular kind of male presence in their lives — elderly, solitary, vulnerable, and witty, part father and part brother, someone who seemed to need female attention and did not object to a little pampering.'[5] Thus, suitably pampered, he went over to Chicago to stay with his daughter Hattie and preached on four Sundays at his old church. This was a sad affair as the number in the Unity congregation had steeply declined and those remaining were 'much cast down'.[6]

Back in New York, he continued the quiet life. The church prospered and the Rev. Savage, with preaching duties supplemented by Collyer, continued to attract a good attendance. Notwithstanding his earlier reticence about foreign travel, on April 16, 1898, Collyer sailed to Naples on the North German Lloyd Steamship *Aller* to begin an extended European holiday. As in 1892, his proposed visit to Yorkshire was carefully coordinated with the itinerary of his friends, Sarah Orne Jewett and Annie Fields, who were travelling in France and

[4] Holmes, 2: 285

[5] Paula Blanchard, *Sarah Orne Jewett; Her World and her Work,* (Cambridge MA: Perseus Publishing, 1994), 310. It is possible that an added dimension to Sarah Orne Jewell's relationship with Collyer was an affinity with Yorkshiremen; an ancestor in the male line, Maximilian Jewett (1607-1684) was born in Bradford, Yorkshire, and was an early settler in Rowley, Essex County, Massachusetts (via www.ancestry.com).

[6] Letter to Annie Fields, November 9, 1897. Holmes, 2: 286.

England with Sarah's sister, Mary, and her nephew, Theodore.[7] The main purpose of Collyer's trip was to give the address at a memorial service for Robinson Gill at Timble in mid-August, and it was at that point that he would join up with the Jewett party. Before then, he would travel and explore.

As it happened, two fellow passengers on the *Aller,* Louisa Dresel and Sarah Clarke, were members of the same group of women writers and artists as Jewett. On discovering that her two friends had sailed on the same ship as Collyer, Sarah Jewett wrote to Miss Dresel; 'I fancied you and Miss Clarke having a delightful time with him.'[8] Alas, no introductions were made and it appears that both parties travelled all the way to Naples unaware of each other's presence on board.

For the journey from Naples to Paris, Collyer retained the services of a courier, Max, who; 'took all possible care of me. He told no end of yarns about my high dignity in the church, so that notes would come addressed to The Very Reverend Bishop, etc., though I warned him this was not my title, but being himself a Catholic, when Archbishop Keane came to see me in Rome and held out both hands in welcome and we sat down for a long chat in the garden, it was no use assuring Max I was not a bishop. ... We took the Simplon Pass at Domodossola. It was the journey of a life-time. The snow when we struck the summits of the Pass was three feet on the level and six to ten in the drifts, but it was a glorious day full of sunshine which lay golden on the vast white snow-clad mountains, white with a glory I shall never see again. There were relays of men cutting a road through the drifts, so that we were only hindered by the snow-slides. These came down twice, and we missed one which would have buried us by only five minutes, which was another mercy, but (we) would have been dug out, so Max said. ... I would not have gone over if I had foreseen what I *hind* see now, but am ever so glad I did it.'[9]

Collyer continued; 'I came to London from Paris where my brother (Thomas) and son (Robert) came to meet me from Angers, and we spent four

---

7 Theodore was the son of Sarah's younger sister, Carrie (Caroline), and her husband, Ned (Edwin) Eastman. Unfortunately, Ned died of peritonitis at the age of forty-two in March 1892, and Carrie died following surgery for an abdominal abscess in April 1897, leaving Theodore an orphan at the age of sixteen. (Blanchard, *Sarah Orne Jewett,* 305).

8 *The Correspondence of Sarah Orne Jewett, Letter 32.* The letter to Louisa Dresel (May 16, 1898) confirms that she was on the same crossing as Collyer but there is no documentary evidence that they met. www.public.coe.edu/~theller/soj/let/dresel.html

9 Holmes: *Life and Letters,* 2: 289-294.

days all together there in very pleasant fashion.' In London he stayed 'in marble halls' with Sir Edwin and Lady Lawrence while he fulfilled several engagements. On June 5 he took the communion service for Rev. Brooke Herford at Rosslyn Hill Church in Hampstead, and in the evening at the recently erected Highgate Hill Church. On the next Sunday he preached at the Essex Street Church after which service; 'I shall have kept my promise to the churches'.[9] He also accumulated sufficient fees to cover much of his travel expenses.

With these commitments behind him, he took the train to Leeds, eager to visit his sister, Maria[10]. Her house stood; 'on the rise of Beeston Hill, with Leeds below full of smoke and grime, but dear old Leeds all the same, where my folks came to live fifty-nine years ago. My father's dust lies in the old church yard, my mother's in the pretty cemetery on the hill. There was no cemetery when my father was buried 30 years before my mother died. Both names are on the stone.'[9]

From Leeds he had an excursion to Otley where he met John Dickinson and had a walk around the town prior to giving his 'Robert Burns' talk in the Mechanics Institute in the evening. Dickinson noted that; 'He called to see his old shop mate Joe Mason who worked with him sixty years ago in the blacksmiths shop in Ilkley. It was very pleasant to hear them talk in the old broad dialect, and Collyer so tender and sympathetic. At parting he said, "Thou'll want a bit o'beef, Joe, this Feeast", and gave him a sovereign.'[11] Collyer also went over to Blubberhouses, stayed with Sam Pullan at Bottom Farm and preached at Hardisty Hill Methodist Church the next day. He then went over to Ilkley and preached at Addingham, staying afterwards with Mr. and Mrs. Gill, 'and drank in the glory of the land from that bench on the rock in the door yard, and drank tea—a good old-fashioned Yorkshire 'drink-in'.'[9]

Meanwhile after a long sojourn in France, Annie Fields, Sarah Orne Jewett, Mary Jewett and Theodore Eastman, crossed the Channel and visited Cambridge together. After seeing the sights, Annie and Sarah left the others and headed by train to Ilkley, a slow 170 miles journey. They arrived late on Tuesday evening, August 16, feeling hot and tired, and retired to the Crescent Hotel where thanks to the fresh, cool northern air, they passed a comfortable night.

---

[10] Maria and John Shires were still living in Greenmount Street, Hunslet.

[11] Ed. by Ronald Harker, *Timble Man: Diaries of a Dalesman* (1988). Hendon Publishing Co., Nelson, Lancashire. p.96.

Annie Field continues the narrative in the diary she kept of the 1898 trip.[12] 'Started directly after luncheon for Timble where dear Robert Collyer was to speak about Robinson Gill who gave the library we helped to dedicate (as it were!) six years ago. It is a long drive from Ilkley, perhaps ten miles, up & up, out of the Wharfedale valley. ... past Denton and up to the great moor. In spite of the heat of the day there was an exquisite breeze blowing here; the heather was purpling all about us and the freshness of everything revived us wonderfully. There are few scenes more impressive than that of those wide moors, silent, dark even in sunshine with their furry cover, soft, thick, as if to keep the bones of the old earth warm. As far as eye can reach they rise and rise and swell, not into mountain heights of peaks but with the soft roll of a wide high sea. We kept on for a long distance descending at last into the little village of Timble.'

'The service had begun, for the day was waning and the driver and Theodore had walked up several hills, and we all walked down one. However, we were in season for the address (*by Collyer*) and very good and interesting it was, telling the people how the sterling honesty and determination of the man had made him what he became, a power in the world. He said the mark of Robinson Gill on his work was sufficient. Two years before his death[13] he was deceived by some wicked men for whom he signed notes and lost a great deal of money. This trouble and the greater sorrow of the death of a grown son, caused his death probably at the last. He did not tell the tale in a sad way, but in a noble encouraging tender fashion which the people drank in as if it were the water of life. There were some tears but the whole was bright and loving and strong and good for every one of us.'

Ilkley, Thursday August 18; 'Brother Robert (*Collyer*) came in the afternoon and we walked out with him to see the old monuments of the town. He stopped to see a large number of persons, or they stopped him by the way. At the place where the old castle stood he said to a woman "they have taken away the few stones of the old wall which used to be just here."[14] "I don't know she said but there is a bit of wall here below which you can see." We followed her a bit down the slope while she found it for us. It enabled us to understand the Roman

---

[12] Annie Fields (1898) *Diary of a Trip to France.* http://www.public.coe.edu/~theller/fields/Diary-1898.html

[13] In Brooklyn on August 16, 1897

[14] The 'Old Castle' was the local name for the Manor House built on the site of the Roman fort. There were several remnants of the wall around the fort when Collyer lived in Ilkley.

position pretty well & as we stood there for the sake of friendliness to the woman Robert Collyer said "You're not as old as I and I suppose you do not remember where the other stones were which seem to have disappeared. "Naw," she said "thank heaven, I'm not as old as you are by a long way and I don't know anything about them." — When the people here are brutal they are very brutal. I was dismayed — but he took it very sweetly and I could not help thinking that she looked more out of repair than he did by far, with poor teeth and far less strength!"

'Friday August 19 : Drove with Brother Robert to The Strid where we stopped, ran down to the river's edge which was quiet and free from visitors and beautiful as the warm sweet day could make it although the water was low.[15] There we sat while he took our Wordsworth at our request and read the story (of the Strid) so simply & beautifully…[16] Then we went on to the village of Burnsall far up Wharfedale and surrounded by the moors where we took luncheon with Mr. Bland who has a small Inn.[17] Brother Robert had sent word we were coming. They were thrown into great excitement by the news and when we arrived hungry as hounds there was not the smallest sign of anything to eat. …The practical business falls much upon his poor overworked wife and this I think he does not understand. "There's one thing I do in the house." he said. "More than anyone else, I take all that kind of labor out of their hands, that is the talking."

'He carried us to see the little church with the Saxon font and other very curious monuments but on the way he began to recite his own verses. Brother Robert had warned us of this weakness, because the verses though very good in feeling were not of especial value. …we were tired and hungry, and

---

[15] A narrowing in the River Wharfe with rapids and deep undercutting of the stone sides.

[16] "The Founding of Bolton Priory, A Tradition" (1807) by the poet, William Wordsworth (1770- 1850). The poem tells of an inconsolable mother (Lady Alice de Romilly) whose son had drowned in the Strid. In her sorrow she gave the land for the building of Bolton Priory and discovered her grief was eased thereby.

[17] John Atkinson Bland owned the 'Manor House Private Hotel' in Burnsall. Bland was a literary enthusiast and loved to indulge in descriptive writing and composing poetry. He was often described, mainly by himself, as 'The Wharfedale Poet' or 'The Wordsworth of Wharfedale'. It is said that in later years he would frequently rest against a stone gatepost and recite poetry to unsuspecting pedestrians on the riverside path. Eric Lodge, *A Wharfedale Village: A History of Burnsall* (Otley, Yorkshire: Smith Settle, 1994), 190.

Theodore began dancing about, as a boy will — "You're not listening" he said, I will begin again!" Finally, he proposed to take us a walk on the moors where we could sit down and hear more. "I won't go a step" said Brother Robert "till we've had luncheon!" So we marched back to the house and it was two o'clock before the feast was spread. They had sent to Skipton for mutton! when their own bacon and eggs and simple things they used themselves would have answered well enough.'

Bolton Abbey (Priory) as Collyer and his guests would have seen it in 1898. (Author's collection)

'We took a different road home, past Appletreewick, and altogether on the other side of the river over what seemed to me a much easier road than the other one of the morning. It was a lovely afternoon as we drove back past Bolton Abbey where we stopped. It was showering but with the gold sunlight coming quickly out upon the shining grass and old cedars — What a wonder of beauty the place seemed! Like all things and places where Nature plays the chief part it is impossible for the mind of man to conceive and to remember the full loveliness of it. She is always more beautiful than one believes real. This afternoon, the sun and shadow, the sound of the river around the stepping stones, the noble arches of the ruin, the soft turf in the enclosures, the entrancing pictures framed in by the architecture at every turn, all these things were as fresh as if we had never seen them before. I think the presence of the old Cistercian monks in their white gowns did not seem far away. One could have walked out from behind one of the arches without surprising me.'

'We reached Ilkley at last before sundown just tired enough to be glad to rest. We found a rather rude note from Ayscough Fawkes of Farnley Hall declining to show his Turner pictures.'[18]

'Saturday — dear Brother Robert left us to return to Leeds. We accompanied him half-way in order to see Ripon (*Cathedral)* and Fountains Abbey which we consider more than a fair exchange for Farnley Hall, which we none of us regretted for an instant.'[19]

Collyer returned to his sister's house in Leeds, but his excursions were not finished. At the end of August, he journeyed up the Aire valley to the village of Bradley (between Keighley and Skipton) where he once again lectured on 'Burns' to a large audience in the Wesleyan Chapel.[20] He gave the lecture as a favor for Mr. Thomas Smith, a fellow member of the Young Men's Reading Group in Ilkley. Collyer was best-man at his wedding in 1850 – a long-standing friendship sustained by regular correspondence.

---

[18] Ayscough Fawkes (1831-1899), grandson of Walter Fawkes (1769-1825) of Farnley Hall (near Otley), a Yorkshire landowner, writer and Member of Parliament. Walter Fawkes befriended British painter, J. M. W. Turner (1775-1851) and became owner of a large collection of his work.

[19] They would have travelled by the North Eastern Railway from Ilkley to Leeds via Otley; the Jewett party leaving the Leeds train at Arthington junction where they would transfer to a main line train to Ripon.

[20] 'Bradley notices', *West Yorkshire Pioneer and East Lancashire News,* September 2, 1898.

Of more significance, Collyer preached at the Wesleyan Church in Ilkley at the invitation of Rev. Joseph Dawson; 'to a noble audience which filled the church and all the chairs and benches they could pile in. ... Nothing in all the five months (of this vacation) has given me greater delight than this, that the old mother church should take me in her arms and give me a good hug. It was just what I longed for, but did not hope for, so here I am like the patriarch, old and satisfied.'[21]

Wesleyan Church, Wells Road, Ilkley, opened in 1869. This church replaced an earlier Methodist chapel in the Addingham Road that Collyer attended as a young man (Author's collection).

[21] Holmes, *Life and Letters,* 2: 293.

31: Degrees of Retirement

Collyer returned to New York in mid-September 1898 to find the Church of the Messiah in crisis. The health of the Pastor, Minot Savage, had collapsed and he was incapable of church work. Collyer had to fill the breach. While some Sunday services were taken by visiting preachers, the majority had to be taken by Collyer himself. It was not just Sunday services, however, there were funerals, weddings, baptisms, church meetings and the continuing pastoral duties – he was back to full-time work.

In January 1899, the church officers were compelled to make 'locum' arrangements. Collyer suffered a severe bout of the 'grippe', — influenza, and was confined to the house, mainly to his bed, for over two weeks.[1] He referred to this as 'the longest imprisonment of my life', but he was not given any further respite and he returned to his former onerous workload. This situation continued through the summer, but Rev. Savage was gradually improving and by October he was able to take back his full share of the work. Collyer returned to preaching on one in four Sundays, but the Sunday School kept him busy every week. He seemed to relish 'busy-ness', however, and began to think less, instead of more, about his advancing age and his declining powers.

Christmas celebrations and New Year resolutions came – and went, then in February 1900, disaster struck their home in the Strathmore - they were re-visited by fire. Collyer describes it in a letter to his Timble friend, John Dickinson; 'The fire started on the floor below us and shot up. We had just time to get out, and by good fortune it was six in the evening. We went down by an iron stair at the rear of the great building. They got the water tower up to our

[1] Holmes, *Life and Letters,* 2: 295.

level – eight stories, and poured tons of water into our pretty and perfect home so that we were more drowned than burnt. It was a heavy frost and everything was sealed up in ice for some days. Everything of value was removed finally and we found more than we hoped for. The plenishing *(furniture)* has gone to the cabinet maker, the pictures to the restorer, and the damaged books have gone to the binders, and we are in a furnished apartment for $35 per month until we can make another nest. The three paintings of our Washburn Valley and the watercolor of the old factory are only damaged in their frames. The old family clock, with the inscription on the face, 'Francis Shaw. Padside', came back from the clock-man yesterday as good as new, and is ticking away at a great rate in our new quarters.[2] We forgot the canary, to our sore grief, but my son *(Robert)* and nephew *(John Roberts)* climbed up in the night to bring back his tiny remains. He was still alive – just alive. They gave him drops of whisky on sugar, and he came back to life, and is now singing new songs of deliverance all day long. He is a great pet of the household and just swears if any stranger sits down in my chair, until the said stranger clears out. We got the whole insurance, and think this will just about cover the loss.'[3]

There was no insurance against loss of confidence, however. Collyer was badly shaken by this episode; the suppressed horror of seeing his house, and his church, destroyed almost 30 years ago, came to the fore. It was some time before he rallied – even as late as June 14, he writes to a friend; 'I am not quite my old self yet.'[4] Indeed, the family never returned to the Strathmore; in October they removed to an apartment in the Van Corlear building at 201 West 55th Street.

In November 1900, Collyer's letters strike a much happier note; his son Robert, who at the age of thirty eight was still living at home, announced his engagement to Gertrude Savage, the thirty four years old daughter of Collyer's fellow minister at the Messiah church. They married at the historic, and beautiful, Unitarian church in Billerica, Massachusetts, on July 17, 1902, and honeymooned in Nova Scotia.[5] Before the year was out, Robert and Gertrude

---

[2] Padside is a hamlet at the head of Washburndale.

[3] Dr. Collyer burnt out of home. *The Wharfedale and Airedale Observer,* April 26, 1901.

[4] Holmes, *Life and Letters,* 2: 301-310.

[5] The town is named for Billericay in Middlesex, England. Rev. Ralph Waldo Emerson occasionally preached at the church in Billerica when he was minister at the Second Unitarian Church in Boston (1829 – 1832). When the latter church closed after uniting with the First Church in Boston in 1844, the Billerica congregation bought the redundant pulpit, which still graces their church today.

returned to Collyer's household, Gertrude taking the place of Martha Roberts as housekeeper, an arrangement much to Collyer's liking. Indeed, he was more than grateful for their love and support when, a year later, on September 23, 1903, he suffered another death in the family. His daughter, Harriet ('Hattie') Eastman, died unexpectedly at the age of 45 and Collyer was once again plunged into the depths of loss and grief.[4]

In December 1903, Collyer's mood lifted with the celebrations surrounding his eightieth birthday. With this milestone, however, he felt there were now explicit grounds for the church to give him full retirement; instead they elected him 'Pastor Emeritus' and kept him on his present salary 'as long as he remains with us'.[4] This reads very much like a continuing attachment, not a retirement, and three years later his 'attachment' became tangible.

Collyer studies a music score. A photograph taken about 1905, from Holmes (1917).

In February 1906, Dr. Savage had a complete breakdown and relinquished his post. Without any warning, the eighty-three years old Pastor Emeritus had to take over the reins once again. On this occasion, however, Collyer was preaching to a much-diminished congregation; Dr. Savage's resignation led to the departure of most of the congregation that had joined the Messiah church over the ten years of his ministry. Collyer was faced with the demoralizing prospect of preaching to a small rump of attenders, some of whom had been with the old patriarch since the halcyon days of twenty years before. The church elders were forced to face the reality of a sparsely attended church and the ensuing dire financial consequences; they advertised for a new Pastor. Accordingly, in December 1906 the society unanimously agreed to offer the vacant pulpit to Rev. John Haynes Holmes, a man who restored viability to the church and ultimately became Robert Collyer's biographer.

The Rev. Holmes took over in February 1907 and by the summer Collyer was back in England for what would inevitably be his final visit. He outlined in a letter to his son Samuel why he felt compelled to go; 'I had only dreamed that I might go over once more, but they are building a free library there for which Andrew Carnegie gave them three thousand pounds, and they want me to open it. I cannot say them nay – and they have employed an artist to make two medallions in bronze they will set up in the library, life size one of Andrew and the other of meself, so you will see I must go. The Court of the Victoria University of Leeds are also head-on to bestow on me the degree of Lit.D., which same is a great honor, and ask me to be present to receive it. So that is another magnet to draw me over the sea. And the other is, I want to see my sister, your Aunt Maria, once more, who is now a widow. This began to pull at my heart when her husband died two years ago.'[6]

Accompanied by Martha Roberts, his niece, Collyer set sail from Boston on the *Saxonia* on August 7, arriving in Liverpool nine days later. They immediately travelled to his sister's house in Leeds which was to be their base for the entire visit. After a week of rest and recuperation, Collyer and his niece went to Otley to meet up with John Dickinson who wrote in his diary; 'August 23. Went up to station to meet Dr. Collyer and his niece Miss *(sic)* Roberts. Hearty greetings. I had acquainted several people of the town of Dr. Collyer's visit and there was quite a reception in the Market place. Dr Collyer came to our house to dinner *(lunch)* and stayed to tea. He is still bright and genial as

---

[6] Holmes, *Life and Letters,* 2: 317.

ever and has an inexhaustible fund of anecdote. To think that once he was a poor boy at Blubberhouse factory working over seventy hours per week.'[7]

Collyer at home in 1906 (Author's collection).

Collyer preached in Chester on September 1, in Birmingham on September 8, and the following Saturday afternoon, accompanied by his sister and niece, Collyer attended a magnificent garden party hosted, in his honor, by Lord Airedale at Gledhow Hall, in Leeds.[8] He preached at Mill Hill Chapel in Leeds

[7] Ronald Harker, *Timble Man: Diaries of a Dalesman* (Nelson, Lancashire: Hendon Publishing Co., 1988), 139-140.

[8] 'Leeds Unitarians and Dr. Collyer'. *Yorkshire Post,* Monday Sept 16, 1907.

on September 15. The theme of his sermon was 'Looking towards sunset' which included the enigmatic statement; 'And in looking into my own life, I can see where I have missed my way and want to try again. I am only a learner, I still want to learn, and turn my lesson to some noble use, so what can this incompleteness mean which haunts me but the intimation of completeness?' He preached the same sermon at the Essex Street Chapel in London the next Sunday (September 22). Apparently, advanced age was no handicap to Collyer's peripatetic preaching activities.

The following Thursday he was in his smartest suit and bow-tie for the degree ceremony at Leeds University. Dressed in scholar's robes, he was led in procession by the Chancellor, Vice-Chancellor, and members of the University Court and Council dressed in their colorful academic gowns. The Dean of the Faculty of Arts, Professor Phillips, presented Rev. Collyer to the large congregation of civic dignitaries, academics and friends. He gave a sketch of Collyer's career and achievements and said that he was now to receive a degree *honoris causa* because he was regarded by our kinsmen across the seas as a great power for righteousness. The Vice-Chancellor then conferred upon him the degree of Doctor of Letters and asked Collyer to respond. This he did with typical aplomb and fine words; he underlined his love of books and indicated that his personal library now numbered some 3-4,000 volumes. Collyer concluded with great humility; 'And so through all his life of sunshine and shadow, he had just been a great reader, and if ever he failed so he could not read, he would do what Southey did — go through his study patting his books on the back as if they were children and giving them his blessing.'[9] So this man of books was eventually awarded his Letters.

Collyer's next engagement was the opening of the new Public Library in Ilkley on October 2. There, Collyer was presented with an illuminated scroll signed by twelve Ilkley worthies, and had a bronze bust of himself unveiled to great acclaim. The bust, together with one of Andrew Carnegie, was created by Frances Darlington, daughter of an Ilkley solicitor who had achieved notable success as a sculptor. Carnegie had provided £3000 towards the provision of a free library and his act of philanthropy was deserving of recognition.

[9] 'A Yorkshireman from afar. His Degree at Leeds University', *Yorkshire Post*, Friday Sept 27, 1907.

Collyer opened the Free Library situated at the near end of the Town Hall Building. Author's collection.

John Dickinson of Timble attended and gave a breathless account of the occasion; 'Just in time for the meeting at the new Town Hall. Mr. Benson, a Councillor, reserved us a good seat at the front and we heard Dr. Collyer's address and other speeches. Bade adieu to Dr. Collyer who rode off triumphant amid cheers of the multitude. He seems beloved and honoured by all who come in contact with him..... We feel a tender love for the old man..... We shall never see his like again.'[10] Collyer sailed for home from Liverpool on the magnificent, and ill-fated, *Lusitania,* on October 6.[11]

---

[10] Harker, *Timble Man,* 140.

[11] This was the *Lusitania*'s second crossing from Liverpool and the ship arrived at Sandy Hook on 11 October 1907 in the Blue Riband record time of 4 days, 19 hours and 53 minutes. The *Lusitania* was sunk on 7 May 1915 by a German U-boat off the southern coast of Ireland, killing 1,198 passengers and crew. The sinking was a prelude to the United States declaration of war on Germany.

The bronze busts of Collyer (left) and Carnegie created by Frances Darlington in their original positions in the entrance vestibule of Ilkley Free (Public) Library. The busts were later moved to alcoves on either side of the entrance. Unfortunately, the bust of Carnegie was stolen about thirty years ago. It was probably melted down for the value of its metal. As a consequence, Collyer's bust was moved into storage for safe keeping.

On Collyer's eighty-fifth birthday in December 1908, Andrew Carnegie, 'a friend of long-standing' gave a private dinner party in his honor. There were numerous guests drawn from the worlds of politics, the arts and the church, including such luminaries as Bishop David Greer - Episcopal Bishop of New York; Mark Twain (Samuel Clemens) – writer, publisher and lecturer, who in 1907 had been awarded a D.Litt by Oxford University; Norman Hapgood – investigative journalist and social reformer, editor of Collier's Weekly; William Vaughn Moody – dramatist and poet; Oswald Villard – a pioneer civil rights leader, editor of New York Evening Post; Horace White - lawyer and politician, benefactor of Cornell University where his uncle, Andrew Dickson White, was the first President; Sir Caspar Purdon Clarke – Director of the Metropolitan Museum of Art; and Woodrow Wilson – President of Princeton University, and future President of the U.S. While it is possible that Collyer and Mark Twain shared experiences of receiving honorary degrees in England the year before, it is doubtful if Collyer told Andrew Carnegie that he had seen him in Ilkley library.

Ornamental key presented to Collyer at the opening of the Free Library in Ilkley on October 2, 1907. The key was made by a local jeweller, Mr E. Earnshaw of Brook Street. Postcard in the author's collection.

In January 1911, Collyer derived particular pleasure from the award of another Honorary Degree, this time from Meadville Unitarian Theological School in Chicago. The School represented the acme of Unitarian teaching in

America, and for Collyer the degree represented the ultimate stamp of approval from the church establishment. The humble, self-educated blacksmith had finally been accepted into the upper echelons of Unitarianism. The award reflected his personal contribution to the Church, but the School authorities will also have been impressed by the substantial donations made in his name - $25,000 in 1900 for 'The Robert Collyer Library Fund', $50,000 in 1901 for 'The Robert Collyer Endowment' and another $50,000 in 1901 for 'The Robert Collyer Endowment for the President's Chair'.[12]

[12] Holmes, *Life and Letters,* 2: 324.

32: End time

In the late Summer of 1912, Collyer was staying with his daughter, Emma, at the Delphine Hotel in East Gloucester when he fell and badly bruised his arm and side, a fall that also gave him a 'nasty shake'.[1] He appeared to recover completely, however, and on his return to New York resumed his usual routine. On November 1, however, he was heard to fall heavily in his bedroom, and Gertrude Savage found him lying on the floor having been momentarily unconscious. He recovered almost immediately and loudly protested that he was 'fine, and did not need a doctor'. This was a serious premonition of what was to follow; a few days later he felt ill and took to his bed, and the family watched as gradually the right side of his body became heavy and paralyzed. By this time his physician, Dr. Wylie, had been called. Wylie was understandably cautious but mildly optimistic about the prognosis; Collyer was still a powerful man, otherwise in good health, and there was the possibility of at least a partial recovery.[2]

For some time, he held his own. His speech was impaired, but he was determined to talk to his visitors, and his conversation was coherent. Over ensuing days, however, it became apparent that his general condition was deteriorating, albeit slowly. On Sunday November 24, the seriousness of his condition was conveyed to the congregation at the Church of the Messiah. The

---

[1] It had become Collyer's habit to take a late summer holiday in East Gloucester, Massachusetts, with his daughter, Emma Hosmer, who came over from her home in Chicago. East Gloucester was only a short distance from his former holiday destination, Manchester-by-the-sea.

[2] Holmes, *Life and Letters,* 2: 333.

next few days saw further deterioration and by Friday he had lapsed into unconsciousness. Robert and Gertrude maintained their vigil and watched him through Friday night. As Saturday progressed, they felt that the end was near; Dr. Wylie was called. Half an hour before midnight on the last day of November, his shallow breathing stopped, and he died - peaceful to the end.

On Sunday December 1, Collyer's death was reported on the front page of the *New York Times* including a long biographical piece – the newspaper editors had plenty of notice about the impending death and had already prepared their copy.[3] At the Church, a bunch of white lilies and the vacant platform chair where Collyer usually sat, spoke of his passing. The events of the next few days are clearly delineated through the columns of the *New York Times*. The funeral plans were announced on Monday, December 2.[4] A private service was held in the morning at the Collyer home; it was conducted by Rev. J. Haynes Holmes and the Rev. Minot Savage of Cleveland, Ohio, in the presence of Mr. and Mrs. Robert Collyer Jnr, Mrs. Emma Hosmer of Chicago, and Mr. Samuel Collyer from Seattle. Early in the afternoon the body was removed to the Church of the Messiah where it lay in state until early in the evening.[5]

On Tuesday 3, the doors of the Church were opened at 9.30am and before 10 o'clock the church was nearly filled. The church was a mass of flowers; the coffin was covered in red and white roses and violets provided by the family, and the platform and pulpit covered with wreaths of chrysanthemums, roses and white lilies, gifts from friends and relations, and clubs and societies. The Pastor, Rev. Haynes Holmes, gave the sermon. Rev. Dr. Merle St. Croix Wright spoke of Robert Collyer's influence on the Messiah church and emphasized that when he arrived from Chicago the church had only twenty-nine regular attenders. After the service, a special train took the funeral party to Woodlawn Cemetery where his body was laid to rest next to his beloved wife and daughter. The *Times* report mentioned that the family of Dr. Collyer had received a cablegram from Mayor Briggs of Keighley, England.[6] It bore the simple message; 'Keighley, Dr. Collyer's birthplace, condoles" – a testimony to Yorkshire remembrance, concern, and thrift.

On Friday, December 6, Collyer's will was filed for probate in the Surrogate's Court. Although he left less than $10,000, his bequests were many

---

[3] 'Rev. Robert Collyer dead at age of 84' *(sic)*. *New York Times,* Sunday December 1, 1912.

[4] 'Collyer Funeral Plans'. *New York Times,* Monday December 2, 1912.

[5] 'Collyer Funeral Service.' *New York Times,* Tuesday December 3, 1912.

[6] 'Rev. Dr. Collyer buried.' *New York Times,* Wednesday December 4, 1912.

and detailed; he listed gifts of money to his grandchildren and items destined for members of the family and a few friends – several paintings, a Dutch oak cabinet, a gold watch, an ivory headed cane and a gold-handled walking stick, being just a few. The residue of his estate was divided between his surviving children, Samuel and Robert Collyer and Emma Hosmer.[7]

Sunday, December 8, the day of the Memorial Service at the Church of the Messiah, would have been Collyer's eighty-ninth birthday. It was a long service, filled as it needed to be with the reading of numerous messages of condolence sent to the family, and tributes from clubs and organizations with which he had been associated through thirty-three years of attachment to the Messiah church. Pastor Haynes Holmes put a sermon to one side and instead gave a masterful summary of Collyer's life and ministry, after which the choir gave full-throated voice to Collyer's hymn, '*Unto thy temple, Lord, we come.*'[8] The old Yorkshireman got a right good send-off.

The new Unity Church in Chicago also chose the birthday, December 8, for its memorial service.[9] Alongside the pulpit, stood the old anvil decked in roses. Addresses were given by William Eliot Furness, who had been present when Collyer gave his first ever Unitarian sermon in his uncle's church in Philadelphia; Benjamin Adams and Samuel Greeley, both Trustees of the Unity Church through the long years of Collyer's pastorate; and the sermon was given by the current pastor, Rev. Frederick Hawley. An original hymn composed by the pastor was sung by the choir and people. For a church with an uncertain future, it was a time for looking back to a golden age.

The most poignant memorial service was undoubtedly that held at Cornell University on February 3, 1913.[10] For over twenty years, Collyer had preached an annual sermon in the Sage Chapel, and on this day it was filled to overflowing with staff and students. In front of the pulpit stood a large photographic portrait of Collyer and hanging down from the lectern was the horseshoe that initiated his link with Cornell. The Acting President, Thomas F. Crane, gave the history of how the man and the institution had been brought together in loving relationship; Professor George Burr, a long standing friend of Collyer, spoke of his particular attachment to Cornell and the highlights of

---

[7] 'Dr. Collyer's Will Filed.' *New York Times,* Saturday December 7, 1912.

[8] 'Memorial for Dr. Collyer'. *New York Times,* Monday December 9, 1912.

[9] The new Unity Church (now Second Unitarian Church) opened in 1906 at 656 W Barry Ave, Chicago.

[10] Holmes, *Life and Letters,* 2: 340.

the twenty years of visits; and Rev Haynes Holmes talked of his impact in New York, City and State. The tributes were heard in reverential silence; many of the Faculty had heard Collyer's preaching, and the students were intrigued to learn about the blacksmith turned preacher. As the service ended and the dignitaries began to file out of the Chapel, the silence was broken by the steady tolling of a distant bell.

Afterword

Although Robert Collyer had a national reputation as an orator, it seems likely that he would have preferred to be remembered as a great writer. His passion for books was evident from an early age; from humble beginnings in the Young Men's Reading Group in Ilkley, he rose to be President of the Chicago Literary Club and counted numerous authors among his personal friends. All his life he had an insatiable appetite for book collecting and reading. In old age, despite having a library of thousands of books, he continued to purchase them. He was a true bibliophile. He did not, however, become a writer of note.

He did publish nine books largely based on collections of sermons or other homilies and co-authored a local history book.[1] Some of his religious books sold in large numbers and ran to several editions, but they did not elevate him into the ranks of great writers. He also produced lectures which

---

[1] *Nature and Life* (Chicago: Horace B. Fuller, 245 Washington Street, 1867). This book ran to at least 11 editions.; *A Man in Earnest: Life of A. H. Conant* (Chicago: Horace B. Fuller, 245 Washington Street, 1868). An abridged version under the title *Augustus Conant* was published in 1905, (Cambridge, U.S.A: American Unitarian Association, The University Press); *The Life That Now Is* (Boston and New York: Lee and Shepard, 1871), *The Simple Truth: A Home Book,* (Boston and New York: Lee and Shepard, 1878); *Talks to Young Men (With Asides to Young Women)* (Boston and New York: Lee and Shepard, 1888); a combined edition of *The Life that now is* and *Nature and Life* (1888) was published by the British Unitarian Association, Essex Hall, Essex Street, Strand, London. *Things New and Old* (New York: E.P. Dutton and Co., 31 West 23rd Street, 1893); *Father Taylor* (Boston: American Unitarian Association, 25 Beacon Street, 1906); *Where the light dwelleth* (London: The Lindsey Press, 5 Essex Street, Strand, 1908). *Some Memories* (Boston: American Unitarian Association, 25 Beacon Street, 1908). With J. Horsfall Turner, *Ilkley: Ancient and Modern* (Otley, Yorkshire, UK: William Walker and Sons, 1885). A further book, *Thoughts for Daily Living – from the spoken and written words of Robert Collyer* was a collection arranged by Imogen Clark, (Boston: American Unitarian Association, 1911).

were delivered as Sunday evening addresses *in lieu* of a service of worship. The talks were on a wide variety of subjects and included brief biographies of such literary giants as Hawthorne, Whittier, Thoreau, Charles and Mary Lamb and Robert Burns. Some of the manuscripts survived fires and house moves and these lectures and addresses along with three poems,[2] a poetic memorial to Lucretia Mott, and two hymns, were published posthumously under the title, 'Clear Grit'.[3]

According to his biographer, the Rev. J. Haynes Holmes, Collyer did attempt to write a novel for publication called *John Watkinson's Wife,* and it was described in a sub-title as *A story of Old Ilkley.* Holmes states: 'Its early chapters showed clearly that the author's forte was not in the field of fiction, and it is not surprising that it was never finished. The paper in which it was published, *The Lakeside Magazine*, perished at the early age of six months, and it was a family joke in the Collyer household that the story had been fatal!'[4] Unfortunately this statement is also largely fiction; the magazine referred to should have been titled *The Lakeside Monthly,* which started life in 1869 as *The Western Monthly,* and was published in Chicago.[5] Collyer had several short articles published in this journal but none were about *Old Ilkley*. The magazine ceased publication in 1873 after seven issues had been produced.[6]

It could be that as late as 1899, when he was seventy-five years old, he still harbored a desire to write a novel. In that year he wrote to a friend, the author Sarah Orne Jewett, seeking her opinion of 'the novel of the future'. She provided no opinion; instead, she sent him two quotations from Flaubert, in French, that had guided her attitude to writing. This was singularly unhelpful advice to a man with no knowledge of the language.[7]

---

[2] The same poems were also published separately as *Three Bits of Rhyme by Robert Collyer.* (New York: E. Scott, Printer and Publisher, undated).

[3] Ed. John Haynes Holmes, *Clear Grit: A collection of Lectures, Addresses and Poems,* (Boston: American Unitarian Association, 1913).

[4] John Haynes Holmes, *The Life and Letters of Robert Collyer,* (New York: Dodd, Mead and Co., 1917), 2: 188

[5] *The Western Monthly* (Chicago, Reed, Browne & Co., 1869)

[6] Hathi Trust Digital Library, https://catalog.hathitrust.org/Record/000531704

[7] Sarah Orne Jewett to Mrs Annie Fields: 'Dearest, -- The letter by Mr. Collyer was from a person who sought to know my opinion of the novel of the future! But he never will. I copied for him those two wonderful bits of Flaubert, -- "Écrire la vie ordinaire comme on écrit l'histoire"; and the other, "Ce n'est pas de faire rire -- mais d'agir a la façon de la nature, c'est à dire de faire rêver." I keep these pinned up on the little drawers at the back of the secretary, for a constant reminder.' See the '*Letters of Sarah Orne Jewett*',

Collyer's meagre output of published poems hardly warrants the epithet 'The Poet Preacher', given to him by at least one author in England.[8] Nor were the poems of any real merit; rhymes do not make poetry.

Collyer is credited with four published hymns; the first, written for the dedication of the new Unity Church, *Unto thy temple, Lord, we come,* was the most successful and has been included in 28 hymnals, and remains available in some contemporary hymnals.[9] *With thankful hearts, O God, we come* was written for the dedication of the re-built Unity after the Fire but has only been in one hymnal, and the other two are *Ye mourners cease to languish* – in 15 non-current hymnals, and *O Lord our God, when storm and flame,* in one old hymnal.[10] Thus, three of the four hymns Collyer wrote have disappeared from contemporary collections. He cannot therefore be considered a hymn writer of note when these four hymns constitute his complete oeuvre.

Thus, this saintly orator had feet of clay when it came to writing poetry and prose. Does this affect our estimation of Robert Collyer the person? Let someone who knew him have the final say – Rev. John Haynes Holmes wrote; 'He had that rare combination of basic spiritual qualities which makes the great *man,* as distinguished from every other form of greatness. Men never looked upon him to marvel at his power, or stand in awe of his accomplishment. The famous personalities of his time – Emerson, Longfellow, Thoreau, Whittier, O. W. Holmes, E. E. Hale, Lucretia Mott, Julia Ward Howe, Andrew T. White and many others – with whom he associated on terms of easy and happy intimacy, sought in him no stores of learning or faculties of genius. All recognized his unquestioned ability and rejoiced in the fresh romance of his career. But what brought men to him in the beginning, and held them at the end, was himself. What he *was* – that was the great thing.'[11]

Letter 94, at http://www.public.coe.edu/~theller/soj/let/letters.htm. A translation provided by Paula Blanchard in *Sarah Orne Jewett: Her World and her Work,* (Cambridge MA, Perseus Publishing, 1994), reads 'Write about daily life as you would write history', and 'It is not to provoke laughter, nor tears, nor rage, but to act as nature does, that is, to provoke dreaming.'

[8] William Smith ed., 'Robert Collyer, the poet preacher' in *Old Yorkshire,* (London: Longmans, Green & Co., 1881), 239.

[9] For example, at https://www.blueletterbible.org/hymns/u/Unto_Thy_Temple_Lord_We_Come.cfm

[10] see www.hymnary.org

[11] Holmes, *Life and Letters,* 2: 374.

Bibliography

Alred, David, *Washburn Valley Yesterday*. Otley,Yorkshire: Smith Settle, 1997.

Andreas, Alfred T., *History of Chicago from the Earliest Period to the Present Time.* Chicago: The A.T. Andreas Company, 1885.

Armstrong, Alison, *Country walks around Addingham.* Addingham, Yorkshire: Addingham Civic Society, 1992.

Armstrong, Warren, *The Collins Story.* London: Robert Hale Ltd., 1957.

Bacon, Margaret H., *Valiant Friend: The life of Lucretia Mott*. New York, Walker and Co. 1980.

Bean, Theodore W., ed., *History of Montgomery County, Pennsylvania.* Philadelphia: Everts & Peck, 1884.

Bishop, Morris, *A History of Cornell*. Ithaca, Cornell University Press, 1962.

Blakeborough, Richard, *Wit, Character, Folklore and Customs of the North Riding of Yorkshire.* London: Henry Frowde, 1898.

Blanchard, Paula, *Sarah Orne Jewett; Her World and her work*. Cambridge MA: Perseus Publishing, 1994.

Bowen, Frank C., *A century of Atlantic travel 1830-1930*. London: Sampson Low, Marston & Co., 1930.

Bradley, Tom, *The Old Coaching Days in Yorkshire* re-printed Otley, Yorkshire: Smith Settle, 1988.

Bradley, Tom, *Yorkshire Rivers. No.10 The Washburn.* Leeds: Tom Bradley, 1895.

Briggs, G. S., *Congregational Church Otley 1821-1921 – A centenary retrospect.* Privately published, 1921.

Brown, Alfred J., *Broad Acres: A Yorkshire miscellany.* London: Country Life Ltd, 1948.

Campbell, William B., *Old Towns and Districts of Philadelphia. Philadelphia History IV.* Philadelphia: City History Society, 1942.

Cawley, James and Margaret, *Along the Old York Road.* New Jersey: Rutgers University Press, 1965.

Chapple, John A.V., and Arthur Pollard, *The letters of Mrs Gaskell.* Manchester: Manchester University Press, 1966.

Chapple, John, and Alan Shelston, *Further Letters of Mrs Gaskell.* Manchester: Manchester University Press, 2000.

Clemmer, Abram, *The Jenkins Town Lyceum.* Jenkintown, PA: Old York Road Historical Society Bulletin, 1952.

Coleman, Terry, *Passage to America: A history of emigrants from Great Britain and Ireland to America in the mid-nineteenth century.* London: Pimlico edition, 1992.

Collard, George, ed., *A Yorkshire Christmas.* Stroud, Gloucester: The History Press, 1989.

Collyer, Robert, *Some account of the Chicago Ministry-at-Large from its foundation to the present time.* Chicago: Privately published by the Trustees, 169 Randolph Street, 1860.

Collyer, Robert, *Nature and Life.* Chicago: Horace B. Fuller, 1867.

Collyer, Robert, *A Man in Earnest: Life of A. H. Conant.* Chicago: Horace B. Fuller, 1868.

Collyer, Robert, *The Life That Now Is*. Boston and New York: Lee and Shepard, 1871.

Collyer, Robert, *The Life that Now is: Sermons.* Boston: Lee and Shepard, 1874.

Collyer, Robert, *The Simple Truth: A Home Book.* Boston and New York: Lee and Shepard, 1878.

Collyer, Robert, *Talks to Young Men (With Asides to Young Women)*. Boston and New York: Lee and Shepard, 1888.

Collyer, Robert, *Things New and Old*. New York: E.P. Dutton and Co., 1893.

Collyer, Robert, *Father Taylor.* Boston: American Unitarian Association, 1906.

Collyer, Robert, *Where the light dwelleth*. London: The Lindsey Press, 1908.

Collyer, Robert, 'Prefatory Sketch' in *Memorials of Robert Spears: 1825-1899.* Belfast: Ulster Unitarian Christian Association, 1908.

Collyer, Robert, *Some Memories.* Boston: American Unitarian Association, 1908.

Collyer, Robert, *Clear Grit: a collection of Lectures, Addresses and Poems*. Boston: American Unitarian Association, 1913.

Collyer, Robert, and J. Horsfall Turner, *Ilkley: Ancient and Modern.* Otley, Yorkshire, UK: William Walker and Sons, 1885.

Conway, Moncure D., *Autobiography: Memories and Experiences of Moncure D. Conway.* New York: Cassell and Company, 1904.

Cook, Robert, *Civil War America: Making a nation, 1848-1877*. London: Longman, 2003.

Copp, Carrie V. Speck, *Some Historic Facts of Cheltenham Township*. Jenkintown, Pennsylvania: Old York Road Historical Society Bulletin, 1944.

Cordley, Richard, *A History of Lawrence, Kansas, from the first settlement to the close of the Rebellion*. Lawrence, KA: E.F. Caldwell, Laurence Journal Press, 1895.

Cromie, Robert, *The Great Chicago Fire.* New York: McGraw-Hill Book Company,1958.

Denney, Robert E., *Civil War Medicine: Care and comfort of the wounded.* New York: Sterling Publishing Co., 1995.

Dickens, Charles, *American Notes for general circulation.* Reprinted in Penguin Classics, London: Penguin Books, 1985.

Dixon, Mike, *Ilkley — History and Guide.* Stroud, Gloucester: The History Press, 2002.

Dixon, Mike, and Radick, Gregory, *Darwin in Ilkley.* Stroud, Gloucester: The History Press, 2009.

Dodd, William, *The Factory System Illustrated in a series of letters to the Right Hon. Lord Ashley. Appendix A; Mr. Drinkwater's report on flax mills.* London: John Murray, 1842.

Dusinberre, William, *Civil War issues in Philadelphia 1856-1865.* Philadelphia: University of Philadelphia Press, 1965.

Eiseley, Loren, *Darwin's Century: Evolution and the men who discovered it.* London: Gollancz, 1959.

Engels, Frederick, *The condition of the working-class in England: From Personal Observation and Authentic Sources*. Reprint of 1892 English edition, Moscow: Progress Publishers, 1973.

Erickson, Charlotte, *Invisible Immigrants.* Ithaca and London: Cornell University Press, 1972.

Faris, John T., *Old Roads out of Philadelphia*. Philadelphia: J. B. Lippincott Co., 1917.

Fay, Charles R., *Life and Labour in the Nineteenth Century*. Cambridge: Cambridge University Press, 1943.

Filby, P. William, and Mary K. Meyer (eds), *Passenger and Immigration Lists Index: Volume 1 A-G.* Detroit, Michigan: Gale Research Co., 1981.

Foote, Shelby, *The Civil War: 1 Fort Sumter to Perryville*. London, Pimlico, 1992.

Fox, Stephen, *Transatlantic: Samuel Cunard, Isambard Brunel and the Great Atlantic Steamships*. New York: Harper Collins, 2003.

Gaskell, Elizabeth, *The Life of Charlotte Brontë,* Angus Easson, ed., Oxford: Oxford University Press, Oxford World's Classics, 1996.

Giles, Calum, and Ian H. Goodall, *Yorkshire Textile Mills: The Buildings of the Yorkshire Textile Industry 1770-1930.* London: Her Majesty's Stationery Office, 1992.

Goodwin, Doris K., *Team of Rivals*. New York: Simon & Schuster, 2005.

Grainge, William, *The History and Topography of the Townships of Little Timble, Great Timble and the hamlet of Snowden, in the West Riding in the County of York.* Otley, Yorkshire: William Walker & Sons, 1895.

Greeley, Samuel S., B.F. Adams and W.G. Lewis, *Historical sketch of Unity Church, Chicago*. Chicago: Privately published, 1880.

Greeley, Samuel S., in *Memorial Services for Rev Robert Collyer D.D. held in the Unity Church, Chicago*. Chicago: Privately published by the Unity Church, 1912.

Harker, Ronald, *Timble Man: Diaries of a Dalesman.* Nelson, Lancashire: Hendon Publishing, 1988.

Harper, Ida Husted, *The Life and Work of Susan B. Anthony*. Indianapolis and Kansas City: Bowen Merrill Co., 1899.

Hartley, Marie, and Joan Ingilby, *Life and Tradition in the Yorkshire Dales.* London: J. M. Dent & Sons Ltd, 1968.

Hartley, Marie, and Joan Ingilby, *Making Ironwork.* Skipton, Yorkshire: Dalesman Publishing Ltd.,1997.

Henshaw, Sarah E., *Our branch and its tributaries; being a history of the work of the Northwestern Sanitary Commission and its auxiliaries, during the war of the rebellion.* Chicago: Alfred L. Sewell, 1868.

Hochschild, Adam, *Bury the Chains: The British struggle to abolish slavery.* London: Macmillan, 2005.

Holmes, John Haynes, ed., *Clear Grit: A collection of lectures, addresses and poems by Robert Collyer.* Boston: American Unitarian Association, 1913.

Holmes, John Haynes, *The Life and Letters of Robert Collyer.* New York: Dodd, Mead and Co., 1917.

Honeyman, Katrina, *Child Workers in England 1780-1820: Parish Apprentices and the Making of the Early Industrial Labour Force.* Abingdon and New York: Routledge, 2007.

Hoole, Kenneth, *Railways in the Yorkshire Dales.* Clapham, North Yorkshire: The Dalesman Publishing Co. Ltd., 1978.

Ingrams, Richard, *The Life and Adventures of William Cobbett.* London, Harper Collins, 2005.

Jennings, Bernard, ed., *A History of Nidderdale.* Huddersfield, Yorkshire: The Advertiser Press Ltd, 1967.

Karamanski, Theodore J., *Rally 'round the Flag: Chicago and the Civil War.* Lanham, MD: Rowman and Littlefield, 2006.

Krakauer, Jon, *Under the Banner of Heaven.* New York: Anchor Books, 2004.

Kring, Walter D., *Henry Whitney Bellows.* Boston: Skinner House, 1979.

Lemmon, William, *Methodism in Addingham.* Privately published, 1983.

Lodge, Eric, *A Wharfedale Village: A history of Burnsall.* Otley, Yorkshire: Smith Settle, 1994.

Lubbock, Basil, *The Western Ocean Packets.* Glasgow: Brown, Son & Ferguson Ltd., 1956.

Lyttle, Charles H., *Freedom moves West: A history of the Western Unitarian Conference*. Boston: The Beacon Press, 1952.

Maddocks, Melvin, *The Atlantic Crossing.* Amsterdam: Time-Life Books, 1981.

Mason, Kate, *Addingham: from Brigantes to bypass*. Addingham, Yorkshire: Addingham Civic Society, 1996.

McIlvaine, Mabel, ed., *Reminiscences of Chicago during the Civil War*. New York: The Citadel Press, 1967.

McPherson, James M., ed., *The Atlas of the Civil War* New York, Macmillan, 1994)

Meyer, Frederick B., *Dwight L. Moody* in *The Sunday at Home*. London: The Religious Tract Society, 1900.

Mitchell, Sally, ed., *Victorian Britain: an Encyclopedia*. London: St. James Press, 1988.

Murray, Jim, *The Great Fire.* New York: Scholastic Inc., 1995.

Oates, Stephen B., *A Woman of Valor: Clara Barton and the Civil War*. New York: The Free Press, 1995.

Parkinson, Thomas, *Lays and Leaves of the Forest: A collection of poems, and historical, genealogical and biographical essays and sketches, relating chiefly to men and things connected with the Royal Forest of Knaresborough* . London: Kent and Co., 1882.

Popham, Frederick S., *A History of Christianity in Yorkshire*. Wallington, Surrey: The Religious Education Press, 1954.

Reach, Angus, *The Yorkshire Textile Districts in 1849*. Helmshore, Lancashire: Helmshore Local History Society, 1974.

Rosenberger, Homer T., *Montgomery County's greatest lady: Lucretia Mott*. Norristown, Pennsylvania: The Bulletin of the Historical Society of Montgomery County, 1948.

Rothschild, Elaine W., *A History of Cheltenham Township*. Cheltenham: Cheltenham Township Historical Commission, 1976.

Rowe, Mortimer, *The Story of Essex Hall*. London: The Lindsey Press, 1959.

Rusterholtz, Wallace P., *The First Unitarian Society of Chicago: A brief history*. Chicago: Privately published by the First Unitarian Church, 5650 South Woodlawn Avenue, 1979.

Sandburg, Carl, *Storm over the Land,* extracts from *Abraham Lincoln: The War Years 1861-1865* London: Jonathan Cape, 1944.

Sawislak, Karen, *Smoldering City; Chicagoans and the Great Fire, 1871-1874*. Chicago, The University of Chicago Press, 1995.

Schrier, Arnold, and Joyce Story, *A Russian looks at America: The journey of Aleksandr Borisovich Lakier in 1857*. Chicago: Chicago University Press, 1979.

Simmons, Jack, *The Victorian Railway*. London: Thames and Hudson, 1995.

Smith, William, ed., '*Robert Collyer, the poet preacher*' in *Old Yorkshire*. London: Longmans, Green & Co., 1881.

Smith, William, *A Yorkshireman's trip to the United States and Canada*. London: Longmans, Green and Co., 1892.

Speight, Harry, *Upper Wharfedale*. London: Elliot Stock, 1900.

Spencer, Gwladys, *The Chicago Public Library: Origins and Backgrounds*. Chicago, The University of Chicago Press, 1943.

Stevenson, Robert Louis, *Essays of Travel: The Amateur Emigrant.* London: Chatto & Windus, 1909.

Thackrah, Charles Turner, *The Effects of Arts, Trades and Professions and of Civic States and Habits of Living on Health and Longevity: with suggestions for the removal of many of the agents which produce disease and shorten the duration of life*. London: Longman, Rees, etc., 1832.

Uglow, Jenny, *Elizabeth Gaskell: A Habit of Stories*. London, Faber and Faber, 1999.

White, Jerry, *London in the Nineteenth Century*. London: Jonathan Cape, 2007.

Whitehead, Thomas, *History of the Dales Congregational Churches.* Keighley, Yorkshire: Feather Brothers, 1930.

Whitehead, Thomas, *Illustrated Guide to Nidderdale and a History of its Congregational Churches*. Keighley, Yorkshire: Feather Brothers, 1932.

Willard, James F., and Colin B. Goodykoontz, eds., *Experiments in Colorado Colonization 1869-1872.* Boulder, The University of Colorado, 1926.

Wilson, Andrew N., *Famine in Ireland* in *The Victorians.* London: Hutchinson, 2002.

Index

Acknowledgements

This book has been many years in gestation. It began with an interest in nineteenth century photographs of Ilkley, the town in Yorkshire where I have lived for over fifty years. One of the early items in my collection was a postcard of 'Robert Collyer's old smithy', thereby identifying him as an Ilkley blacksmith, and yet in the local library there was a bronze bust labelled 'Rev. Robert Collyer D.D., LLD'. When I later learnt that Collyer had emigrated to America in his twenties, became an eminent preacher in Chicago and New York, and had acquired University degrees, I was intrigued.

I soon discovered that Collyer had produced several books, mainly collections of sermons, and all published in America, but I was hungry for autobiographical details and set about acquiring them. I searched the stock lists of antiquarian booksellers when I visited the States but found only three books on my 'wants' list. Several years later, and now in the internet era, an Ilkley bookshop owner, the late Andrew Sharpe, told me that he had started to use *abebooks.com* to advertise his books and suggested that I should give it a try. I remember that same evening sitting at my home computer and logging into *abebooks*. Within twenty minutes I had found all but one of Collyer's books for sale and, even better, identified the two-volume biography by John Haynes Holmes published in 1917. I was on my way.

Over the next twenty years I purchased dozens of books that would shed light on Collyer's progress from artisan to major pulpit figure; his involvement in the Civil War, the Great Fire in Chicago and its aftermath, Trans-Atlantic travel in the second half of the nineteenth century, and so on. I set out to obtain copies of public and private records that informed Collyer's story. I received assistance from many people in this quest. The majority remain anonymous, but some are recorded in correspondence spanning thirty years. I wish to thank them all, unnamed and named. Among the latter I should mention; Cynthia Brown, Superintendent Registrar at the Town Hall, Keighley; M.Y. Ashcroft, County Archivist, Northallerton; W.J. Connor, Leeds District Archivist; and Marian Berry, Assistant Archivist at the Bradford District Archives. Turning to the U.S., in Pennsylvania they include; Steven Smith, Reference Librarian, The Historical Society of Pennsylvania; Robert J. Plowman, Director, National Archives (Mid-Atlantic Region), Philadelphia; Brian McCloskey, Administrator, The Commission on Archives and Historical Society of the Eastern Pennsylvania Conference of the United Methodist Church, Philadelphia; Joseph McPeak, Library Supervisor and Richard C. Boardman, Head, Map Collection, The Free Library of Philadelphia. I wish to give special thanks to David Rowland, President, Old York Road Historical Society, who not only provided invaluable help in bringing my article on Robert Collyer and the Old York Road to publication in the Society's Bulletin, but also gave me new scans of photographs for this book. David's own research led me to identify Collyer's former house in Mill Road, Cheltenham, PA., and I am grateful to John C. Mellor for a contemporary photograph of his house. One of my medical classmates, Prof. Stephen Leech, provided photographs and other information about Elkins Park and old Abington, PA. Likewise, Gould P. Colman, University Archivist at the Carl A. Kroch Library, Cornell University, provided me with invaluable information and a photograph of the Fewston Bell. Similarly, photographic help and additional information about the Chicago-Colorado Colony was provided by Erik A. Mason, Curator of Research and Information at Longmont Museum, Longmont, CO.

Other important archives in the United States were identified by Alison Cowden, Librarian at the Institute of United States Studies, University of London, and I have appreciated the assistance given by; Joseph A. Stroble, The Methodist Library, Madison, New Jersey; Kristi C. Heesch, Public Information Assistant, Unitarian Universalist Association, Boston, Mass.; Kathryn M. Harris, Supervisor, Reference and Technical Services, Illinois State Historical Library, Springfield, Ill.; and Marie E. Lamoureux, Assistant Head of Readers' Services, American Antiquarian Society, prior to a visit I made to the Society's library in Worcester, Mass.

After completing the writing of the book, I called on family members and friends to serve as sub-editors. I am greatly indebted for all their suggestions. To gain a perspective from America, I enlisted the help of my sister, Ann M. Dixon, long time resident of Maryland and Florida, and John Guinness in Cleveland and his sister, Margie, in New York. Other readers of the manuscript were my wife, Judy, who had to adopt an unusually critical stance; a well-read nephew, Christopher Rush; and Ilkley friends, Gary and Hilary Williams, all of whom gave me the benefit of their comments and corrections. The latter also kindly undertook a photo reconnaissance of Chicago in the footsteps of Collyer during a vacation in America. Finally, I owe special thanks to my niece, Joanna Hill, for using her skills in graphic design to produce the cover.

Those of you who have read this book before reading the Acknowledgements, will have formed your own view on its content and balance, aspects that are usually influenced by an editor. A self-published work can by-pass such influence and fall into self-indulgence. I hope that you, dear reader, have been suitably engaged by the narrative and not overwhelmed by detail, the result of forty years of intermittent research. I also hope, that like me, you have warmed to the eventful life of Robert Collyer.

Collyer's old anvil in the Second Unitarian Church, West Barry Avenue, Chicago, Photograph by Hilary Williams, 2016.

About the Author:

Mike Dixon M.D., F.R.C.Path., is an Emeritus Professor of Pathology at the University of Leeds. He has published over 400 scientific research papers, review articles, books and book chapters, and made major contributions to our knowledge of ulcer disease and cancers of the digestive system. He retired in 2006 since when he has concentrated on golf, gastronomy, gardening, grandchildren – and local history.[1]

Mike qualified in Medicine at Edinburgh University in 1965 and after junior posts in Respiratory Medicine and General Surgery embarked on training in Pathology. In 1968 he was appointed Lecturer in Pathology in the Edinburgh Medical School. Two years later, following the death of his father-in-law in a road traffic accident, he moved to a Lecturer post at Leeds University Medical School and took up residence in his wife's family home in Ilkley, West Yorkshire. After an early dip into local history, he learnt that Ilkley had been home to Robert Collyer, the blacksmith turned preacher, whose fascinating story has been a continuing interest over the past forty years.

1. *Ilkley: Images of England series* (Stroud, Gloucester: Tempus Publishing Limited, 1999); *Ilkley – History and Guide* (Tempus Publishing Limited, 2002); with Gregory Radick: *Darwin in Ilkley* (Stroud, Gloucester: The History Press, 2009); *Ilkley Revisited,* (The History Press, 2010).